The Philosopher's Game

MATCH YOUR WITS AGAINST THE 100 GREATEST THINKERS OF ALL TIME

Edwin Schlossberg & John Brockman

ST. MARTIN'S PRESS NEW YORK

To Katinka Matson

Library of Congress Cataloging in Publication Data

Schlossberg, Edwin.
   The philosopher's game.

   1. Philosophical recreations.   I. Brockman, John,
1941-   joint author.   II. Title.
GV1507.P43S34   793.7'3   76-62793

ISBN 0-312-60463-7

Design by Anita Duncan

CONTENTS

INTRODUCTION

The English biologist J. Z. Young once wrote that humans create their world and are molded by their use of it. He was talking about how we invent tools and technologies and then learn to perceive ourselves in their image. In this sense Isaac Newton's seventeenth-century mechanistic physics led to our image of the body as a clock, the heart as a pump. Similarly, Norbert Wiener's recent work in cybernetics helped to bring about the notion of the brain as a computer.

The interesting thing about such metaphors is that they transform reality for us. We don't say "your heart is *like* a pump," or "your brain is *like* a computer." Your heart *is* a pump. Your brain *is* a computer. The real world is thus essentially a human invention. All the concepts by which we live, the names we use for self-description, the ideas we have at hand to explain the world, have initially fallen from the tongues of certain special individuals through the ages. The words of the world are the life of the world. Nature is not "created" out of a nameless void. It is, quite simply, "said."

The Philosopher's Game has been written to take you on a journey through history, to visit briefly with 100 of those thinkers whose words and ideas are the foundation of our world.

The book presents 100 mini-chapters, each dealing with the work and ideas of a great thinker. All of the chapters include (1) a story—incomplete—about the subject; (2) a choice of three answers—quotations—to complete the story; (3) a listing of the correct and incorrect answers, with attribution and annotation; and (4) a brief biographical sketch of the subject. The basic ideas and information necessary to arrive at a correct answer are contained within the story. Only one answer is "correct" because it represents the actual words of the subject; the two incorrect answers are derived from other sources.

You can play *The Philosopher's Game* alone, or you can read it aloud and play it with a group of people. If you have a competitive spirit, keep score and find out how you rate on a scale of 0 to 100. Or, play the game against your friends and family.

However you choose to use this book, we hope it will bring you hours of rewarding and enjoyable experience.

Have fun!

Edwin Schlossberg
Chester, Massachusetts

John Brockman
New York City

THE AUTHORS

Edwin Schlossberg holds a doctorate in science and literature from Columbia University. He has taught at Columbia University, MIT, and the University of Illinois, and has designed the Learning Environment for the Brooklyn Children's Museum. He is the author of *Wordswordswords* and *Einstein and Beckett*, and the coauthor of *Projex*. Dr. Schlossberg lives in Chester, Massachusetts.

John Brockman is the author of several works of philosophy. His books—*By The Late John Brockman, 37*, and *Afterwords*—are the subject of a collection of essays, *After Brockman*. Mr. Brockman is the editor of *Real Time 1, Real Time 2*, and *About Bateson: Essays on Gregory Bateson*. He lives in New York City.

Edwin Schlossberg and John Brockman are coauthors of *The Pocket Calculator Game Book*.

1. I CHING

"Take note, Lin Tseng. We do not want this text to predict or even seem to predict the future." Chuang Huang looks over the shoulder of his scribe and continues: "The examples of wisdom should be written to be compared and contrasted with the events in one's own life. We must create descriptions of the basic forms of human interaction and develop a process to select one over another by chance. The key to it all is that the chance must not suggest the will of the gods nor any other such ineffable source. It must be the sheer interest of chance."

For several years Chuang Huang and Lin Tseng have toiled long hours every day on this book entitled *Changes*. They have chosen that title in accordance with their belief that change is the only constant in life. Their aim is to create a book that will present the various changes everyone may experience.

Still, they fret that the work will be misread and misunderstood. "People will read it and believe that rules of life come from the outside, rather than the inside," Lin Tseng says.

Indeed, Chuang Huang recognizes this danger. He knows that each generation has its "true believers," those people unwilling or unable to think for themselves, to take responsibility for their own actions. "I know many people will use the book the wrong way," he replies, "but I refuse to abandon it merely to protect the abuser from their own self-abuse."

"If this is the case," Lin Tseng says, "how will it be effective? How will the words in our book make any difference to the reader?"

"It's not the words themselves that will make a difference, Lin Tseng. The difference comes not from the meaning of the words but from the act of contemplating a position from a different perspective, an act that will be suggested by the reading of the words.

"For example," he continues, "take your own position as my subordinate. This human relationship is so widespread that we should compose a particularly effective line about change with regard to it. I shall write it so that no one will have trouble 'getting it' when he spreads the yarrow sticks or throws the coins."

Chuang Huang paces back and forth for several moments before beginning to dictate to Lin Tseng. . . .

(A) *"Pardon free truth, and let thy modesty
which conquers all, be once overcome
by thee."*

(B) *"The earth's condition is receptive
devotion
Thus the superior man who has breadth
of character
carries the outer world."*

(C) *"Who would not throw his better
thoughts about him,
And scorn his dross within him:
that, without him?
Cast up, my soul, thy clearer eye,
behold,
If thou be full melted, there's
the mold."*

Answer (A):   From Ben Johnson's, "To William Camden," in his *Epigrammes*. Johnson (c. 1573-1637) was one of the wittiest and most interesting of the English metaphysical poets.

Answer (B):   CORRECT! From the *I Ching*, or *Book of Changes*.

Answer (C):   From Francis Quarles' "Epigram 6." Francis Quarles (1592-1644) bridged the gap between the religious poetry of the sixteenth century and the metaphysical poetry of the seventeenth century.

The *I Ching* is an ancient Chinese book of divination based on the study of sixty-four named hexagrams, each made up of two trigrams containing three divided or undivided lines. It represents one of the earliest human attempts to come to grips with the universe. As well as an oracle, it is a book of wisdom and poetry, and a guide to Confucianism and Taoism.

Legend tells us that Fu-hsi (2948-2838 B.C.), the first of the Five Emperors, was inspired to create the first eight trigrams from which the *I Ching* developed by taking note of the markings on the shell of a tortoise. King Wan (1171-1122 B.C.) is given credit for the explanations of the hexagrams, and his son, Duke Kau, for the explanations of the separate lines. Although Confucius has been credited with the commentaries, he himself said that he simply collected the material. Most likely, they are the work of many, his pupils and others, over a period of time from about the sixth to the third century B.C.

The undivided lines of the hexagrams represent the Yang principle—masculine, creative, positive; the divided lines represent the Yin principle—feminine, receptive, negative. Each hexagram is accompanied by a certain text. The *I Ching* can be used as an oracle by asking it a specific question, throwing three coins (or stalks) six times (one for each line of the hexagram), and consulting the appropriate hexagram.

2. RIG-VEDA

It is the second millenium in northern India, an Aryan tribesman sits alone on the side of a mountain. His eyes scan the innumerable stars that glow in the darkness of the autumn night. He is awed by his insignificance and by his ignorance.

His is a local world: the shelter of community, the warmth of the cave, the fire. The idea of travel, the possibility of other cultures, have not occurred to him. A hunter and a warrior, he protects his family from deadly enemies. His life is stark and immediate.

The tribesman wants to compose something that will place him in this universe. A hymn. His words are not symbol-laden. He makes words from things that he h̶ experienced directly, observed directly—natural forces that have been named. His hymn, his Veda, is chanted simply and directly, to express his awe of the universe. He sings to the gods and goddesses about faith, about the mystery of the night, about the creation of the world. . . .

(A) *"Have you ever watched the spider and noted how fantastically she spends her time? With speed and foresight she spins her marvelous web. When the fly falls headlong into the web, she rushes up, sucks the little creature's blood and leaves the body to dry for us as food. Then along comes a man and brushes it away and in an instant the web, the spider and the fly are gone. The web represents the world, the fly the subsistence which God has placed there for man."*

(B) *"Who verily knows and who can declare when creation started and when it was born? The gods were invented after its start. Who knows then when the world started? He the creator, whether he made it or not, whose eyes control the world, he knows how the world began, or perhaps not."*

(C) *"And I will add that considering the traces of God's grace which surrounds us, I am very sanguine, or rather confident (if it is right so to speak), that our prayers and our alms will come up as a memorial before God, and that all this miserable confusion tends to good."*

Answer (A): A symbolic epigram from Attar's (1120-1230) *Conference of the Birds*, a philosophical, religious poem written in the twelfth century.

Answer (B): CORRECT! From *Rig-Veda*.

Answer (C): From John Henry Cardinal Newman's *Apologia Pro Vita Sua*. Newman (1801-1890), British prelate and leader of the Oxford Movement, wrote this work as a defense of dogma against the liberal spirit that began to pervade the Roman Catholic Church in late nineteenth-century Italy.

The *Rig-Veda* is a basic text of the Hindu religion. Western scholars believe that it was composed between 1500 and 1200 B.C. Indian traditions maintain that the date is much earlier, since the material was chanted long before it was transcribed.

The hymns of the *Rig-Veda* represent experiences of Aryan tribes as they moved into what is now India and established themselves among hostile tribes of the north. Far from being simple, the hymns are remarkably complex and interwoven.

There are ten books in the entire *Rig-Veda* containing a total of 1017 verses. The most prominent god in the hymn is Indra, a warrior. The word "Veda" means knowledge. The entire text reveals the deep respect for knowledge held by these ancient people.

3. MOSES

"Your life is the answer to questions about it." Moses reflects upon the words of God. The strains, the bruises accumulated on his march through life ache in his mind as he humbly ponders the answer to the question posed by his existence.

Moses sits on a rock atop Mount Pisgah. It is the morning of a clear, sunny day in the thirteenth century B.C. Beside him stands Joshua, his aide. These two strong men are looking down at the rich, fertile land below, a marked contrast to the harsh, dry desert where they have spent so many years with their people. Moses is the leader of the Hebrew tribes, their guide. He has led them from Egyptian persecution, wandered with them through the desert, fought with them in battle, shared in their struggle for life.

To Moses, the top of Mount Pisgah is the point between past and future, between difficulty and hope, between the possibility of continuation and the otherwise certain destiny of extinction.

"Joshua," Moses says, rising slowly to face the younger man, "on this day I have heard the word of God. I shall not lead my people beyond this mountain. God has chosen you to take them across the Jordan River to the Promised Land."

Joshua's face freezes with shock at the words of his leader. "Joshua," Moses continues in a forceful voice, "remember that laws make life bearable. My own mind is not eased by our system of laws because I have known and experienced life prior to their inception. I am worried at what will happen when you lead the people away. Sacred cows? Idols? Will the tribes turn to primitive forms of worship after I am gone?"

"Moses," Joshua replies to the elder man, "the people have not only the laws but the example of your strength and character as well."

Moses, ignoring the compliment, responds, "But are the laws of diet and behavior, of worship and atonement sufficient? Will these laws carry my people through the ages?"

The men descend the mountain as Moses ponders these questions. Below the leaders of the tribes are assembled. Finally, Moses stands before them. In a thundering voice he speaks. . . .

(A) "Great actions are not always true sons
Of great and mighty resolutions;
Nor do the old'st attempts bring forth
Events still equal to their worth;
But sometimes fail, and in their stead
Fortune and cowardice succeed."

(B) "Set your heart unto all the words wherewith I testify against you this day; that ye may charge your children therewith to observe to do all the words of this law. For it is no vain thing for you; because it is your life, and through this thing ye shall prolong your days upon the land."

(C) "Do you think that anything could be at any time or in any place which was not in the supreme truth, and which did not receive from it that what it is, in so far as it is, or which could be other than what it is in the truth?"

Answer (A):   From Samuel Butler's *Hudibras*, Part I, Canto I, lines 885-890. Butler (1612–1680) wrote the poem as a satire on the cruelty and hypocrisy of Puritan England.

Answer (B):   CORRECT! From *Deuteronomy* 32: 46-48.

Answer (C):   From Saint Anselm's *Dialogue on Truth*, Chapter 7. Anselm (1033-1109) was Archbishop of Canterbury and one of the great theologians of his time.

Moses, called the great lawgiver of Israel, was an important figure in Judeo-Christian history. The authorship of the first five books of the Bible is attributed to him. Exodus, Leviticus, Numbers, and Deuteronomy, sometimes called the Book of Laws or the Books of Moses, tell his story and record the laws he gave his people.

According to the Bible Moses was born in Egypt during a period of Egyptian persecution of the Hebrew tribes. He was saved from drowning by the pharaoh's daughter who raised him as her own child. As Moses grew up, he became aware of the persecution of the Israelites by the Egyptians. God spoke to Moses from a burning bush and told him that he was to lead his people out of Egypt, through the desert, to the Promised Land. During this long, arduous journey, God appeared to Moses many times, giving him the Ten Commandments, the criminal code, and the liturgical laws, which served as the bases for Judaism and which were later incorporated, in part, in the Christian religion.

Moses never reached the Promised Land but died after glimpsing it from the summit of Mount Pisgah. He was buried in Moab.

4. UPANISHADS

It is a remote part of India in the year 725 B.C. Ideas and culture do not exist. Everything that happens is a mystery. Little is gathered together to be seen as a pattern. There are no roads. No buildings. No gathering places for more than a few.

The animals prowl at will. Because they prey on people, the animals are worshiped by the inhabitants in the hope that this will protect them. There are even greater threats than the animals—great floods, mountains cracking apart, raging fire.

People gather in small groups and discuss what these forces must be and what they themselves are in relation to the great forces. This very questioning separates them from the environment which they have feared and in which they have survived. The separation itself frightens them. It is worse than the fear of animals and fire. In their conversations, they suggest a larger world, one into which they can fit, one in which they form a part, an essential element. They worship through song. These songs, later written down as the *Upanishads*, praise the forces that threaten them. The *Upanishads* express ideas which evoke fear. At the same time they recommend rules to avoid both the fear and the ideas themselves.

(A) *"Housed everywhere but nowhere shut in, this is the motto of the dreamer of dwellings. In the last house as well as in the actual house, the day-dream of inhabiting is thwarted. A day-dream of elsewhere should be left open therefore, at all times."*

(B) *"These rivers, my dear, flow, the eastern toward the east, the western toward the west. They go just from the ocean to the ocean. They become the ocean itself. As there they know not 'I am this one,' 'I am that one'—even so, indeed, my dear, all creatures here, though they have come forth from Being, know not 'We have come forth from being.' "*

(C) *"Wherefore again and again in the same way it must needs be, since the first-beginnings of things are made by nature and not fashioned by hand to the fixed form of one pattern, that some of them fly about with shapes unlike one another."*

Answer (A): From Gaston Bachelard's *The Poetics of Space*. Bachelard (1884-1962) was a French philosopher.

Answer (B): CORRECT! From the Upanishads, Tenth Khanda.

Answer (C): From Lucretius' *On the Nature of Things*. Lucretius (c. 97-54 B.C.) was a Roman philosopher and poet.

The *Upanishads* (c. 800-500 B.C.), written in Sanskrit, are a series of metaphysical dialogues or treatises which form part of the sacred literature of Hinduism. They were written after the Vedas, the oldest Hindu Scriptures, in part as a commentary on them. Although many writings have been called "Upanishads," the term properly applies to the oldest class of text.

The *Upanishads* mark a turning point in Hinduism from an extroverted, life-accepting religion to a more introverted, esoteric form. The texts explore the deeper cosmological and personal significance of Hinduism. They represent an attempt to define the concept of the absolute and to describe the dual search for the eternal self within and the eternal ground of the universe outside the individual.

5. HOMER

It is a clear, sunny afternoon in Smyrna. The year is 675 B.C. In a tavern by the sea sit several Greek patricians. They are exiles, driven from Greece to Asia Minor because of the loss sustained by their army. The men are desolate, irritable. Their discussions erupt into angry fights or drift into the silence of drunken stupor.

"Do we really believe we are heroes?" Glaukos asks in derision. "Here we sit," he continues, "drunk on the rotten fruit of this strange land. We should begin to think about returning home to conquer our enemies. Better to take back our lands and possessions and drink their blood instead of this foul wine."

"Words, Glaukos, words," Petrocolus calls out from across the room. "You think you can shame us into honorable actions. It will take more than a tragic description to stimulate the hero in us to emerge once again and take arms against our enemies."

Near the back of the room, a blind man sits by an open window, holding a lyre and mumbling hoarsely to himself about life and death, valor and grief, the gods and men. Only his dog seems interested in his words. Yet, he continues. He too is an exile who feels anger at being deprived of examples of heroic deeds. He is a poet who wants to sing of valor, of destiny and achievement, not of failure and waste.

Glaukos notices the man. "Blind poet," he shouts in a cynical voice, "come and sing to us about heroes, about the approval of gods, about the glory of battle. Surely you can see we need such songs!"

The poet stumbles toward the Greek patricians, reaches out, feels a barrel, and sits down. He begins to sing. His song is not of the present and present-day heroes, but of the past, of legends. His voice is strong. His aim is to stimulate the minds and hearts of these men by comparison with the past. His magical voice fills the tavern and carries through the open windows, reaching the ears of men whose muscles begin to tingle with the energy they receive through the song of Homer. . . .

(A) *"Let man put a good edge to his spear,
        and his shield in order,
    let each put good fodder before his swift
        footed horses,
    and each man look well over his
    chariot,
        careful of his fighting . . .
    There will not even for a small time be
        any respite
    unless darkness come down to separate
        the strength of the fighters. . .
    they kindled the fire's smoke along the
        shelters, and each man made
        sacrifice
    to some one of the immortal gods,
        in prayer to escape death."*

(B) *"Minds that are great and free
    Should not on fortune pause;
    'Tis crown enough to virtue still,
        her own applause."*

(C) *"Heav'n but the Vision of
        fulfill'd Desire
    And Hell the Shadow from a Soul
        on fire,
    Cast on the Darkness into which
        Ourselves,
    So later emerged from, shall soon
        expire."*

Answer (A):   CORRECT! From Homer's *Iliad*.

Answer (B):   From Ben Jonson's "An Ode to Himself." Jonson (c. 1573-1637) was an English metaphysical poet.

Answer (C):   From Omar Khayyam's "Quatrains" from the *Rubaiyát*. Omar (?-1123) was a Persian poet and philosopher.

Homer, the towering figure of Greek literature, was the first European poet. His influence on later Greek and present-day Western literature has been enormous.

Homer was born in Asia Minor, probably in Chios or Smyrna sometime before 700 B.C. Beyond this, little is known about his life. Legends say that he was blind, and scholars agree that the *Iliad* and the *Odyssey*, his two great works, were composed for an aristocratic society, and that the poems were probably sung or recited for a noble audience.

There has been much debate as to whether the same person wrote both works. According to the narrative, the poems follow one another. The *Iliad* is the story of the siege of Troy by the Greek heroes. The *Odyssey* follows one of the heroes, Odysseus, on a ten-year journey home after the fall of Troy.

Together these two poems form the prototype for what we now think of as an epic poem. Indeed the Western idea of a hero is, to a great extent, drawn from the men Homer describes.

6. LAO-TZU

"In every action there is a reaction, in every challenge a response."

"To yield is to be preserved whole."

"Water is the most yielding of substances yet has the power to move rocks."

This text expounds the doctrine of inaction, or *wu-wei*. The wisdom in the words is profound. Self-effacement. Wonder at the universe. The lack of objective being. The practical refusal to talk without knowledge. Knowing without understanding. Such new ideas are enormously influential in the Chinese mind.

The text first appears in China in the sixth century B.C. It is composed of 5000 archaic characters. Its authorship is a mystery. The major thinkers of the day do not want to take credit for it, since the mysterious text has more power without the attachment of their names. The young men do not want to take credit for it because its wisdom would be inappropriate to their station. Throughout China, people begin to copy and learn the 5000 characters, the *Tao Te Ching, The Doctrine of the Power of the Way*. They call the unknown author Lao-tzu, the "old man," and a legend arises that he spent eighty-one years in his mother's womb before emerging whitehaired and speaking.

At a stream near the foot of a mountain people gather thinking they have found Lao-tzu and strain to get a glimpse of a scroll. Every day the old man has appeared to hang another scroll and wash away the characters. After he erases the words, he leaves the scroll hanging in the sun to dry. He is known to some as the sage, to others as the hermit.

"What words do you erase?" they ask the old man.

"These are the words of ancestors which are so simple that no one will understand them," he replies. Many among the crowd recognize these words. "Old man," they entreat, "are you Lao-tzu?"

"An old man, yes. I am an old man. But so are you."

The hermit hangs his scroll on the tree. He erases all the words but a few and walks away. As he does so, the crowd begins to wade into the river to get close enough to the tree to read the remaining words on the scroll. . . .

(A) "They that fear the hoar frost, the snow shall fall upon them. The fear of the adversities of this world causes some to run the risk of eternal misfortune."

(B) "Truthful words are not beautiful; beautiful words are not truthful. Good words are not persuasive; persuasive words are not good. He who knows has no wide learning; he who has wide learning does not know.

"The sage does not hoard.
"Having bestowed all he has on others,
    he has yet more;
"Having given all he has to others,
    he is richer still.
"The way of heaven benefits and does
    not harm; the way of the
    sage is bountiful and does not contend."

(C) "In the beginning the gods did not at all reveal all things clearly to mortals, but by searching, men in the course of time find them out better."

Answer (A): From the *Second Letter of Gregory VII to the Bishop of Metz,* March 15, 1081. The letter details the views of Pope Gregory (1020-1085) on the relative positions of church and state.

Answer (B): CORRECT! From *Tao Te Ching.*

Answer (C): From the writings of Xenophanes. Xenophanes (570-480 B.C.) was a Greek philosopher and poet.

Lao-tzu (c. 604-531 B.C.) was a Chinese philosopher and the legendary author of the *Tao Te Ching (The Doctrine of the Power of the Way),* which is the basis for Taoism, one of the main philosophical systems of ancient China.

According the legend, Lao-tzu spent his later years at the Chinese Imperial Court at Loyang as Palace Secretary and Keeper of the Archives. He is reported to have married and had a son. Although he did not actually found a school, he attracted many people who came to him as disciples. Confucius was a younger contemporary of Lao-tzu, and the two men supposedly met and talked.

During his last years, Lao-tzu, disgusted with the Imperial Court, decided to withdraw from the world. Before doing so, he wrote down in 5000 archaic Chinese characters the *Tao Te Ching,* which teaches that one succeeds by being rather than by doing, and by attitude rather than act.

7. PYTHAGORAS

"Such goings on," Philander remarks to Zenocrates as they wander and pick their way through the ruins of the secret meeting place in Athens where Pythagoras and his followers had carried out their mystical activities and their search into the nature of the universe.

The year is 310 B.C. The Pythagorean sect had been stamped out a hundred years before for deviance from accepted beliefs and practices. Philander and Zenocrates are young pupils at the Academy founded by Plato.

"These people," Zenocrates remarks, "actually believed that the souls of living things go from one to another, that all living things are related." "Yes," replies Philander. "Legend has it that Pythagoras saw someone beating a dog in the marketplace and told him to stop, saying 'Do not beat that dog for in him I see the soul and I hear the voice of a dear departed friend.' "

"Strange man," Zenocrates continues. "His people did not eat living things, they would not laugh, nor did they leave a trace of their existence anywhere. They believed that God's mystery was everywhere. They exercised absolute secrecy. No outsiders were allowed into their institute." The two young men continue their walk on this cool, clear day in Athens. A small puppy joins them and frolics at their heels.

"Frightening," Philander says. "On the one hand he was a brilliant mathematician who looked into the harmony of the universe and found relationships between numbers and things, between the unlimited and the limited. On the other hand, he was a quack who insisted on such behavior as absolute abstention from the eating of beans. It is so different from the rational discourse of the Academy. Just imagine, only 100 years ago this kind of thinking was acceptable."

"Still," Zenocrates responds, "Pythagoras remains an extremely stimulating figure. I, for one, certainly would have enjoyed hearing him expound upon his view of reality."

Zenocrates and Philander are startled by a booming voice coming from the enclosed courtyard just ahead. The voice rings with authority and conviction. They listen, stunned. The brief speech ends and they run into the ancient courtyard. No one is there, only the puppy who trots up to them, eagerly wagging its tail. Zenocrates and Philander stare at each other incredulously as they ponder the words they have just heard. . . .

(A) "Life . . . is like a festival; just as some come to the festival to compete, some to ply their trade, but the best people come as spectators, so in life the slavish men go hunting for fame or gain, the philosophers for the truth."

(B) "It is true that in practice events take place in the world sporadically at points of stress—not generally or simultaneously throughout the planet. So, even if the consequences anticipated by the model were, through human inertia and political difficulties, allowed to occur, they would no doubt appear first in a series of local crises and disasters."

(C) "The world is a terrible place but the Universe is a fine thing."

Answer (A): CORRECT! From the writings of Pythagoras, only fragments of which still exist.

Answer (B): From *Limits to Growth,* a contemporary book on planetary planning by Donella H. Meadows, Dennis L. Meadows, Jorgen Randers, and William W. Behrens III.

Answer (C): From Edwin Arlington Robinson's *Collected Poems.* Robinson (1869-1935) is best known in his poetry for his characterizations and his insights into the tragic elements of human nature.

Pythagoras (c. 582-507 B.C.), a Greek philosopher, was born in Samos, the son of Mnesarchos. He eventually left Samos because he disagreed with the government, probably traveling through Egypt before settling in Croton, a wealthy Greek town in southern Italy. Here Pythagoras founded a religious society to which he gave his name and became an influential figure in the city until the people turned against him and forced him to depart. He went to Metapontion where he died.

Pythagoras's philosophy is a unique combination of religion and mathematics. His religion advocated, among other primitive ideas, abstention from certain foods, like beans. He believed in the transmigration of souls.

Pythagoras held that all things are numbers, that is, that the universe could be seen as a series of numerical relationships. Several interesting discoveries resulted from this theory. Pythagoreans were the first to realize that tones are numerically related. They were the first to understand that the earth is a sphere which revolves around a fixed point, which they called the Great Hearth. The Pythagorean theorem, one of the basic theorems of plane geometry, was another important discovery.

The sect was stamped out during the great age of Greece (the fourth and third centuries B.C.).

8. SAPPHO

The sound of flutes rises lightly above the island of Lesbos. The year is 550 B.C. In the courtyard of the island's school, the white sun plays upon the golden heads of the girls who dance to and sing the poems of the time. Sappho, their teacher, walks about this school of the muses, assisting each girl in turn to perfect and expand her skills, as well as to develop understanding of them through practice. The girls possess a delicate rage to learn, which is matched only by the intensity of Sappho's relationship with them.

The courtyard of Sappho's school is set atop a hill. From the nearby army camp below, the first stirrings of an infantry drill can be heard. The girls flock to the walls to view the uniforms, the swords, the plumed helmets. Sappho is angered. Once again, the girls are neglecting themselves and their arts to watch the performances of the men. Although married to Cercolas, a rich man from Andros, and terribly in love with Phaon, a young boy, Sappho has dedicated her school to the worship of Aphrodite, the Greek goddess of love.

Later, alone with Melina, her favorite student, Sappho reveals her disappointment. "Why must you abandon your work? Why do you not respect yourselves and your feelings?" The young woman explains that the girls were only responding to the soldiers' outward signs of success. Sappho listens quietly as she combs Melina's long flaxen hair. She understands all too well the irony of the girls' abandonment of themselves. Once again, the pressures of the outside world have turned the girls from contemplation to idleness. Sappho places the comb on the table next to her, draws Melina close, holding her in her arms while kissing her gently on the lips. It is a kiss of fulfillment, not passion. A kiss to express her love for all women. Melina draws back, looks at her with deep love, and listens to the words Sappho whispers. . . .

(A) *"Pain has the element of blank;*
It cannot recollect
When it began, or if there were
A day when it was not.

"It has no future but itself.
Its infinite realms contain
Its past, enlightened to perceive
New periods of pain."

(B) *"I saw a man pursuing the horizon;*
Round and round they sped.
I was disturbed at this;
I accosted the man.
'It is futile,' I said,
'You can never—'

" 'You lie,' he cried,
And ran on."

(C) *"Some say a cavalry corps,*
some infantry, some, again,
will maintain that the swift oars

"of our fleet are the finest
sight on dark earth; but I say
that whatever one loves, is."

Answer (A): From Emily Dickinson's "Pain Has the Element of Blank", in *Selected Poems and Letters of Emily Dickinson*. Dickinson (1830-1886) was an American poet who helped to create the New England ethic of poetry.

Answer (B): From Stephen Crane, "I Saw a Man Pursuing," *Poems of Stephen Crane*. Crane (1871-1900), was an American poet and novelist, most famous for his novel, *The Red Badge of Courage*.

Answer (C): CORRECT! From *Sappho*.

Sappho (sixth century B.C.), the Greek lyric poet whom Plato called the "Tenth Muse," lived in Mytilene on the island of Lesbos. Although she is the subject of numerous legends, little is known about her life. She was said to have been small, dark in appearance, and not beautiful. Born of an aristocratic family, she had three brothers. By her husband Cercolas, she had a daughter, Cleis. Sappho was probably the leader of a group, or school, of women dedicated to the worship of Aphrodite. Sappho's relationship with her students has been compared to that of Socrates to his disciples, and her poetry certainly provides evidence of her intense feelings toward women.

Only fragments of her poems survive. According to ancient critics, she wrote nine books. A seven-stanza invocation to Aphrodite is the only poem intact today. Sappho composed in her own dialect, Aeolic. She may or may not have written her poems down. Most likely she sang or recited them to the accompaniment of a lyre.

There is a legend that Sappho fell in love with Phaon, a young boy, and committed suicide by jumping from a cliff. It is probably no more than legend.

Sappho's poems, which are personal, intense, and passionate, are wonderful examples of pure love lyrics, characterized by simple, beautifully articulated stanzas. Her work influenced many later poets.

9. BUDDHA

Soft. Hot. Moist. Her passionate kisses fall onto his eyes, his cheeks, his lips. Down his neck to his broad, bare chest. Her lips and quivering tongue caress him with desire, with raw, naked lust. Her hands begin moving slowly down his chest to his hard stomach, as her soft silken body touches his while together they sit, leaning against the pipal tree. With one hand, she removes her garment, revealing the wonders of her body. With the other hand, she feels him grow hard and large.

Mara now expertly straddles him and slowly, deliciously lowers herself upon him until he is deep inside her. She sits astride him, looking longingly into his eyes. Her body slowly begins to undulate with pleasure. Up and down, up and down, frantically building until in a burst of climactic ecstasy and relief, she melts into him.

As Mara holds him close she realizes that something is wrong, that this man who has helped her obtain so much pleasure has remained detached throughout, never responding emotionally to her passion. Yet, the last time she had seen him, some six years before, they had loved lustily. They had been filled with pleasure, he taking delight in her skillful lovemaking. "Siddhartha," Mara whispers close to his ear, "what is wrong?"

Siddhartha Gautama, son of a king, a worldly man of luxury, has practiced abstinence from all wordly behavior for six years. It is now 528 B.C. He has been sitting with Mara all night under this tree in Bodh Gaya, while Mara has tried to lure him back to "human life."

The temptation is great. The fact that his body has sexually risen to her pleadings helps him to realize that a discussion and physical battle are parts of the same issue. Mara has stopped talking. Her youthful, ripe body begins to stir once again. Her fresh kisses are awakening his sexual energy, dormant for so long. He feels himself grow within her. His resolve is melting.

Just then, the orange sun rises above the eastern horizon. The eyes of the universe are back upon him. He knows he is saved. Mara feels him go limp inside her. "Siddhartha," she pleads, "is there no way you can respond to me?"

"No way exists for me that involves desire," he responds. "Life is pain caused by desire, which must be destroyed through proper action, through abstinence, through concentration, through resolve. You must try to understand. . . .

(A) "It is obvious that the good of the greatest number cannot be obtained until we know in some sort of what that good must consist. In other words we must know what sort of an animal man is, before we can contrive him maximum happiness, or before we can decide what percentage of that happiness he can have without causing too great a percentage of unhappiness to those about him."

(B) ". . . the man who loves others and is incessantly active on their behalf, is a man who simply seeks to impose his will on others. As long as his love does not depend on his own Solitude—i.e., as long as his love is not completely detached and selfless—it is merely an endeavour at tyranny over others."

(C) "Where there is nothing to grasp there is no more grasping. Where there is an object there is a subject—but not where there is no object. The absence of an object results in the absence of a subject, and not merely in that of grasping. It is thus that there arises the cognition which is homogeneous, without object, indiscriminate and supramundane."

Answer (A):   From Ezra Pound's "The Serious Artist," in *Literary Essays of Ezra Pound*. Pound (1885-1969), best known for his *Cantos*, was one of the most influential poets of this century.

Answer (B):   From Peter Munz's *Relationship and Solitude*. Munz (1922-   ) discusses the relationship between mythology, ethics, and metaphysics.

Answer (C):   CORRECT! From *The Mahayana* in *Buddhist Texts Through the Ages*.

Buddha (563-483 B.C.), founder of Buddhism, was born Gautama Siddhartha, the son of the King of Sakya, a warrior caste in present southern Nepal. On his birth, it was said that he was destined to become either ruler of the world or a great teacher. Siddhartha's father wanted his son to succeed him as ruler and therefore protected him from anything that might inspire him toward religion or teaching. Consequently, his childhood was wrapped in luxury and ease. As a young man he married and had a son.

At twenty-nine Siddhartha began making clandestine excursions in a chariot beyond the shelter of the palace grounds. The sights that met his eyes were his introduction to suffering, and his ultimate destiny.

Siddhartha soon left his wife and son to become a wandering religious man in search of enlightenment. He studied various disciplines along the way, but was afraid that their severe deprivations might destroy him before he attained enlightenment. Finally, one day, he sat down under a pipal tree in Bodh Gaya and, despite many evil temptations, vowed to remain there until he became enlightened. One night, under a full moon, he was enlightened and became Buddha. He was thirty-five years old at the time and spent the next forty-five years of his life teaching others what he had learned.

10. CONFUCIUS

The Chief Judge of Lu sits alone in his simple study. A single hummingbird is feeding from the fragrant flowers on the tree outside his window. The streets are quiet. Indeed, since he assumed his post, there have been no crimes, no cases to be judged.

The judge ponders his ideas of social order and begins to write. His system of mortality will, he hopes, engender a stable, orderly society. He sees human beings as social creatures, bound together by the principle of *jen* (humanity, sympathy). His *jen* is expressed in five relationships: a ruler to his subjects, a parent to a child, an older brother to a younger brother, a husband to a wife, a friend to a friend. The relationships can operate in society only through strict adherence to *li*, a combination of etiquette and ritual.

Many think that Confucius is a mystic, a magician, or a consultant to kings. Few realize that he considers himself to be the transmitter of ancient wisdom in light of the present world. This morning he is studying the doctrines of Yao, Shun, and Yu—the Sheng, the Divine Sages. He feels that he is standing at the edge between the great past and the uncertain future. China, in the fifth century B.C., is wracked with internal strife. The leaders are helpless to cope with the situation. The spiritual followers of Taoism are disillusioned with the absence of an understanding, a protocol to take them through the rigors and trivia of daily life. They have turned to Confucius, and through him to the ancient texts, for guiding rules of the day.

A lord of the province is ushered into the study. He walks with an angry stride. Behind him follows a small, trembling man.

"Chief Judge," he says, "this man has stolen three stalks of grain from my granary. He says I gave him permission. But I told him he could take only one. Is there no trust left in the world?"

"You are free to go," Confucius says to the small man.

The lord is beside himself with rage. "You have no sense of justice. I expected you to have his hands cut off. At least, you can lecture him about the words of truth and honesty that no longer seem to be spoken."

Confucius looks both men in the eyes and says . . .

(A) *"A gentlemen, when things he does not understand are mentioned, should maintain an attitude of reserve. If language is incorrect, then what is said does not concord with what was meant: and if what is said does not concord with what is meant, what is to be done cannot be effected. If what is to be done cannot be effected, then rites and music will not flourish, then mutilations and lesser punishments will go astray. And if mutilations and lesser punishments go astray, then the people will have nowhere to put hand or foot. Therefore the gentleman uses only such language as is proper for speech and only speaks of what it would be proper to carry into effect. The gentleman, in what he says, leaves nothing to mere chance."*

(B) *". . . as in the case of language, the empirical material is too abundant to be all accepted indiscriminately or to be all used on the same level. Here again, it must be accepted as a fact that the material is the instrument of meaning, not its object. For it to play its part, it must be whittled down. Only a few of its elements are retained—those suitable for the expression of contrasts or forming pairs of opposites."*

(C) *"A free man shall not be fined for a small offence, except in proportion to the measure of his offence; and for a great offence he shall be fined in proportion to the magnitude of the offence, saving his freehold; and of a merchant in the same way, saving his merchandise, and none of the fines shall be imposed except by the oaths of honest men of the neighborhood."*

Answer (A): CORRECT! From the *Analects* of Confucius.

Answer (B): From Claude Levi-Strauss' *The Raw and the Cooked*. Levi-Strauss, the influential twentieth-century anthropologist deals in his work with the science of mythology from a structural perspective rather than using analogues to other cultures.

Answer (C): From "The Magna Carta". The Magna Carta, signed in England in 1215, was one of the first documents giving freedom and rights to common people.

There are few hard facts available about the life of Confucius (551-478 B.C.), one of the most important, influential philosophers in the history of the world. He was born in Lu, a feudal state (modern Shantung province). He was married in his youth and fathered two children, a son and daughter, and perhaps more. When he was twenty-four, his mother died and Confucius went into mourning for the traditional three-year period, removing himself from active life.

At thirty, Confucius began his extremely successful career as a teacher, eventually becoming Minister of Crime and Chief Judge of Lu. It was said that while he held this post there were no crimes or cases to be judged. Rival factions eventually toppled him from his post, and Confucius spent the remainder of his life on the road with several of his disciples, teaching and lecturing. He died at the age of seventy-three.

Confucianism, the system of ethical precepts developed by Confucius for the proper management of society, became one of the best known and most important of all ethical systems. It influenced Chinese life and government into the twentieth century. The sayings and dialogues of Confucius were collected by his disciples in the *Analects*. Confucius also compiled the *Six Classics*, some of the earliest known works of Chinese literature.

11. HERACLITUS

"Each pair of opposites forms a unity and a plurality. All opposites join in a variety of interconnections." The odor coming from the speaker is overwhelming. One student faints. On this day in Ephesus, in 500 B.C., Heraclitus has dared his followers to gather around him as he buries himself in cow dung. "Men are worth less than shit," he proclaims. This event is but one of the many provocative ways in which Heraclitus dramatizes his ideas.

Heraclitus the Obscure, as he is called, revels in the contradiction that his students will listen to him despite the nauseating stench. His is a world of opposites. He believes in the power of riddles to free the mind of the puzzler. "Each pair of opposites forms a unity and a plurality," he repeats as he extricates himself from the dung heap. "All opposites join in a variety of interconnections." Heraclitus laughs to himself as he walks to the baths. Separate and together, the tensions between things fascinate him.

"All is change," he mumbles to the students walking at his side. They do not notice the shocked, disgusted stares of the passing crowd. "The hidden connection in things is the important one. The unimportant connection is the one which we all assume—like me and shit, for example." No one laughs but Heraclitus.

Hecktor, one of the young men at his side, has begun to question his apprenticeship to this strange, erratic man. Indeed, a rumor that members of the establishment plotted Heraclitus' death because of his riddles has caused several followers to depart. "Why must you always talk in riddles?" he implores, knowing that to wait for an answer is to hear another riddle, another aphorism. "Don't you realize that they call you a river of misery and stupidity?"

"You cannot step into the same river twice," Heraclitus answers, grinning at him. Hecktor does not understand and continues questioning him until they arrive at the baths. At this point Heraclitus holds up a dung-coated hand and says, "Let me say two things before I bathe. . . .

(A) "Scattered petals lie
    on the rice waters:
        Stars in the moonlit sky.

"Night that ends so soon:
    in the shallows still remains
        one sliver of the moon."

(B) ". . . the whole system of the world is built on a lie. And although it's as plain as the shining sun, the don't-knows have lived with that lie so long they just can't see it.
    "By dignity. By becoming hard and strong. We must build strength for our real true purpose."

(C) "If one does not expect the unexpected, one will not find it out, since it is not to be searched out, and difficult to encompass.
    "I search out myself."

Answer (A): Two Japanese haiku from *Anthology of Japanese Literature*, edited by Donald Keene. A haiku is a Japanese verse form of seventeen syllables.

Answer (B): From Carson McCullers' *The Heart Is a Lonely Hunter*. McCullers (1917-1967) was an American novelist and short-story writer whose works dealt mainly with the American South.

Answer (C): CORRECT! From fragments attributed to Heraclitus.

Heraclitus (540-475 B.C.), Greek philosopher and mystic, was born in Ephesus of a noble family. He inherited the office of Basileus but passed it on to his brother. He was known as Heraclitus the Obscure because of his style of speaking in aphorisms and riddles. In general, he was thoroughly contemptuous of his fellow citizens and said so.

Heraclitus was famous in his own time for his belief that everything is in a perpetual state of flux. The only reality is the reality of change; permanence is an illusion. More important was his theory of the unity of One (reality), which, he stated, was made possible through the conflict or strife between opposites (expressed on the human level in warfare). All things contain their opposites; life and death, being and not being are in all things. Therefore, the only permanent state is the state of transition from one opposite to the other, or "becoming." Heraclitus believed that fire was the primordial element and essence of reality.

12. SOPHOCLES

The old playwright sits on the cold stones, far above the players who rehearse his new work on the stage below. A few miles away, the crumbling city of Athens is a reminder to him of his own frail, aching body. The city holds a tenuous future for him.

The year is 460 B.C. Sophocles is a famous poet. He has increased the theatrical excitement begun by Aeschylus, whose innovation was to employ two actors, rather than one, in his plays. It is a period in which artists are greatly respected, and Sophocles is revered as one of the great artists of his time. Yet, he is disturbed. His mind has formed insights about the nature of success and expression. He remembers the classic myths in which the hero is undone, not by outside forces, but by his own faults of character. He believes those faults are both cultural and self-generated. His heart sinks at his awareness that the world he appreciates so much is doomed to fade away.

Watching the actors, Sophocles ponders the myth of Oedipus. He has been searching for a way to use Oedipus' life as an example to humanity of the agony of self-knowledge and self-expression. Slowly, it becomes clear to him. The pieces finally come together. He stands erect, raising his hands to his mouth, and shouts for silence. The startled actors stop rehearsing and look up to the top of the stands in the amphitheatre where Sophocles speaks. . . .

(A) *"If a man walks with haughtiness
of hand or word and gives no heed
to Justice and the shrines of Gods
despises—may an evil doom
smite him for his ill-starred pride
    of heart!
If he reaps gains without justice
and will not hold from impiety
and his fingers itch for
    untouchable things.
When such things are done, what man
    shall contrive
to shield his soul from the shafts
    of God?
When such deeds are held in honor,
why should I honor the Gods in the
    dance."*

(B) *"To see that beyond this dream there
    is another,
one has only to open one's eyes for
    a moment. Every child
knows that the void beyond life is
    peopled with figures.
The darkness that hems us about is
    only our dullness.
If we stretch a hand through this
    darkness a thousand
hands stretch forth in answer.
    Already one has grasped mine
in trust and friendship.
    Why should I let go?"*

(C)   *"Airy dreams*
    Sat for the picture. And the poet's
       hand
  Imparting substance to an empty shade,
    Imposed a gay delirium for a truth.
  Grant it. I still must envy them an
     age
  That favored such a dream, in days
    like these
    Impossible, when virtue is so
     scarce."

(Answer (A):   CORRECT! From Sophocles' *Oedipus the King.*

Answer (B):   From Jean Giraudoux's *The Enchanted.* Giraudoux (1882-1944) wrote plays that often stressed the messages of the gospels.

Answer (C):   From William Cowper's "The Task." Cowper (1731-1800) was an English poet who developed a style which served as a transition from the metaphysical poets to the romantics.

Sophocles (496-406 B.C.), Greek playwright, was born in Colonus, a village near Athens. Sophillus, his father, was a wealthy man who provided his son with an excellent education. Sophocles rewarded him by blossoming into a handsome, charming, and extremely talented youth. He was a skillful dancer and had such a beautiful singing voice that he was selected to lead a boys' choir in celebration after the naval victory over the Persians at Salamis.

Sophocles was an important citizen in Athens and took an active part in the life of the city. He served as general, priest, and treasurer. His career as a popular dramatist began early. In 468 B.C., he was awarded first prize for drama in a competition with Aeschylus, his older contemporary, and he went on to win again and again, at least twenty times in all. It is believed that he wrote a total of 123 plays, of which, although there are hundreds of fragments, only seven exist complete: *Ajax, Antigone, Oedipus Rex, Trachiniae, Electra, Philoctetes,* and *Oedipus at Colonus.*

After having been a part of the full brilliance of Athens, Sophocles was greatly embittered by the decline of the empire, which finally collapsed two years after his death.

The plays of Sophocles set new standards by which later tragedies have been judged. He made several innovations in the traditional form of Greek drama: he added a third character, he enlarged the chorus, he utilized painted scenery, and he was the first playwright to compose a self-contained play, rather than a trilogy.

13. PLATO

Plato strolls through the Academy in Athens. The year is 383 B.C. His Academy is the center of Greek thought. As he walks, the brilliant afternoon sunlight sparkles on the golden hair of the beautiful youth at his side. Plato is reminded of the day when he, as a lad, walked at the side of his own mentor, the great Socrates.

The boy wants to engage Plato in a dialogue about ideas and reality, being and becoming, the need for concepts and ideals which do not disregard actuality.

"Reality," the boy begins, "is concrete and hard like the rocks beneath our feet. The words for real things are learned and then compared to the things themselves, as the mind becomes trained to work in the world."

"No!" screams Plato. He stares at the boy with wide incredulous eyes. His face is red with the fury the boy has learned to dread. "This is not what you have learned from me!" he shouts. "You know that ideas and things are different. Ideas are the perfection of things. Physical things are beneath the purity of ideas. The goal of thought is to separate and purify the realm of the mind, to keep it distinct from the impurity of the physical world." They walk on. Plato is silent and dark with anger.

Late that night, softened by the tenderness of the boy, Plato whispers, "Listen, so you may tell others how Plato describes reality. . . ."

(A) *"He recognized that the heavens and all the stars contained therein were bodies, because they are extended according to the three dimensions, length, breadth, and thickness. He asked himself if their extension was infinite or bounded. He had grave doubts about any answer and so made himself a part of the world and not above it."*

(B) *"The calendar in the sky seemed to stand insistently out of the haze, yellow like a page of old parchment. No answers to things exist unless they are named."*

(C) *"He has lived in a cave all his life. He had never seen the outside world, nor had he seen the mouth of the cave. He only knew of the outside world from the shadows of passing men and animals, shadows that passed by on a sunlit wall inside the cave. He never saw the men or animals, but only experienced and learned about them from their shadows. His, and our, reality is a relative reality. Perfection of reality itself occurs only in the realm of the ideal."*

Answer (A):   From Ibn Tufayl's *Alone on a Desert Island*. Tufayl, born near Granada in the early twelfth century, was a physician and metaphysician in the Muslim world.

Answer (B):   From Ayn Rand's *Atlas Shrugged*. Rand (1905-   ), is an objectivist philosopher concerned with notions of reality that confront an individual desiring unlimited power.

Answer (C):   CORRECT! From Plato's *The Republic*, Book I.

Plato (427-347 B.C.), Greek philosopher, was born in Athens. His family was rich and aristocratic. Because his father died when he was quite young, Plato was raised in the home of his stepfather.

At the age of twenty Plato became the student of Socrates. It was expected that he would enter politics, as was customary for young men of his background. However, the death of Socrates at the hands of the Democrats turned Plato away from that endeavor.

In 388 he founded his Academy. Similar to today's Western university, it offered courses in mathematics, astronomy, physical sciences, and philosophy. Plato was director of the Academy as well as its leading lecturer. Aristotle was his most famous student.

Plato's writings constitute one of the most influential bodies of work in the history of the human race. His attempt to understand and describe experience and thought have served as the basis for almost every system of mathematics and philosophy, either in support or contradiction of his ideas. Plato uses the dialogue as the format for presenting his thought, a form that conveys not only his ideas but also the spirit in which they were conceived.

14. ARISTOTLE

"But what is unity, then?" the students ask Aristotle as they sit in the gardens of the Lyceum in 323 B.C. Aristotle has founded the Lyceum as a place to develop and enhance understanding. In 35 B.C., he returned to Athens after serving as the tutor to Alexander the Great. His own work in anatomy, biology, physics, and philosophy is already considered by his peers to be of major importance in the direction of classifying natural phenomena.

"We are not so interested in unity," Aristotle responds, "as we are in its parts and in its causes. The whole is an idea which can be likened to all the stars. We can see them all, but can only look at a few at a time." A scribe writes down every word. Aristotle has little time to write himself. His concern is to translate and transmit information—and to ask, to question further.

"We know in three ways," he continues, "theoretically, productively, and practically, through signs and symbols. The first way is metaphysics, the second sense experience of motion, the third, ethics. Our knowledge is used to gain understanding, to promote happiness and the true good. By erecting contradictions and tensions between things we learn of them. It is only through the efforts of the Prime Mover that anything can be known at all."

Aristotle is interrupted as a courier races into the garden. Gasping for breath, he tells Aristotle that Alexander the Great is dead. An ominous silence falls over the students. Knowledge is for them both exciting and dangerous. They all remember the fate of Socrates in his quest for knowledge. Without Alexander, Aristotle is in danger from leaders of the anti-Macedonian movement. The students fear for his life. Aristotle, sensing their mood, asks, "What do you believe is the purpose of man?" Hearing no response, Aristotle begins to answer his own question. . . .

(A) *"Man's need to believe that he is prompted by human and constructive impulses is so great that it always makes him disguise (to himself and others) his most immoral and irrational impulses, making them appear as though they were noble and good."*

(B) *"Man is the source of his actions; deliberation is concerned with things attainable by human action; and actions aim at ends other than themselves. For we cannot deliberate about ends but about the means by which ends can be obtained."*

(C) *"I don't fear man. I do better. I respect and admire him. And pride: I am ten times prouder of that immortality which he does possess than ever he of that heavenly one of his delusion."*

Answer (A): From Erich Fromm's *Man May Prevail*. Fromm (1900-   ), the noted psychoanalyst and the author of *The Art of Loving*, among other works, analyzes foreign policy in this book.

Answer (B): CORRECT! From Aristotle's *Nicomachean Ethics*.

Answer (C): From William Faulkner's *A Fable*. Faulkner (1897-1962), a major American literary figure, received the Nobel Prize for literature in 1950.

Aristotle, (384-322 B.C.), Greek philosopher and one of the giant figures in the human struggle to bring order to the world, was born in Stageira, the son of Nicomachus, a physician. After his father's death, he was raised by a guardian who sent him, at the age of seventeen, to Athens to study with Plato in his Academy. After the death of his mentor (347 B.C.), Aristotle left Athens and traveled to several Greek cities, stopping in each one to establish a school.

In 343-342 B.C. he became tutor to the thirteen-year-old Alexander the Great. Three years later he left the Macedonian court and returned briefly to his birthplace before moving to Athens. Here, he spent the next twelve years of his life, lecturing, writing, and teaching in the Lyceum. In 323 B.C., upon the death of Alexander the Great, with whom he had been associated, Aristotle was forced to leave Athens to escape the anti-Macedonian movement in the city. He fled to Chalcis where he died at the age of sixty-two.

Aristotle was active in almost every discipline of human learning. Only fragments of his earlier works are still extant, but there remains a substantial body of his later writings, summaries of lectures he delivered on various topics. Some of Aristotle's best-known works are *Organum*, *Metaphysics*, *On the Heavens*, *History of Animals*, *On Parts of Animals*, *On the Soul*, *Politics*, *Nicomachean Ethics*, *Rhetorics*, and *Poetics*.

One of the major differences between Aristotle and his teacher Plato is that whereas Plato was concerned with the unity and interdependence of human knowledge, Aristotle searched for what distinguished one branch of knowledge from another.

15. MENCIUS

The lazy, elegant students gather in the large room to meet their new tutor. Mencius, the famed Confucian philosopher, has come to train them to become leaders of China during this difficult period. China, in the fourth century B.C., has been wracked by wars caused by cruel and insensitive government leaders. Mencius believes that his lectures to the sons of noblemen will result in a higher level of leadership, thus improving conditions in the future.

The smell of perfume is in the air as Mencius, plainly dressed, walks into the room. He is struck by the fine silks, the jewels of the young men. They, in turn, are impressed by the strength and composure of this man. He appears to have great integrity.

Mencius sits on a low stool and begins to talk: "You must begin to learn not what to do but what not to do." A student raises his hand to speak. Mencius ignores him and goes on. "You must look at yourselves as the basis for the mistakes you see in others."

One of the students gets up to take off his cloak. Mencius yells at him to sit and be quiet. The young man looks at him in disbelief. No one has ever spoken to him in this tone of voice. He is angry and shouts that Mencius is an old fool. "You don't even have a single jade ring!" he cries. "What does humanity, justice, propriety, and wisdom," Mencius replies, "have to do with jade rings?" The young man is silent.

Another student asks Mencius the meaning of his words. Because the student explains that he has never heard anyone speak of such things before, Mencius is wary that the boy is teasing him. He looks across the room at the other boys and realizes that these concepts are totally foreign to them.

Mencius is silent while he composes his reply. He wants to be direct and inspiring to these future leaders. The young men wait in earnest for understanding of the new ideas which seem to be very important to this man who has quickly earned their respect. Mencius answers . . .

(A) "I define myself in terms of you: I know myself only in terms of what is 'other' no matter whether I see the 'other' as below or above me. There is no meaning to words except in the way in which we relate to one another."

(B) "A mental image is not a model. A mental image of a blue sky is not a model. A great deal is required of a mental image to become a model. And does it make sense at all to talk about mental images as models?"

(C) "If one can recognize suffering, feel shame, defer to other's wishes and know the difference between right and wrong, one has a chance at becoming more than one is. Words are the edge not the middle."

Answer (A): From Alan Watts' *The Book.* Watts (1915-1973), a contemporary master of philosophy, offers a synthesis of Eastern thought in this work.

Answer (B): From Henryk Skolimowski's *The Twilight of Physical Description.* Skolimowski is a contemporary systems planner who writes about systems and approaches to world planning.

Answer (C): CORRECT! From *The Book of Mencius.*

Mencius (372-289 B.C.), Confucian philosopher and contemporary of Plato and the Chinese mystic Chuang-tzu, was born in the feudal state of Ch'ao (present-day Shantung province). After the death of his father, he was raised by his mother. He belonged to the governing class and spent the major part of his life traveling from one feudal court to another, teaching his doctrines and those of Confucius as a remedy for the disintegrating condition of society.

According to a well-known story about the childhood of Mencius, he lived with his mother near a cemetery and would play on the graves. His mother, who disapproved of this, moved herself and her son to a house near the market. Mencius, in turn, pretended he was a merchant. This also displeased his mother, so they moved again, this time to a house near a school. Here Mencius teased the students and mocked the ceremonies of court life. His mother was pleased.

After she died, Mencius mourned for three years. (She later became the symbol of maternal devotion in Chinese folklore.) Late in his life, he went into seclusion to devote all his energy to perfecting and refining his philosophy. The *Book of Mencius* (one of the *Shih shu,* or four books) is the only text of his works. His philosophy is considered second only to Confucius'.

Mencius believed that human beings are naturally good but are corrupted by their environment. Therefore, he felt it to be the essential obligation of rulers to provide for the welfare of their subjects. If they fail to do so and their subjects become corrupt, Mencius taught, they should be deposed.

16. CHUANG-TZU

The old man sits on the green bank of a river in southern China. Fish swim in clear waters. The air is fresh. Clouds drift by in the blue sky. Chuang-tzu is pondering the notion of usefulness. He is a mystic, a philosopher, a master of Taoism. The year is 290 B.C.

Chuang-tzu's purpose in life is purposelessness. The edges of his experiences are clear and invisible. He sees beauty and ugliness but never makes a distinction except to explain the absence of distinction.

A man approaches seeking advice. He bows before speaking. "Chuang-tzu," says the man, "I have worked, loved, and fathered many children. Yet nothing gives my life meaning. I do not know who I am."

The man pauses. Chuang-tzu's expression has not changed as he continues to gaze at the fish in the river. "Chuang-tzu," pleads the man, "can you help me?"

Chuang-tzu thinks to himself, "I do not recognize this question since it suggests that a human being has a meaning. Words are like traps: once you have captured the quarry, you can forget the trap." He looks up at the man . . .

(A) *After a moment of silence, he answers: "Anyone can try to become a man of knowledge; very few actually succeed, but that is only natural." The man listens. He proceeds: "The enemies a man encounters on the path of learning to become a man of knowledge are truly formidable. Most men succumb to them."*

(B) *"What ordinary people do and what they find happiness in—I don't know whether such happiness is in the end really happiness or not. I look at what ordinary people find happiness in, what they all make a mad dash for, racing around as though they couldn't stop—they all say they're happy with it. I'm not happy with it and I'm not unhappy with it. In the end is there really happiness or isn't there?*

"I take inaction to be true happiness, but ordinary people think it is a bitter thing. I say: perfect happiness knows no happiness, perfect praise knows no praise. The world can't decide what is right and what is wrong. And yet inaction can decide this. Perfect happiness, keeping alive—only inaction gets you close to this!"

(C) *He picks up a stone and throws it into the river. He speaks. "Set not thy heart on the pleasures of sense that thou mayest not for all thy heedlessness have to swallow the iron ball (in hell) and that thou mayest not cry out in the midst of fire, 'This is pain.'"*

Answer (A): From Carlos Castaneda's *The Teachings of Don Juan: A Yaqui Way of Knowledge.* Castaneda (1931-   ) is a philosopher and novelist who explores nonordinary states of consciousness.

Answer (B): CORRECT! From *The Complete Works of Chuang Tzu.*

Answer (C): From the *Dhammapada (Path of Virtue),* an ancient, basic text of Buddhist law and religion.

Chuang-tzu (c. 369-289 B.C.), founder, along with his predecessor Lao-tzu, of Taoism, was born in the southern state of Meng in ancient China.

It is known that he served as a petty officer in his native state, and that he refused the position of prime minister offered him by King Wei because the job would have prevented him from living as he was naturally inclined: Chuang-tzu lived a hermit's life, separate from and indifferent to society.

He was not interested in protecting or changing the world around him, which he saw as artificial, but in achieving a transcendental state that would allow him to live in harmony with nature, having literally forgotten the fact of his own existence.

The collection of his writings, called the *Chuang Tze,* contains thirty-three chapters of his work. Witty, imaginative, profound, it is considered one of the most important philosophical works ever written.

17. BHAGAVAD-GITA

A youthful writer sits cross-legged on the floor of his hut. The thatched roof shelters him from the Indian rains. It is the first century B.C. He has been reading and studying for many years. His writing reaches out to embrace and synthesize the cultural and religious ideas that surround him.

His work, which later generations will call The *Bhagavad-Gita*, is destined to become a foundation of the Hindu religion and the favorite bible of the Indian people.

His concerns include the essence of culture, the finiteness of energy, the idea that truth is the limit of the universe and that the universe is forever. He believes that discipline, not action and thought, create the proper attitude for conducting one's life.

The writer wants to be free from opposites, free from possessions, fixed in goodness. He practices self-control, lest he fall under the control of others. He wonders if he can express the essence of religion in a few lyrical sentences.

"Abandon yourself," he writes, "and find the mystery of the universe within and through your abandoned self." He pauses to glance out the doorway at the rain-soaked fields, then continues. "Overcome conditions of birth through your behavior. Devote yourself to God." The rain ceaselessly paints a pattern of sound on the roof.

He is disturbed because these words are not a clear guide to all human activities. Late that night, after writing for many hours, he bends over his scroll and begins to inscribe the words that he hopes will become the guide to thought and action for all. . . .

(A) *"History is not a line but a dial. If you stand at the center of the dial and face toward six o'clock you have to turn your back on midnight. At midnight is music and spirituality. As the hands sweep around it is growing later and later and once again we find ourselves looking out and opposite from the dark of midnight."*

(B) *"To whom praise and blame are equal, restrained in speech,*
Content with anything that comes,
Having no home, of steadfast mind,
Full of devotion, that man is dear to me."

(C) *"Yet not so much predictions from without, as verifications of the foregoing things within. For with little external to constrain us, the innermost necessities in our being, these still drive us on."*

Answer (A): From William Irwin Thompson's *At the Edge of History.* Thompson (1938-   ) is an essayist who writes concerning the transformations of contemporary culture.

Answer (B): CORRECT! From *Bhagavad-Gita.*

Answer (C): From Herman Melville's *Moby Dick.* Among American writers, Melville (1819-1891) is considered the major allegorical novelist of the nineteenth century.

The *Bhagavad-Gita,* a Sanskrit poem which is part of the epic *Mahabharata,* is one of the great classics of Hinduism. It is presumed to have been written in the second century B.C. by an unknown poet, and its present form is thought to be the result of its development and change at the hands of a variety of writers over the course of its history.

The *Gita,* which means song, is in the form of a dialogue between Lord Krishna and Prince Arjuna, which takes place the night before the commencement of the great battle of Kurukshetra.

The effect of the *Gita* upon the Hindu religion is inestimable. It is especially notable in that it preaches a respect for authority which, until the time of its composition, had never been a doctrine or principle of Hinduism.

18. VERGIL

Octavius has conquered Antony at Actium. Antony and Cleopatra are dead, suicides. Octavius, now called Augustus, is Emperor of Rome. He is now in a position to aid his close friend, the poet Vergil.

Octavius' patronage and friendship over the years have been greatly appreciated by the poet who first journeyed to Rome in 41 B.C. As tribute, Vergil plans to commemorate the emperor's triumphs, to talk of the bitterness and glory of battle, the irony of life and death, the need for valor, the essence of conflict and resolution. He is experimenting with many forms and techniques in his attempt to capture contemporary Roman history, to create a solid work on which future generations can depend for understanding Augustus and his times.

Vergil is a masterful scholar who is familiar with the ancient works and the ways in which history has been created and recited. Using Homer as a model, he decides to tell Augustus' story by basing it on the adventures of Aeneas during and immediately after the Trojan War. That war allows him to explore the irony and paradox of battle, because, though magnificent, it did nothing to advance civilization, although public belief is much to the contrary. Success and failure in battle, Vergil believes, are tied together by a tangled web that only the words of a poet can unravel.

Vergil presents the plan to the emperor. Augustus is pleased. Work is to commence immediately. As a gift, Vergil presents the emperor with a sample of his work, containing the essence of the enigma of valor and pride, of courage and defeat. . . .

(A) "Crowns may flourish and decay
Beauties shine, but fade away.
Youth may revel, yet it must
Lie down in a bed of dust.
Earthly honors flow and waste
Time alone doth change and last.
Sorrows mingle with contents, prepare
    rest for care
Love only reigns in death: though art
Can find no comfort for a broken
    heart."

(B) "If you wish with your whole hearts
To follow a man who dares all, even
    to death,
Then follow me—you see the state of
    affairs.
Our gods have left us, every one,
    their altars
And shrines are deserted, the prop
    and stay they gave
To our Empire are no more. The city
    you go to succor
Is a blazing shambles—come then,
    let us die!
Let us charge into the thick of
    things—the defeated
Have but one hope of safety, not to
    hope for it!"

(C) "Now by yourselves and thunder
    daunted arms,
But never daunted hate, I you
    implore,
Command, adjure, reinforce your
    fierce alarms:
Kindle, I pray, who never prayed
    before,
Kindle your darts, treble repay
    our harms.
Oh, our short time, too short,
    stands at the door!
Double your rage, if now we
    do not ply
We lone in hell, without due
    company,
And worse, without desert,
    without reverence shall lie."

Answer (A):   From John Ford's *The Broken Heart*. Ford (c. 1586-1640) was one of the most successful Tudor playwrights.

Answer (B):   CORRECT! From Vergil's *Aeneid*.

Answer (C):   From Phineas Fletcher's "Apollonists." Fletcher (1582-1650) wrote this epic poem in an attempt to revive the Greek and Roman epic form.

Vergil (full name Publius Vergilius Maro, 70-19 B.C.) was born in the Roman province of Cisalpine Gaul, the son of a yeoman farmer. Vergil is thought to have begun his formal education at twelve years of age, studying in Milan, Naples, and Rome before returning to his father's farm where he spent the next decade working and writing poetry.

In the early part of Vergil's life, Rome suffered through much civil strife and discord, the outcome of which was Caesar's assassination in 44 B.C. and the triumph of Augustus Caesar, the first Roman emperor.

After arriving in Rome in 41 B.C., Vergil became a member of a literary circle sponsored by Augustus Caesar and Maecenas. By 30 B.C. Vergil had completed two volumes of poetry, *Ecologues* (37 B.C.) and *Georgics* (30 B.C.), both dealing with pastoral themes.

The *Aeneid*, one of the great epic poems in world literature, occupied Vergil for the rest of his life and was still not completed to his satisfaction when he died in 19 B.C. Vergil instructed that it be burned, but by the intervention of Emperor Augustus, the poem was preserved intact and protected from the finishing touches of other poets of the time. The *Aeneid* is composed of twelve books. It tells the story of Aeneas who, after the fall of Troy, spends years wandering around the world and Hades before landing in Italy, where he sets up what was to become the Roman state.

19. JESUS CHRIST

The twelve men who sit at the supper table are in a serious mood. The political climate has been changing. Their success in the outlying districts has become a cause for concern among the established leaders here in the Jewish capital, Jerusalem. The dangers in continuing their operations are becoming obvious. The Roman governor of the occupation troops will most certainly side with the establishment, most of whom are appalled at the upstart's popularity with the common citizenry.

As the men eat at the food-laden table, Jesus the Nazarene speaks, addressing himself to their concerns: "We have some great problems. As you know, our ideas go against the beliefs of many people. They are frightened by our stand against vengeance, they do not understand our proposed social program of sharing what one has rather than hoarding."

"That's not all," interrupts Peter the fisherman. "I worry about our image. Jesus, just look at the stories about you. They are becoming difficult to bear, even for me! Walking on water? Bread out of stone? Wine out of water? Virgin birth? The simple country people love it, but what will they say in Jerusalem?"

"So?" replies the thirty-three-year-old rabbi. "What can I do? Are my acts more important and useful as symbols or as facts? Is it better to convey the truth through stories and symbolic messages, or is it better to convey the truth through descriptions of what really happened?" The point Jesus has raised becomes the focus of a bitter discussion, an intense argument. Beyond all the political issues, each man present knows that their leader is really someone directly connected with the people to whom he speaks. His charisma, his incredible personal power, has up to now inspired the masses and brought them this far in their quest. But, at the same time, it has evoked jealousy and anger in Jerusalem.

"One point we are all missing," Jesus says, filling Judas Iscariot's cup with wine and addressing him, "is not how the question of my life is being interpreted, but the irony of how my death will be understood. Consider the following," he continues while sipping his wine. . . .

(A) "In truth, in very truth I tell you, a grain of wheat remains a solitary grain unless it falls into the ground and dies; but if it dies, it bears a rich harvest. The man who loves himself is lost, but he who hates himself in this world will be kept safe for eternal life. If anyone serves me, he must follow me; where I am, my servant will be."

(B) "I am but one man. I am the voice of my people. Whatever their hearts are, that I talk."

(C) "Either they will refuse to believe you, or, if they do believe you, they will blame you, . . . because it was you who brought the matter up. It is certain that not a single man would follow a rebellion of that sort."

Answer (A):   CORRECT! From John 12:24-26.

Answer (B):   Kintpuash, as quoted in Dee Brown's *Bury My Heart at Wounded Knee*. Kintpuash, also known as Captain Jack, was the chief of the Modoc Indians, a northern California tribe.

Answer (C):   From T. H. White's *The Once and Future King*. White (1906-1964), a British novelist, based this work on the Arthurian legend.

According to tradition, Jesus of Nazareth, or Jesus Christ, was born in A.D. 1, although scholars now believe that the date was somewhat earlier, around 4 or 8 B.C. The Bible, specifically the four gospels in the New Testament, is the main source for information about his life. Although the gospel writers differ on several points, certain basic facts above Jesus' life are traditionally accepted.

Jesus was born in Bethlehem and raised in Nazareth. At the age of thirty, he began teaching and preaching throughout Galilee, gaining recognition and attracting numerous followers, among them the men known as the Twelve Apostles. During this time, Jesus is reported to have performed countless miracles. At the age of thirty-three, he made a triumphant entry into Jerusalem, capital of the Roman-occupied Jewish state. His evident popularity seriously disturbed those in power, who searched for a way to eliminate him. Judas Iscariot, one of Jesus's apostles, betrayed him to the religious leaders, who found him guilty of heresy. It was Pontius Pilate, the Roman governor, who imposed sentence, and bowing to popular will, condemned Jesus to be crucified, ostensibly for sedition.

According to the gospels, on the third day after his crucifixion, a tomb was found open and empty, evidence that Jesus had been resurrected and had joined his Father in heaven. Jesus appeared later to the apostles, who continued to propagate his teachings and founded the Christian church.

20. SAINT AUGUSTINE

"It is difficult to be good, to be free from guilt. Those who live sheltered lives, whose existence runs the risk of corruption and evil, can barely know the joys of conversion. We admire most those who have sinned and redeem themselves through action because we know that doing this is the hardest. . . . Coming from an uneventful life it is hard to embrace the goals of religion . . . . and it is harder even to embrace them once one has opened the door to sensual and worldly pleasures."

The young man sits at the side of his mother's bed. She is dying. The year is 386. All night he has talked on and on, baring his troubled soul as his mother looks at him with weak, tired eyes. Augustine is trying to convince himself of the path he should take. He has come to realize the futility of his past behavior, in his dissolute student days in Carthage. His present situation is causing him great distress. Although he has renounced most sinful activities, and even given up his mistress, he still lusts after women. Worse, he cannot control himself. For months he has tried to abstain from sexual pleasures but found it impossible to do so.

"Mother," Augustine says. "I want her so badly." Augustine is talking about his mistress. On the one hand he feels great love and loyalty toward her and the son she has borne him. On the other hand he feels his weakness, his lack of charity and true belief weighing heavily upon him. "I must redeem myself," he says with quiet resolve. His mother does not hear. Her eyes are closed. She is breathing quietly.

Augustine picks up Saint Paul's Epistles, which are lying by his mother's bed, and begins to read. In the words, he realizes that Christ was not only a gifted teacher but a redeemer who would show him God's mercy and grace. This sudden and startling vision swells within Augustine, filling him with the strength he needs to understand and practice his acceptance of God's power and grace.

Many years later in Hippo, Augustine recalls this night, as he writes down a confession of his vision and conversion . . . .

(A) "Wounded by the fatal lances of his own nostalgia, and that of others, he admired the persistence of the spiderwebs on the dead rose bushes, the perseverance of the rye grass, the patience of the air in the radiant February dawn."

(B) "I no longer wished for a better world, because I was thinking of the whole of creation, and in the light of this clearer discernment, I had come to see that though the higher things are better than the lower, the sum of all creation is better than the higher things alone."

(C) "Death, judgement, heaven and hell, was now to be considered in the light of God's need for supermen to negotiate His passage quickly through the heavens, then how much more value might He give to courage than to charity, how much harsh judgement to justice itself if the act to be considered was not expeditious but merely just, yes if speed were of the essence then Hell's Angels were possibly nearer to God than the war against poverty."

Answer (A): From Gabriel Garcia Marquez's *One Hundred Years of Solitude*, a cinematographic novel. Marquez (1928-   ), is an acclaimed South American writer.

Answer (B): CORRECT! From Augustine's *Confessions*.

Answer (C): From Norman Mailer's *Alive on the Moon*. Mailer (1923-   ), an American writer well known for his innovative journalistic style, is most famous for his war novel, *The Naked and the Dead*.

Saint Augustine (354-430), one of the four Latin Fathers, Doctor of the Church, was born in Tagaste, North Africa. His mother, Saint Monica, was a Christian, and his father a heathen.

Augustine went to Carthage to study when he was sixteen and was soon proficient in the art of rhetoric. He journeyed to Rome around 376 to teach the subject. It was here that he fell under the influence of the Manicheans, a religious sect believing in a dualistic conflict between light and dark. Later he went to Milan and met Saint Ambrose, who became an instrumental figure in Augustine's decision to convert to Christianity. Augustine was baptized on Easter in 387.

Returning to Tagaste in 388, Augustine founded a monastic community. In 391 he was selected to be a priest of the Christian church in Hippo. He remained there, eventually becoming bishop. Augustine died in 430, while the Vandals were laying siege upon the town.

Saint Augustine wrote widely on the problems and questions facing the Christian church of his day. He was among the first Christian thinkers to study the intellectual aspects of Christianity. He also introduced and standardized what were to become official teachings of the church. His three major works are his *Confessions* (397-401), in which he condemns his dissolute youth and discusses his conversion; *On the Trinity* (400-416), in which he carefully systematizes Christian doctrine; and *The City of God* (413-426), which is a statement of the relationship that should exist between church and state.

21. MUHAMMAD

Muhammad stands before his followers as they camp outside the besieged walls of Mecca. "If Mecca falls," he cries out to them, "our religion shall finally have a home. Allah is one and with us. Submit to Allah's will and walk with me through the gates of Mecca to proclaim the glory of Allah!"

This preparatory moment is the culmination of the vision that had come to Muhammad many years before in the cave at Mount Hira. After his revelation, he began preaching and was joined by legions of followers who fought with him to establish themselves as supreme over other religions and other cities. Muhammad's goal is to make his religion the dominant one in Arabia, a religion of pure devotion and strict discipline. Muhammad's destiny is to become the Prophet of Islam.

Ali, Muhammad's son-in-law, stands at his side. He is nervous because he knows that Mecca will be the turning point of Muhammad's career. Failure means disaster. Also, he sees the look in Muhammad's eyes, the same glow he remembers seeing in 622, the day of a nearly successful assassination attempt on the life of Muhammad. Ali advises that the attack be canceled, that the band remain in the desert to wander and slowly convert followers.

Muhammad, looking toward the walls of Mecca, shrugs off this advice. He turns to the troops and begins to preach with an enthusiasm he hopes will instill in them the will of Allah. . . .

(A) *"When heaven is rent asunder and gives ear to its Lord and is fitly disposed; when earth is stretched out and casts forth what is in it and voids itself and gives ear to its Lord and is fitly disposed, thou shalt encounter Him. God shall surely admit those who believe and do righteous deeds into gardens underneath which rivers flow."*

(B) *" 'We shall hear from hence when the dogs are loosed.' And with that they heard a commotion and could see a dwarf riding a big sturdy horse, wide nostriled, ground devouring, strong mettled. And in the dwarf's hand was a whip and near the dwarf was a lady on a handsome pale white horse. 'These shall be signs that we gain the threshold and advance with certainty.' "*

(C) *"This striving towards perfection which manifests itself, in spite of the absence of any personal, immediate, and proportional reward, constitutes the secret virtue which assures the continued progress of the world."*

Answer (A): CORRECT! From the *Koran*.

Answer (B): From the *Mabinogion*, one of the finest masterpieces of Celtic genius, written in 1300.

Answer (C): From Georges Sorel's *Reflections of Violence*. Sorel (1847-1922) was a French engineer and socialist thinker.

Muhammad (570-632), Prophet of Islam, was born in Mecca into a family belonging to the tribe that ruled the city. His father died when he was a baby, and he was raised by his uncle. At twenty-four he married Khadija, a rich widow much older than he, and became a successful merchant.

When Muhammad was forty, he had a revelation in a cave at Mount Hira, in which he saw himself commanded by God to become the Arab prophet and preach the true religion to the people, who still worshipped pagan gods. In general, his preachings were received with hostility, and in 622 Muhammad learned of a plot to assassinate him. He fled in the night from Mecca to Medina. This flight, the Hegira, marks the beginning of Islam. In Medina, Muhammad, who thought himself to be the successor to Jesus Christ and the last prophet, established a theocratic state and ruled an empire which grew to vast proportions over the next ten years.

He had many wives and a troublesome harem. He died in the arms of his last wife, Aisha, on June 8, 632.

The *Koran*, the sacred book of Islam, records the revelations of Muhammad during his lifetime as prophet. It is based on a collection originally put together by his secretary, Zaid Ibn Thabit.

22. PLATFORM SUTRA OF THE SIXTH PATRIARCH

The Fifth Patriarch is old and tired. Many years before, he sat in the same Ta-Fan Temple in Shao-Chou and received the Precepts of Formlessness. Now, in the short time he has left, he must devote himself to finding a successor, one whose *dharma*, or essential nature, will allow for sudden enlightenment.

In this pursuit, he has called upon the monks to write mind verses, words which will describe their state of understanding and knowledge of their own minds. While the monks meditate on this task, the head monk, Shen-hsui, walks boldly to the sun-soaked white wall of the chamber and writes the following words:

> The body is the Bodhi tree,
> The mind clear as a mirror,
> We must continually polish it,
> We must not let the dust collect.

The Fifth Patriarch strains to read the words. His eyesight is failing. Hui Neng notices his distress and reads the words into his ear. The Fifth Patriarch is pleased by Shen-hsui's mind verse. He understands that it is written in a way that will communicate with the common people. All the same, he is distressed. Shen-hsui lacks flashing insight, poetic sophistication and illumination. His words do not enlighten, they only explain. "This will not do," he decides.

Hui Neng is also concerned. He instinctively realizes that Shen-hsui's verse is inadequate. He walks to the wall and begins to write two mind verses that will earn him the position of the Sixth Patriarch. . . .

(A) "We are as clouds that veil the midnight
        moon;
How restlessly they speed, and gleam,
        and quiver,
Streaking the darkness radiantly—yet
        soon
Night closes round, and they are lost
        forever."

(B) "Bodhi has no tree
Mirror without stands
The nature of Buddha is clean
How can there be dust?

"The mind is the tree
The body is the mirror
The clear mirror is spotless
How can there be dust?"

(C) "Why did the lamp go out?
I shaded it with my cloak to save
        it from the wind and
that is why the lamp went out.

"Why did the flower fade?
I pressed it to my heart with
        anxious love, that is why the
flower faded."

Answer (A):   From Percy Bysshe Shelley's "Mutability". Shelley (1792-1822) was an English romantic poet.

Answer (B):   CORRECT! From *The Platform Sutra of the Sixth Patriarch*.

Answer (C):   From Rabindranath Tagore's "The Gardener." Tagore (1861-1941), one of India's greatest poets, awarded the Nobel Prize in 1913.

    Legend tells us that a man named Hui Neng (658-713) gave a lecture one day in the Ta-Fan Temple in Shao-Chou. His pupil, Fa-hai, wrote it down. It was this lecture that became known as the *Platform Scripture* (or *Sutra*), and it is one of the earliest known statements of classic Zen Buddhism, or Ch'an Buddhism. The lecture supposedly caused Hui Neng to become the Sixth Patriarch, because in it he far surpassed his rival in his intuitive grasp of the truth of enlightenment.

    Ch'an Buddhism and the *Platform Sutra of the Sixth Patriarch* advocate the abandonment of the study of texts. The emphasis is on concentration and introspection to achieve enlightenment. The text relies on riddles and paradox to shock the mind and awaken the self to more profound questions.

23. MANYŌSHŪ

Otomo Yakomochi sits cross-legged on the rice straw mat, blossoms falling slowly around him. He sips from a cup of hot saké. In the corner, a lovely woman lies a-sleep. The year is 768. Otomo is feeling timeless, remembering the changing limbs of the willow tree. In his mind he hears the fish jump on this early, bright morning.

Otomo, a Japanese court official, has just completed his compilation of the Manyōshū. This anthology now contains 4000 poems collected in twenty books and includes works written as early as the fifth century. Otomo, a poet and member of an old, distinguished family, has contributed 500 poems himself.

Otomo remembers how past generations have turned to the poems of the Manyōshū for sustenance in moments of wistful recollection. "How amazing it is," he thinks, "this continuance of respect for the delicate and evanescent beauty of the human mind in combination with the interplay of nature." He gazes at the woman sleeping in the corner, dreaming of a world no more sensuous than the petals that lie in her hair.

"How extraordinary," he reflects, "that nature and emotions, the culture of princes, the honor of soldiers, even now enter my mind through the words of these 4000 poems, many of which I know by heart. Generations have passed, people have experienced new and different worlds, yet these poems seem to bind all the emotions and feelings and exert the most amazing sense of continuity of living. Is this because the poets are the most ingenious of all time, or because their words constantly affected the next generation and instilled a respect that would not be there without the poems?" The poems, Otomo realizes, are not insights into understanding, but boundaries to these insights.

The morning wind begins to chill Otomo's body. The mat becomes uncomfortable beneath his skin. He takes up the collection of poems and lets the pages fly open. They come to rest at a poem that Otomo recognizes instantly. Once again he feels warm and content as he reads . . .

(A) *"A white gem unknown of men—*
Be it so if no one knows!
Since I myself know its worth
Although no other—
Be it so if no one knows!"

(B) *"In all there is naught empty. Whence,*
then, could aught come to increase it?"

(C) *"Come let us go while we are in our*
prime:
And take the harmless folly of the
time.
We shall grow old apace, and die
Before we know our liberty
Our life is short, and our days run
As fast away as does the sun."

Answer (A): CORRECT! From a poem written by a monk of the Gango-ji Temple, in the *Manyoshu*.

Answer (B): A fragment from Empedocles of Akragas. Empedocles (c. 490-430 B.C.) was a Greek philosopher who flourished in Sicily.

Answer (C): From Robert Herrick's "Corrina's Going a Maying," in his *Hesperides*. Herrick (1591-1674) was a well-respected English poet who achieved greatness with his *carpe diem* ("seize the day") poems.

The *Manyoshu* *(The Book of Myriad Leaves)*, the earliest anthology of Japanese poetry, is noted not only for the quantity of its poems, but also for their exceptional quality and the variety of styles in which they are written. The poets represent every segment of Japanese society, from emperor to peasant. Many are written in the five-line verse known as *tanka*, the main verse form for Japanese poets for the next eight centuries, and still a favorite in Japan. The *Manyoshu* contains superb examples of longer poems as well, evidence of a more sustained literary effort.

24. ARABIAN NIGHTS

King Shahryar sends another exquisite woman to her death. This time he has ordered the woman to be tied to four horses. He laughs as he watches her body pulled apart, limb from limb. The spectacle brings him great relief. This fourteenth-century monarch, the King of Samarkand, has had 500 of his consorts killed in the last few weeks and the pleasure still consumes him. He doesn't know why he wants to kill beautiful women, but the compulsion is always with him. It overwhelms him.

Shahryar is distracted from his meal by a woman, slowly making her way toward him from a corner of the room, winding and slithering on the floor like a snake. Her movements fascinate him. Her femaleness disgusts him. "I will put her to death by having her thrown into a pit of snakes," he thinks, as the woman continues to slip and slide toward his feet.

"Vile creature, what do you want?" the King asks. "Who are you to disgrace a beautiful meal with your evil presence."

"I am Scheherazade, my lord."

"Well, what do you want?"

"I want to tell you stories that will amuse and delight you, entrance and bedevil you, strain and exhaust you."

"Stories! You want to tell me stories. Bah! I know what you want. You want to save your neck. Well, begin! So long as you keep me interested neither you nor any other women will be put to death."

"Thank you, gracious lord," whispers Scheherazade, as she begins to tell him tales of lust and death and war. . . .

(A) *"Nature decimates, weeds out, and slaughters, too! Nature spawns and exterminates millions of creatures every day. A day in the life of the world is just one vast birth and one vast slaughter for the fulfillment of her plans."*

(B) *"If you leave at daybreak*
Silently, lightly, love,
Do not alarm the nightingale.
If you part at dawning
From these arms that hold you dear
That you not be seen in the arms
Of an enviable affair,
Go on woolen tiptoe
Silently, lightly, love
Do not alarm the nightingale."

(C) *"A woman was married to a merchant who was a great traveler. Soon after the marriage, it chanced that he set out for a far country and was absent so long that his wife, from pure ennui, fell in love with a handsome young man, and they loved each other with exceeding fervor. One day the youth quarrelled and fought with another man and was put in jail. When the news came to the merchant's wife, she immediately went to the jail to beseech the magistrate to release her lover. When the magistrate saw the woman, he fell in love with her."*

Answer (A): From Jean Anouilh's *Poor Bitos*. Anouilh (1910-   ) is a French dramatist, concerned with the conflict between the individual and society.

Answer (B): From Lope de Vega's "Si Os Partieredes Al Alba," found in *Poesias Liricas*. Lope de Vega (1562-1635) was one of Spain's most renowned poets and playwrights.

Answer (C): CORRECT! From "The Lady and Her Five Suitors," in *Arabian Nights*.

Arabian Nights, or *The Thousand and One Nights*, is a collection of classic Oriental tales, written in Arabic. Their authorship is anonymous and true origin unknown, although they are thought to have originated in India and Persia in the tenth and eleventh centuries. The philosophy of the stories is essentially Muslim. Most of the tales are set in India. A simple plot device ties the stories together: Queen Scheherazade, in order to prevent her husband, King of Samarkand, from murdering her, tells him a continuing story every night for 1001 nights.

25. AL-GHAZZALI

"Am I wasting my life?" Al-Ghazzali mutters to himself. He paces back and forth in his study. The sun streams through the window, lighting up the faded covers of his scholarly books.

The year is 1091. Al-Ghazzali, who at thirty-three years of age is perhaps the most distinguished professor and theologian in all of Baghdad, is an unhappy man. No longer secure in his ideas concerning the nature of knowledge, no longer comfortable with his academic position or rewarded by his work, he feels imprisoned by the trappings of his life.

"Make it strange," Al-Ghazzali thinks to himself. He has glimpsed the mystical spirit that informs the soul and creates wisdom out of mere knowledge. The skeptical and critical nature of his academic mind has been completely overwhelmed by a new optimism. He suddenly wants to be free, free to wander among the people living the life of an ascetic, free to feel the power of the mystical universe. He decides at that moment to leave the university.

Al-Ghazzali strides from his study. He walks through the courtyard, out the gates of the university, and into the streets of Baghdad. As he walks through the crowds he thinks about writing a new kind of text, one based solely on his own mind, his own experience. He wants to urge a return to the rigorous ethics of Islam and yet include the mystical without disdain. He wants to express his views on individual change, the idea that superficial change is a sign of conquest, not understanding. His text will put his faith into words. It begins to form in his mind. . . .

(A) "In the earthly world I thought it was only an easy prey, this bird, only an easy prey. But now here in hell it has become a gruesome phantombird, pursuing the sinner, honking from its beak of iron, beating its mighty wings, sharpening its claws of copper. It tears at my eyeballs, it rends my flesh. I would cry out, but choking amid the shrieking flames and smoke I can make no sound."

(B) "If we open this door, if we adopt the attitude of abstaining from every truth that the mind of a heretic has apprehended before us, we should be obliged to abstain from much that is true. The educated man does not loathe honey even if he finds it in the surgeon's cupping-glass: he realizes that the cupping-glass does not alter essentially the honey."

(C) "But what if a minister who downgrades the Lord continues to hold his position? And what if the religious who do wrong continue to be in good standing? Then it is time to face the fact that the bad fruits identify the religious organization itself."

Answer (A: From Seami Motokiyo's *Birds of Sorrow*, a Japanese Nō text of the Muromachi period (1300-1600), and one of the strongest plays in the *Uto* (virtue bird) tradition.

Answer (B):   CORRECT! From *The Faith and Practice of Al-Ghazzali*.

Answer (C):   From *The Truth That Leads to Eternal Life*, a text written by the Watch Tower Bible and Tract Society.

Al-Ghazzali, (1058-1111), Islamic theologian, was born in Tus in Persia and raised after his father died by a guardian who saw to it that the boy received a thorough education.

He became a distinguished professor at the University of Baghdad and lectured there for several years. During this time he wrote *The Destruction of the Philosophers*, criticizing philosophical methods and illustrating the contradictions in various metaphysical systems.

In 1095, after a spiritual crisis, he underwent an abrupt conversion to mysticism. He quit the university and spent the next decade wandering, living a solitary life of asceticism and contemplation.

Later he returned to Tus, where he founded a school of Sufism. He taught according to the system he had formulated for the individual's attainment of union with God through mysticism, which he described in *The Revival of the Religious Sciences*.

Al-Ghazzali has been proclaimed the greatest Muslim after Muhammad. His main importance was his success in defending orthodox Islam from Greek influences and reuniting those orthodox teachings with the mystical spirit.

26. SAINT THOMAS AQUINAS

Scratch, scratch, scratch. A man sits in a monastery garden in southern France. It is 1270. He is wearing the rough habit of a monk. In the nearby copying room, several monks are busy transcribing his Latin translation of Aristotle. The noise of their quills is distracting him from his thinking. Scratch, scratch, scratch. Thomas Aquinas is startled by a voice shouting his name from outside the garden wall.

"You are a heretic, Thomas, a heretic!" exclaims an older monk, striding through the gate and into the garden. "You teach the lessons of the godless Averroës and the hated Aristotle who believed in the cause of all as God, but not the God we have come to know and believe. You will be excommunicated and shunned by every true Christian in the world!"

Thomas does not reply. He is not surprised by this outburst, because his is a new, unique theological position. He is a Realist, a Scholastic. He advocates a position that calls for responsibility of the knower; the human mind can detect what to do and what exists. He believes that we know God only by analogy. The old monk, feeling that his criticism of Thomas has satisfied his righteousness, turns on his heels and walks away.

Thomas is noticeably relieved by his departure. Ever since his university days in Paris, he has been tortured by his teachers and peers for his difficulty in speaking. They dubbed him "Dumb Ox." But Thomas has always known that his thinking is pure and respectful of God and that his teachings will enable human beings to function on a fuller, more religious level of being. In time he knows that his work will be accepted.

Later that evening, the old monk returns unexpectedly to see Thomas. "Do you think reason is as strong as faith?" he demands. "Do you believe that through the mind God's truth can be revealed to humans?"

Thomas is slow to respond. He stands up and looks through the open window into the starry night. If he answers "yes," he knows that the answers will need a defense. If he answers "no," he will be denying his thinking and beliefs. He turns to the monk and says . . .

(A) *"Being cannot be understood except because being is intelligible. Yet being can be understood while its intelligibility is not understood. Faith and reason exist as one entity, inseparable and as parts of the total existence of man and God."*

(B) *"A thought limited to existing for itself, independently of the constraints of speech would no longer appear than it would sink into the unconscious, which means it would not really exist."*

(C) *"The main thing is that you and I should exist, and that we should be you and I. Apart from that, let everything go as it likes. I would rather exist even as an impudent argufier, than not exist at all."*

Answer (A):   CORRECT! From Thomas Aquinas' *Summa Theologica*.

Answer (B):   From Maurice Merleau-Ponty's *The Phenomenology of Perception*. Merleau-Ponty (1908-1961), a French philosopher, was primarily concerned with the nature of perception.

Answer (C):   From Denis Diderot's *Rameau's Nephew*. Diderot (1713-1784), the French philosopher and encyclopedist, wrote this important philosophical work in 1761.

Saint Thomas Aquinas (1225-1274) was an Italian philosopher and theologian whose teachings were declared by Pope Leo XIII in 1879 to be the official teachings of the Roman Catholic Church. He was known as the Angelic Doctor.

Born in a castle in Roccasecca, near Naples, Thomas was placed in the Benedictine Abbey of Monte Cassino at the age of five, where he studied until 1239. At fourteen he went to the University of Naples and in 1244 joined the Order of Dominican Friars.

He received his license to teach the faculty of theology at the University of Paris, became a magister, and lectured as a Dominican professor. In 1259 he went to Italy to teach and act as adviser at the papal court.

The rest of his life was spent in Italy, except for a short period when he was called to Paris to defend the Dominicans against accusations from authorities at the university. Thomas successfully defended the Dominicans, proving that the doctrine of Averroës was a misinterpretation of Aristotelian philosophy. In 1272 Thomas returned to Naples where he founded a Dominican house of studies.

In 1274 Thomas was summoned to the Council of Lyon by Pope Gregory X to act as consultant. On his way there he died in a monastery at Fossanuova. He was forty-nine years old.

27. MEISTER ECKHART

The clarity of his thought is painful to many. Often, after one of his sermons, the parishioners are puzzled and confused. "He asks so much of us," a man says to his teen-age son as they file out of the church after a sermon by the vicar general of Bohemia. The year is 1312. "He demands so much concentration, so much attention to the words."

"But, father," the son replies, "he believes that words are not as important as the truth behind them. You heard him say that he would give up God for truth since truth is more important than God and since God in fact is an idea equal to the idea of truth."

"That's exactly what confuses me," the father continues. "He says all these things in his words, his sermons, and yet he is sympathetic to the mystics and to the men who are devoid of God."

The son, disturbed by his father's thoughts, wanders off on his own. He waits until the congregation has left before walking through the empty church and knocking softly on the giant door of the study. Meister Eckhart bids him enter. He greets the youth warmly, and with a paradox: "Friedrich, it is good to see you, if it is you I see."

"It is me," Friedrich replies, "or your image of me that you see. I come here," he continues, "to ask whether what you feel to be true within you is more important than the subtle things that are attributed to God's grace in the world, such as religion and prayer."

Eckhart pauses and smiles. "Friedrich," he says, "your questions are of real concern to me since they plumb the depths of the problems I have encountered with Rome. My convictions are an expression of God's will and, because I know them so well, I can trust myself knowing that this is the truest expression of love of God."

Friedrich looks searchingly at Meister Eckhart, awaiting some confirmation of these ideas. Eckhart searches his heart and mind for words which will capture religion and inner trust. "Friedrich," he says, leaning toward the boy . . .

(A) *"Only thus does man develop conscience, that dependence on himself which will make him in turn, dependable; and only when thoroughly dependable in a number of fundamental values (justice, truth, love) can he become independent and teach and develop tradition."*

(B) *"I have often said that a person who wishes to begin a good life should be like a man who draws a circle. Let him get in the center in the right place and keep it so and the circumference will be good."*

(C) *"For weeks and months, for years, in fact, all my life I had been looking forward to something happening, some extrinsic event that would alter my life, and now suddenly, inspired by the absolute hopelessness of everything, I felt relieved, as though a great burden had been lifted from my shoulders."*

Answer (A): From Erik Erikson's *Childhood and Society*. Erikson (1902-   ) is a psychologist who has stressed the importance of the development of identity without anxiety.

Answer (B): CORRECT! From *The Sermons* in the *Writings of Meister Eckhardt*.

Answer (C): From Henry Miller's *Tropic of Cancer*. Miller (1891-   ) inaugurated a new era of fiction with his flowing and highly realistic narrative technique.

Meister Eckhart (1260-1327), priest, theologian, and mystic, was born Johannes Eckhart in Hochheim in the province of Gotha in Germany. At the age of fifteen, Eckhart entered a Dominican monastery, spending the next nine years studying for the priesthood. He continued his education at the College of Cologne.

After his studies, Eckhart was appointed prior of Erfurt and vicar of Thuringia. Gradually, he became known for his preaching, and was sent to Paris to preach in 1300. He was given a Licentiate and Masters degree from the College of Paris in 1302, and from then on was called "Meister Eckhart."

Eckhart's success continued. In 1303 he was made provincial of the Dominican Order of Saxony; in 1307 vicar General of Bohemia; and in 1312 superior general for Germany. Eckhart's talent and passion for preaching to anyone and everyone, including the most humble and uneducated, made him appear a suspicious character to many. Soon charges of heresy were leveled against him. He was made a professor at the College of Cologne but shortly thereafter he was officially accused of heresy in connection with the Baghards, an unpopular religious group of men. Eckhart appealed to Rome but was denied in 1327. His best known work is his *Defense*, written to answer the charges. Eckhart died soon after. In 1329 Pope John XXII declared twenty-eight of Eckhart's propositions heretical.

Eckhart was the first important figure to write in the German language, and from his time on German was used in the writing of popular tracts. Eckhart was a mystic, fervently believing that man and God were one and that without God, man was nothing. Eckhart has been called the father of German idealism.

28. DANTE ALIGHIERI

Dante is depressed as he sits amidst the heads and torsos in a sculptor's studio in Florence. The year is 1300, and he is thirty-five years old. "When the real world is horrible," he thinks, "the life of the mind is filled with richness and compassion, with relief and rationality." He ponders the work before him, sculptures that represent single moments in the Bible and in the history of Florence. He is always fascinated by the fact that one can make a model of something by using only metal and clay.

As he stands, his flowing robe accidently brushes against one of the clay figurines, knocking it to the floor where it breaks into hundreds of pieces. Looking at the damage, Dante is overcome by sadness. In his mind's flight he has once again neglected the real world, thus causing destruction.

He rushes from the studio and walks for many hours, unable to resolve his anxiety. Turning a corner, he finds two opposing groups of soldiers, Black and White Guelphs, who are preparing to do battle. Dante runs between them, shouting, "What battle is this? For what cause do you risk your lives?" Angered, both sides threaten Dante, who is forced to retreat as the bloodshed begins. Head down, Dante walks away in despair.

When he arrives home, a servant asks what he wants. "What do I want?" Dante replies. "I want to create a model of the universe which makes sense, which includes love, which rejects false reason and worldliness. The world is a pleasant place yet it is filled with sinners waiting to confess. I must understand the discrepancy in act and reason. I must leave this world of disconnected events and create a model, like a sculpture, which holds the universe and all variation in a pattern of harmony and understanding, drawing from the richness of the Christian belief, drawing from the Father, the Son, and the Holy Ghost, drawing from my own love of music, drawing from my own confusion, and being the example of its own organization and resolution. How will I begin?"

Dante dismisses the servant with explicit orders that he is not to be disturbed. He goes to his study, sits down, and begins to write. . . .

(A) *"Midway in our life's journey, I went astray*
from the straight road and woke to find myself
alone in a dark wood. How shall I say
what wood that was! I never saw so drear,
so rank, so arduous a wilderness!
Its very memory gives shape to fear."

(B) *"I shall place my own hand, moreover the right one which—although at the moment it is slightly injured owing to the misforture which recently befell me—is nevertheless my own, and has never once failed me in my whole life, on my heart, of course also my own—but on the inconstancy or constancy of this part of my whole I do not find it necessary here to expiate—and frankly confess that I myself have personally not the slightest wish to write."*

(C) *"In condensing this memoir to manageable length I have omitted many verified historical incidents but I have left in lies and unlikely stories on the assumption that the lies a man tells tell more truth about him—when analyzed—than does the truth."*

Answer (A):   CORRECT! From Dante's *The Inferno,* Part I of the *Divine Comedy.*

Answer (B):   From G. I. Gurdjieff's *Beelzebub's Tales to His Grandson.* Gurdjieff (1878-1949) was a philosopher and mystic.

Answer (C):   From Robert Heinlein's *Time Enough to Love.* Heinlein (1907-   ) is a popular writer of science fiction.

Dante Alighieri (1265-1321), Italian poet, was born in Florence into a family of some nobility. He was probably educated at church schools and the University of Bologna. In 1289, as a member of the cavalry, he took part in the victorious Battle of Campaldino against the Ghibellines.

He was active in the government in Florence, serving as councilman from 1295 to 1301, as chief magistrate, and as ambassador to San Gimignano and to Rome. During this time the White and Black Guelphs were at war. It was Dante's job to negotiate with the Pope in order to make peace between the two factions. The Black Guelphs eventually took over Florence. In 1302 Dante, a White, was convicted of selling church offices and exiled, his property confiscated.

Dante spent the remainder of his life in the service of various princes, wandering from court to court. He died at Ravenna while serving Lord Guido da Polenta. He is buried there.

While in exile, Dante composed his most famous work, The *Divine Comedy,* which he dedicated to Beatrice, his inspiration. (Dante titled the poem "Commedia"; the "Divina" was added to the title in the sixteenth century.)

The Divine Comedy is an allegorical tale, both religious and political in nature. It is the story of the poet's supernatural journey through Hell, Purgatory, and Heaven. Vergil serves as guide through Hell and Purgatory; Beatrice guides him through Heaven.

29. YOSHIDA KENKŌ

Two men sit on the river's edge in Kyoto. It is late fall in the year 1340. The leaves are falling swiftly in the warm wind. The smell of decay mingled with the odor of ripe fruit and with the light of the sun hitting the water envelops the men. They are discussing the universe. It is, they admit, a big subject, but one which they address each year when they meet by the river.

"You see, when the leaves fall we can see the mountain," Kenkō says. He is an old man, a Buddhist monk, long since retired from his worldly life as a court poet.

"But, we can no longer see the ground," replies Ichinagi. The slightly younger man, dressed in rich attire, is a wealthy merchant from the nearby town and a companion of Kenkō since childhood.

"We see a new ground," Kenkō continues, "made of leaves which are caressed by the air."

"But the air is not something we can consider except in its absence," argues Ichinagi.

"I think of you all year and yet only see you at this time."

"You and the earth are different. The years are measured by the rays of the sun."

"Ah, but it is I who measure the rays."

A silence prevails. The two men are smiling. The wind brings a flurry of leaves that nearly cover their legs and dress their heads.

"These leaves are signs of the past," says Ichinagi.

"No," answers Kenkō, "they are on my hands and head right now."

Silence. Their conversations always reach the point of opinion, of right and wrong. Silence always results. Kenkō feels dissatisfied. He does not want the discussion to end in this way. He wants to characterize his problems with Ichinagi, to reveal why they always remain unsolved. He turns to speak to his old friend. . . .

(A) "Children will be able to predict that if water is run from one vessel into the other, the level will drop in the first and rise in the second but they remain incapable of ordering any thoughts that they themselves have made of this process."

(B) "Emptiness accommodates everything. I wonder if thoughts of all kinds intrude themselves at will on our minds because what we call our minds are vacant? If our minds were occupied, surely so many things would not enter them."

(C) "The idea of God lessens man. These words will not be forgotten for they are both true and timely. Every false or confusing belief ultimately does harm to man and today we are coming to understand this."

Answer (A):   From Jean Piaget's *The Child's Conception of Time*. Piaget (1896-   ) is a leader in the observational analysis of structural behavior in children.

Answer (B):   CORRECT! From Kenkō's *Essays in Idleness*.

Answer (C):   From Lancelot Law Whyte's *The Universe of Experience*. Whyte (1896-1972) is a leading thinker about structure and form in nature as it applies to ideas of philosophy and science.

Essays in Idleness is a book of short essays and notes composed by Yoshida Kenkō, (1283-1350), a Japanese monk. It is one of the classics of Japanese literature.

Kenkō secured himself a place at court as a young man because of his talent as a poet. In 1326 he joined the Buddhist order, but rather than retiring from the worldly life, he remained in the city and participated in many of the court functions, which included meetings of a group of prominent poets. During his last years, he lived at a temple near Kyoto, having become famous both as a poet and an expert in Japanese tradition.

Kenkō's *Essays in Idleness*, unknown to the public during his lifetime, later became a model of Japanese prose and remains today an integral part of the school curriculum. The essays are mainly concerned with Kenkō's interest in and respect for tradition, as well as an examination of the evanescent nature of beauty. Kenkō's influence is widespread, and Japanese literature is filled with allusions to these essays.

30. WILLIAM OF OCCAM

A carriage makes its way slowly through the dark Bavarian forest. Sheltered against the cold of the winter night, the man inside is bundled in blankets. He has no coat. He is a fugitive.

William of Occam is shivering. He is tired, very tired. He is fleeing from detention by the Pope who, four years earlier, in 1324, had ordered him held prisoner for expounding heretical doctrines.

During his trial at Avignon, William insisted on the need to clarify and reduce theological language, to explain the nature of reality but not get trapped in the excessive wordiness of those writers currently in favor with the authorities. He wanted to explain events the way they happened empirically, but carefully leave room in his explanations for reason and faith. Thus, Aristotelian logic would contain the essence of practical religious thought and feeling.

William was cleared of charges brought against him at the trial. Nevertheless, he was detained in France because he was unable to reconcile differences with the Pope. Those long years were not wasted. Riding through the dark, William considers the questions he has been asking himself:

"Can God command man not to obey him?"

"Are being and the object of being the same things?"

"Are logic and the thoughts of the mind real, or as in Plato, signs of things?"

"Can feelings of religion be rationalized?"

The traveling bag at William's side contains a tablet upon which he has been inscribing his philosophy as well as notes for further polemics against the Pope. On the first page are writings particularly inspired with the clarity and elegance of his thinking. . . .

(A) *"Belief I define to be the healthy act of a man's mind. It is a mysterious indescribable process. All vital acts are indescribable. We have our mind given us not that it may cavil and argue, but that it may see into something and give us clear belief and understanding whereon we are then to proceed to act. Doubt truly is not itself a crime."*

(B) *"God is responsible for all things.*
"Man acting or nature acting for God can be replaced by God's direct action.
"God is the cause of all action.
"All God's powers can be described in this way without thinking of more ways to describe them.
"Everything that is described and happens is related to everything else and so proves the power of God."

(C) *"Power is persecution. You have said it. It does not lead to peace. You have lost the road again. But wanting more does not always require power."*

Answer (A):   From Thomas Carlyle's *On Heroes and Hero Worship.* Carlyle (1795-1881), a British historian, delivered this work as a series of lectures in London in 1840.

Answer (B):   CORRECT! From "The Possibility of A Natural Theory" in *William of Occam.*

Answer (C):   From Frank Waters' *The Man Who Killed the Deer,* a text about the American Indian.

William of Occam (1285-1349), English philosopher and Franciscan, was born at either Occam in Surrey or Occam in Yorkshire. He attended Oxford and was a student of Duns Scotus in Paris. In 1324, Occam was accused by the Pope of heresy on the issue of transubstantiation and was summoned to the court at Avignon. He was excommunicated and detained there until 1328, when he managed to escape, fleeing to Munich and the protection of Emperor Louis IV, who was also struggling against the Pope. He remained there, writing political treatises, until he died of the Black Death plague in 1349.

Occam defended the doctrine of nominalism, which holds that abstract words do not stand for anything objective. He is most famous for his "Occam's razor," which states: "It is vain to do with more what can be done with fewer."

31. JEAN BURIDAN

"Would God let man have an evil will?" Jean Buridan asks himself this puzzling question as he sits on the steps of the fourteenth-century French cathedral. He stares out at the dust settling in the streets and wonders if this position about the will is too strong, or perhaps too weak.

Buridan looks up. There is a commotion in the center of the square. A hungry-looking urchin is struggling with an immaculately dressed young prince. Buridan rushes forward and breaks up the fight. Another man, a grocer, comes forward, shouting that he has been robbed. The grocer, now at the center of the crowd, sees the urchin and exclaims, "No, this is my son. The other rascal is the thief." Buridan, and the rest of the crowd, are embarrassed. They let the urchin go and apologize to the father.

As Buridan walks back toward the cathedral, he is overcome by the realization that freedom means not only the ability to reflect and choose alternatives, but finally, to make a choice based on reason. He turns, thinking that he will immediately communicate this idea to the crowd still gathered, but realizes that his thought must be told in simple, common terms or the lesson will be lost to these people.

He walks into the crowd, calls for their attention, and begins. . . .

(A) *"If one is an inept craftsman, then things go better. Big things stop up the hole and will not go in, and small things are slender and do not fill the space around. Such work that is motivated by the heart and sent out to the hands is exceedingly deformed."*

(B) *"Couples are things whole and things not whole, what is drawn together and what is drawn asunder, the harmonious and the discordant. The one is made up of all things, and all things issue from the one."*

(C) *"Two piles of extremely delicious and aromatic grain stood on either side of a donkey. He eyed each of them, weighing the pros and cons of each pile. He did this for several days, then weeks. Finally a farmer walked into the barn and discovered the donkey. He was lying dead of starvation between the two piles of grain."*

Answer (A): From Huai-nana Tzu *Placing Customs on a Par*. Huai-nana Tzu (180-122 B.C.) was a prominent Chinese Taoist.

Answer (B): From the writings of Heraclitus (see selection 11 for further information about Heraclitus).

Answer (C): CORRECT! From "Questions About the Four Books of Earth and Sky" by Jean Buridan.

There are few facts available about the life of Jean Buridan (c. 1295-1356), French scholastic philosopher. He was probably born in Artois. He studied philosophy at the University of Paris, where he later became professor of philosophy and then rector.

A nominalist influenced by William of Occam, Buridan was also associated with the official condemnation of nominalist theories in 1340. He is best known for the parable of "Buridan's ass".

Buridan was responsible for originating and developing some of the essential ideas of modern philosophy and sciences.

32. NŌ DRAMA

All day long, Seami has been watching actors and playwrights working in the small theatre beside the house. He is fascinated by the expression of the words uttered by the actors and with the precise stage directions offered by the playwrights and directors. Seami has grown up in this world. His father, Kanami Kiyotsugu, has been experimenting with this form of theatre since 1365.

In the evening, the family gathers for a meal of fish and rice. Seami's cousin, Ihara, has brought his new bride to dinner. She is a lovely, graceful girl with beaming dark eyes. Although Ihara constantly prods her, she has few words to say.

"Noburu," Ihara says to the girl, "speak to my family about the lovely swans you saw today." Noburu remains silent. She looks at her hands and, as though they were wings, slowly moves them over the plate. Her arms vault over her head as she follows them with her eyes. She smiles and emits a slight shout.

The family is delighted. Her performance is greeted with warm applause. As they sit back to relax and discuss the day's activities, Seami is agitated by an inner excitement. Through Noburu's actions he sees the possibility of developing the new theatre to be an expression of the drama of the soul and the mind which cannot be directed from without but must be nurtured from within.

"I will create a series of plays that evoke the mystery of the self," he thinks. "The way is obviously through simple gestures, postures, and phrases that mesh with the tone of the statement rather than its content. Form reveals essence more clearly than content."

Late that night, Seami writes by candlelight. He remembers Noburu as he composes. He hopes to create classic characters. The beauty, the art, will come in the sensitive and resonant expression of the understanding of these characters by the actors. Within a simple form, the texture of emotions will emerge. "I will write some words," he says to himself, "to capture the excitement created in me by Noburu's movements. . . ."

(A) "One thought consumes me,
The anger of lust denied
Covers me like darkness.
I am become a demon dwelling
In the hell of my dark thoughts,
Stormcloud of my desires."

(B) "Please don't interrupt. It is especially rude to interrupt confessions. You see, I long ago decided that these considerations weren't useful to me, particularly since I could not find the proper answers as to how I got here or what I should be."

(C) "They stood together looking out across the country, down over the apple trees, beyond the road, across the lower fields and the woods of the point to the lake. The wind was blowing straight down the lake."

Answer (A): CORRECT! From Seami Motokiyo's *The Damask Drum*.

Answer (B): From Richard Burgin and J. M. Alonso's *The Man with Missing Parts*. The authors are contemporary writers who have been influenced by the writings of Samuel Beckett and Jorge Luis Borges.

Answer (C): From Ernest Hemingway's "The Three Day Blow." Hemingway (1898-1961) was a leading writer of the impressionist and realist school in this century.

The Nō plays are a form of Japanese drama which developed in the fourteenth century. Kanami Kiyotsugu (1333-1384) and his son, Seami Motokiyo (1363-1443), are credited with their invention, development, and refinement. Although probably thousands of Nō plays were written, only several hundred of them are still performed today.

The Nō plays are short, formal tragedies, with no real plot, and often like puzzles. The cast includes a single main character (the *shite*), a second character (the *waki*), usually a priest, and several attendants, a chorus, and musicians. Only male actors perform the Nō plays. Wooden masks are used by the main character and the women, demons, and old people portrayed in the plays. The stage itself is a platform with a walkway, the setting bare and simple.

A Nō play traditionally presents two aspects of the main character—in the first half, a false aspect, and in the second half, the true one. The pace of the play is slow, the actual text being a few hundred lines which are developed into an hour-length play through the devices of singing, dancing, mime, speech, and music. All the actors are exactly positioned and their movements precisely choreographed.

33. NICHOLAS OF CUSA

The year is 1462. The papal legate in the Holy Roman Empire, dressed in long flowing robes, is enjoying the fragrance of the garden in Todi. Although he serves the Pope, he feels the need to explain and explore new ideas and to say what needs to be said about the mind and about the ideas of God. Even more important to him is the way in which such thoughts must be presented.

Nicholas of Cusa is a brilliant man. Often he has cleared away years of confusion with a single sentence or with diagrams, which are his favorite method of explanation. Today he is to receive a young student who is anxious to discuss Nicholas' ideas.

As the student approaches the garden, he observes Nicholas making geometrical designs and mumbling to himself. "I am preparing a diagram of how God can be seen as the unity, the harmonious synthesis of opposites," he explains to the student. "It is fascinating to think that God is just that much greater and more powerful than we can conceive."

The student, Frederico, studies the drawing, which is a polygon inside a circle. "What does it mean, Cusanus?" he inquires.

"It means that although we can approach God and try to understand him, we will always be like this polygon and never quite get there," he answers.

"This is not theology," Frederico argues. "This is geometry. What does God mean to you, Cusanus?"

"God does not mean anything. He is everything," says Nicholas, drawing his robes about him. "The essence of my belief can be summed up in a few words. . . .

(A) *"God is both the center and the circumference of the world."*

(B) *"God has a plan. He would not suffer the soul of man to die but had prepared a plan for his salvation."*

(C) *"Our likeness and our unlikeness both make it impossible for him to understand what my life is really about. And yet I invite his judgement!"*

Answer (A): CORRECT! From Nicholas of Cusa's *De Docta Ignorantia*.

Answer (B): From James Baldwin's *Go Tell It on the Mountain*. Baldwin (1924-   ) is one of the leading black American writers.

Answer (C): From Christopher Isherwood's *A Meeting by the River*. Isherwood (1904-   ), an English poet, novelist, and playwright, focuses on the themes of homosexuality and Oriental beliefs.

Nicholas of Cusa (1401-1464) German philosopher, was born Nicholas Krebs in Kues on the Moselle River, the son of a fisherman. He studied philosophy in Heidelberg, canon law in Padua, and theology at Cologne. In 1426 he became assistant to Cardinal Orsini, the papal legate to the Holy Roman Empire.

Nicholas participated in the Council of Basel. His *De Concordantia Catholica* set forth his program for the reform of the church and empire. Although he supported the idea that the council had superiority over the Pope, the failure of the council to bring about any church reform caused him to swing his support to the papal cause. At the Pope's bidding, he became involved in several projects to unify and reform the church.

In 1448 Nicholas became a cardinal, and in 1458 he was made Bishop of Brixen. Thereafter, he initiated several widespread reforms of monasteries.

Nicholas of Cusa was important for his highly original achievements in science and philosophy. Nicholas believed (before Copernicus) that the earth revolved around the sun and that stars were other planets. He held that the universe was infinite, boundless, and indeterminate. He anticipated the Gregorian calendar reform. His essays, *De Docta Ignorantia (Of Learned Ignorance*, 1440) and *De Visione Dei (Vision of God*, 1453), set forth his mystical religious philosophy. Nicholas believed that wisdom resides in the knowledge that the mind is limited in its ability to know truth.

34. DESIDERIUS ERASMUS

"Let's start a good religious war," the old man proposes to his young novice. "How can we get good Christians and heathens together to fight an old-time battle for the glory of God, and then have them kill each other off until none is left? This is the real question of our day, the one important issue that you, as a young devotee, must face up to."

Shocked, Lucullus never thought he would hear such cruel and inhuman talk from the sage. True, he knows firsthand of the master's sense of humor and satire, but nonetheless, in the year of 1508, Erasmus is considered the major scholar of northern Europe. "Strange behavior," Lucullus mutters to himself.

They continue their walk along the canals of Venice. "You know," Erasmus says, "we make fun of all our traditions because we love them. If we didn't love at least some of it, we would not bother with such satire. Face it, we're human. All of us are compromised at some point, aren't we?"

Lucullus reacts with anger, and answers bitterly, "Not the ones who have truly absorbed Christ's message and learned to truly love their fellow man."

"But, Lucullus, I am a believer too," answers the master, "but I am one who continues to question. Would you have me believe in the whole of the church and its problems and its forgetfulness? Would you have me be a dogmatist rather than a critic?"

This puzzles Lucullus, and Erasmus can see the confusion in the young man's eyes. "Tell me if this makes sense to you. . . ."

(A) *"The Christian religion on the whole seems to have a kinship with some sort of folly, while it has no alliance whatsoever with wisdom. If you want proofs of the statement, observe first of all how children, old people, women and fools, find pleasure beyond other folk in holy and religious things, and to that end are ever nearest the altars, led solely no doubt by an impulse of nature. Then you will notice that the original founders of religion, admirably laying hold of pure simplicity, were the bitterest foes of literary learning."*

(B) *"The manifestation of the universe as a complex idea unto itself as opposed to being in or outside the true Being of itself is inherently a conceptual nothingness or Nothingness in relation to any abstract form of existing or to exist or having existed in perpetuity and not subject to the laws of physicality or motion or ideas relating to non-matter or the lack of objective Being or subjective otherness."*

(C) *"We owe the decline of faith in God to technical progress and the amenities of life. Surrounded by our own works we feel we have created the universe. How can I see God when at every step I see only man? The voice of God was heard in the wilderness in silence, and silence and wilderness are exactly what we lack. We have drowned every sound and crammed every space with our own presence and after that we are astonished that the Lord does not show himself to us."*

Answer (A):   CORRECT! From Erasmus' *In Praise of Folly*.

Answer (B):   From Woody Allen's *Getting Even*. Allen (1935-   ) is a well-known actor, movie writer, and director on the contemporary scene.

Answer (C):   From Andrey Sinyavsky's *Unguarded Thoughts*. Sinyavsky is a contemporary Russian theological and satirical writer.

Desiderius Erasmus (1466-1536), Dutch scholar and humanist, was born in Rotterdam, the bastard son of a priest and a physician's daughter. Both parents died when he was young, and his guardians persuaded Erasmus to become a monk at St. Gregory's. In 1492 he was ordained a priest. In 1493 he became secretary to the Bishop of Cambrai and two years later, went to Paris to study theology.

Erasmus arrived in England in 1499 to study the classics and Christian literature. While there, he became friends with Colet and Thomas More. Erasmus wanted to work on the Bible, and thought that a knowledge of Greek was essential. He returned home, and by 1502 he was proficient in Greek. Four years later, he received his Doctor of Divinity from Turin and began tutoring the sons of Henry VIII.

In 1508 Erasmus published *Adagia*, in Venice, a collection of proverbs by classical writers. This work earned him the reputation as the greatest scholar of northern Europe. In the next year Erasmus wrote his famous satire *In Praise of Folly* in 1509 while staying in the house of Sir Thomas More. In 1516 he published a Greek edition of the New Testament with his notes, a work that had a great influence on church reformers.

Basically, Erasmus tried to avoid personal involvement in the Reformation. He lived first in Catholic Louvain and then in Protestant Basel. Both sides pleaded with him to take a stand. Erasmus finally chose the Catholic side. In 1524 he attacked Luther in *De Libero Arbitrio (On Free Will)*, for which Luther launched an attack on him. In 1526 he broke with the reformists and left Basel when they took over three years later. He returned to the Netherlands where he died at the age of seventy.

35. NICOLÒ MACHIAVELLI

Cesare Borgia sits on the throne observing the gathering before him. Standing at attention are soldiers of fortune, thieves, and murderers. He is planning to use them in his battle against the Medicis. It is early in the sixteenth century.

"Nicolò, what do you think of my troops?" he asks his adviser. Machiavelli does not speak. He has learned many lessons since he began his career working for "The Ten," a group of Florentine magistrates in charge of diplomatic affairs and military operations. Looking at the motley assortment before him, he knows that they are useless. "Men can only be counted upon to fight out of fear of their leader or out of devotion inspired by cruelty," he thinks to himself.

"Well, Nicolò, what do you have to say?" Borgia interrupts his thoughts.

"They will not serve you well, my lord. You will be beaten. Medici is backed by the devoted soldiers of Florence. They are afraid of him. They must serve him."

Infuriated by his adviser's words, Borgia quits the court chamber. Later, he has Machiavelli summoned to his private room. "And now, explain your thoughts to me," he demands.

"My Lord, you are a great leader. Never ask my opinion as if you needed it, or I will tell you what you want and not what you need."

"Nicolò, you are a wise counselor. I expect you to voice your opinions and I will judge them. If they are good you will continue to serve me. If they are bad, you will be put to death."

Machiavelli greets these words with a smile. He is pleased. Borgia understands. The two men continue their discussion as Nicolò expands on his theory of ruling which he hopes Borgia can put to use. . . .

(A) "A man must keep up with the procession of crazes, or his day is swiftly done. But in it there are also considerations a good deal more subtle, and maybe less discreditable. For one thing, a man devoted professionally to patriotism and the wisdom of the fathers is apt to come to a resigned sort of acquiescence in all the doctrinaire rubbish that lies beneath the national scheme of things—to believe, let us say, if not that the plain people are gifted with an infallible sagacity, then at least that they have an inalienable right to see their follies executed."

(B) "All those you have injured you cannot keep as friends—they are your enemies and those whom you have put in power are not your friends or else you will not be able to use strong measures against them. He who fails to govern well will soon lose whatever he has won and even while he holds it will have infinite trouble and annoyance. A wise prince must adopt a policy which will insure that his citizens always and in all circumstances will have need of his government; they will always be faithful to him."

(C) "Wealth rather than military valor comes to be the characteristic feature of the dominant class: the people who rule are the rich rather than the brave. One might say, indeed, that the whole history of civilized mankind comes down to a conflict between the tendency of dominant elements to monopolize political power and transmit possession of it by inheritance, and the tendency towards a dislocation of old forces by new forces."

Answer (A): H. L. Mencken's "Roosevelt, An Autopsy," in his *Prejudices*. Mencken (1880-1956) was one of the preeminent essayists of this century. The clarity of his expression has served as a model for effective editorial journalism.

Answer (B): CORRECT! From Nicolò Machiavelli's *The Prince*.

Answer (C): From Gaetano Mosca's *The Ruling Class*. Mosca, (1858-1931), a Sicilian, formulated many of the logical ideas that have served as the philosophical basis of his criticism of Western capitalism.

Nicolò Machiavelli (1469-1527), political philosopher, was born in Florence, the son of a lawyer.

After Savonarola was executed and the Medici family driven out of Florence in 1498, Machiavelli became a secretary in the Florentine Chancellery, working for a group called "The Ten." He was sent on several diplomatic missions, and his work impressed Soderini, the head of the Florentine government. A close relationship developed between the two men. In 1512 the Medicis returned to Florence, overthrowing the republican regime. Machiavelli lost his job and was arrested because of his affiliations with the ousted group. Later acquitted, Machiavelli was permitted to retire to a small estate outside Florence.

It was during this period that Machiavelli began to write. *The Prince*, which is about how principalities are won and lost as shown by history and contemporary events, was written in 1512-1513 and dedicated to a nephew of Pope Leo X, the ruler of Florence. His *Discourses*, written several years later, is dedicated to the members of the ruling group. As a result of these works Machiavelli began to be accepted again in government circles as a minor political commissioner. He died the year that Rome was sacked by the Emperor Charles V and the Medicis once again driven from Florence.

36. NICOLAUS COPERNICUS

Although he can barely lift his head off the pillow, there are a dozen churchmen around his bed, begging and pleading with him to renounce and recant his infamous idea and not allow it to be published and spread around the world. Every time Copernicus begins to speak, the weak whisper of his voice is drowned out by the ecclesiastical words of the canons and priests who hover over him like bees on this day in the year 1543, in Frauenberg, Poland.

"The world is simple. It is not as complicated as Ptolemy attests," he says, and is seized by a fit of coughing. "Aristotle was wrong in his perception of the universe of spheres in the order in which he placed them. As a canon of the church, I am well aware of the implications of placing the sun at the center of the universe. It is a leap within my own mind, a clear and rational act."

"But, Copernicus," the Bishop exclaims, "God is at the center of the universe. Not man. The world is ordered and comprehensible. We are to describe God's world, and not make man's world the center of the universe. You are becoming a heretic. Your words shall be utterly discredited and ignored. Think, Copernicus, of your own condition. You are so close to the end!"

Copernicus smiles weakly at the Bishop, who has brought his red face so close to his own that he can smell the wine on his breath. "If my ideas are to be ignored, why have all of you come to me now, like this? The human mind must be used to discover the harmony and beauty of the universe. People, yourselves included, will naturally tend to want to destroy an idea at whose base is the need for more intensive and thorough analysis." Copernicus lifts his head once more from the pillow and continues. . . .

(A) *"Events far-reaching enough to people all space, whose end is nonetheless tolled when one man dies, may cause us wonder. But something, or an infinite number of things, dies in every death, unless the universe is possessed of a memory."*

(B) *"Mathematics does not deal with motion and is not abstract for it investigates forms of bodies apart from matter, and therefore from movement, which forms, however, being connected with matter cannot really be separated from bodies."*

(C) *"Consider the motion of the earth. We sail forth from the harbor, and the lands and cities retire. As the ship floats along in the calm, all external things seem to have motion that is really that of the ship, while those within the ship feel that they and all their contents are at rest."*

Answer (A): From Jorge Luis Borges' *Dreamtigers*. An Argentinian writer, Borges (1899-   ) has become well known for his surrealistic fiction and poetry.

Answer (B): From Boethius' *On the Trinity*. Boethius (c. 475-525), a Roman, translated Aristotle and was one of those who preserved the Greek tradition in the West.

Answer (C): CORRECT! From Nicolaus Copernicus' *De Revolutionibus*.

Nicolaus Copernicus (1473-1543), astronomer, physician, and clergyman, was born in Torun, Poland, on the Vistula River. He studied astronomy at the University of Cracow, and then went to Italy, where he studied medicine and canon law, receiving a doctorate in canon law from the University of Ferrara in 1503. From 1506-1512, after returning to Poland, Copernicus worked as a physician to his uncle. In 1512 he became canon of the cathedral in Frauenberg. Until his death he performed religious duties there and practiced medicine.

Copernicus continued his study of mathematics and astronomy during his years in Poland. That study culminated in his major work, *De Revolutionibus Orbium Coelestium (The Revolution of the Planets in the Sky)*, which set forth his heliocentric theory of the universe. However, *De Revolutionibus* was not published until the year of his death, and it is said that he finally saw the printed and bound copy on his deathbed. The work is dedicated to the Pope and, despite the fact that it went absolutely against the official teachings of the Catholic Church, it was not declared heretical until 1616.

37. MARTIN LUTHER

Luther stalks about his room in the tower. The year is 1528. He remains angry over the indulgences, the payments people make to priests to gain redemption from their sins. A ridiculous, decadent practice, according to Luther's convictions.

"Are human beings condemned in life?" Luther asks himself. "What is man's relationship to God? Is God able to make man work continuously in this life for grace, only for man to then find it unattainable? Can the work be as priests explain it?"

A streak of lightning brightens the room, followed by a clap of thunder that resounds in Luther's ears and ends his train of thought. He recalls how, years before, he had narrowly escaped being struck by lightning in a violent storm. His fear had been so great that it caused him to change the entire course of his life. He entered a monastery and, since then, has been searching his mind and heart for ways to understand man and God. This drove him to post his infamous Ninety-five Theses on the door of the church at Wittenberg in 1517, protesting the sale of indulgences. Four years later, Pope Leo X excommunicated him, calling him before the Diet of Worms. Now, he lives in Wittenberg with his wife, an ex-nun, and their children.

Luther descends the winding stairs of the tower in search of a fellow priest to hear his confession. His confessor is irritated. "What a bore this man is," he thinks to himself. "All day long he confesses to anyone who will hear him. Never anything interesting, never anything worthwhile, only articles of faith that he has neglected, or prayers he forgot to say." Yet, today, something seems to be different. He notices Luther's red eyes and strange demeanor.

"I must confess to you," Luther says calmly.

"How have you sinned?"

Luther twists his hands in his lap while remembering all his wishes for man's role with God to be one of real trust and devotion. "I have sinned," he says finally, "because I have not reconciled faith and work."

"This will be done in time," replies the priest, getting up to leave.

"No! Stop!" Luther bursts out, and grabs at the priest's robes to detain him. "It is more important than you think. Don't you see? . . .

(A) *"We must not attribute the power of justifying to charity which maketh a man acceptable unto God, but we must attribute it to faith which apprehendeth and possesseth in the heart Christ the Saviour himself. This faith justifieth without and before charity."*

(B) *"A man should endeavor to make the sphere of his innocent pleasures as wide as possible that he may retire into them with safety, and find in them a satisfaction as a wise man would not blush to take."*

(C) *"A single incongruous part may destroy the harmonious effect of many beauties, without, however, making the object ugly. Ugliness requires the presence of several incongruous parts which we must be able to take in at a glance if the effect produced is to be the opposite of that which we call beauty."*

Answer (A):   CORRECT! From Martin Luther's *Commentary on Galatians*.

Answer (B):   From Joseph Addison and John Steele's *The Spectator*. *The Spectator* was a popular journal of philosophy and opinion which was published and written by Addison (1672-1714) and Steele (1672-1729) in England.

Answer (C):   From Gotthold Ephraim Lessing's *Laocoon*. Lessing (1729-1781), a German critic and playwright, wrote this classic text to establish standards for the appreciation of art.

Martin Luther (1483-1546), leader of the Protestant Reformation, was born at Eisleben, Saxony, the son of a copper miner. He attended the University of Erfurt, and in 1505 began to study law at his father's bidding. However, after a spiritual crisis, Luther quit the law and entered an Augustinian monastery at Erfurt. He was ordained a priest in 1507.

In 1510, while in Rome on business for his order, Luther was shocked by the lack of spirituality evident among many people in high positions in the church. He returned to Wittenberg and became a professor. He led an ascetic life, fearful of the wrath of God. At this point John von Staupitz encouraged him to study the Scriptures. Luther eventually concluded that God was benevolent and that salvation was possible through faith alone. This conclusion eventually led to his break with the Catholic Church.

In 1517 Luther posted his Ninety-five Theses on the town's church door. His attempts at reform were eventually declared heretical, and Luther was excommunicated. He was called before the Diet of Worms and ordered seized. Friends hid him in Frederick II's castle in Wartburg, during which time he translated the New Testament into German.

Luther eventually returned to Wittenberg, despite the dangers, because he feared that his movement would die. He spent the rest of his life there, preaching and writing.

Luther's doctrines created the first major schism within the Roman Catholic Church. He believed that the only essential guide to truth was to be found in the Scriptures, that the individual was responsible to God alone, and that salvation came through faith. He rejected the sacraments except as aids and denied the authority of priests to serve as mediators between the individual and God.

38. FRANCIS BACON

"You have been found guilty of accepting bribes while in office. Such acts demand punishment. Therefore, you are hereby condemned to prison and fined 40,000 pounds."

"But your honor, let me reiterate. The gifts did not affect my judgment."

"That is simply nonsense, Sir Francis. Case closed." The judge retires to his chambers.

Bacon is escorted from the courtroom. He has decided to continue working despite the humiliation of his sentence. While serving in high office, he had composed a new work, the *Novum Organum*, which he hopes will replace Aristotle's *Organum*. It is a great work, the major work of his lifetime. Bacon has written it as a treatise on induction, the method of inquiry which develops a general idea on the basis of observation of specifics. In induction, thinking goes from parts to wholes. By the time of his trial his treatise has already begun to change the entire scientific method used in England in the seventeenth century. It has created a new breed of scientists: collectors and observers who are busy looking at and cataloguing all of nature in hopes of arriving at a theory once the evidence is in.

Bacon is allowed to return to his house before beginning to serve his sentence in the Tower of London. His assistant slowly packs his belongings, picking up a mirror which he starts to place in the valise. Bacon stops him. "Vanity is the beginning of error," he says.

A day later, sitting in jail, Bacon remembers the incident and recalls something he wrote about vanity and the old theories of the acquisition of knowledge. . . .

(A) *"One of my persistent prayers to God and my guardian angel was that I not dream of mirrors. I know I watched them with misgivings. Sometimes I feared they might begin to deviate from reality; other times I was afraid of seeing there my own face, disfigured by strange calamities. I have learned that this fear is again monstrously abroad in the world."*

(B) *"He would give to God, getting down to specifications, the greatest diamond in the world . . . In return he asked only a simple thing, a thing that for God would be absurdly easy—only that matters should be as they were yesterday at this hour and that they should remain so. . . . He doubted only whether he had made his bribe big enough."*

(C) *". . . all perceptions as well of the sense of the mind are according to the measure of the individual and not according to the measure of the universe. And the human understanding is like a false mirror, which, receiving rays irregularly, distorts and discolors the nature of things by mingling its own nature with it."*

Answer (A): From Jorge Luis Borges' *Dreamtigers*. Borges (1899-   ) is an Argentinian writer who has gained great acclaim for his surrealistic stories and poems.

Answer (B): From F. Scott Fitzgerald's "The Diamond as Big as the Ritz," in his *Babylon Revisited*. Fitzgerald (1896-1940) was an American writer of the twenties whose simple language and vivid characters changed the nature of fiction.

Answer (C): CORRECT! From Francis Bacon's *Novum Organum*.

Francis Bacon (1561-1626), English philosopher, was born in London in 1561, the son of Sir Nicholas Bacon, Lord Keeper to Queen Elizabeth I. He became a member of Parliament at twenty-three. He was adviser to the Earl of Essex and it was through the latter's influence that Bacon, who was out of favor, became a member of the Queen's Learned Council. In 1601, when Essex was prosecuted, Bacon took part, an action that brought him much public disapproval. When James I succeeded to the throne, Bacon's fortunes improved. From 1603 to 1618, he held various government posts including those of attorney general, lord keeper, and lord chancellor.

In 1621, Bacon was accused of accepting bribes. He pleaded guilty to this crime, and was fined and sentenced to the Tower of London. He was imprisoned for four days, and then expelled from office and banished from court forever. Bacon spent the rest of his life writing books. He died in 1626 from a cold he caught while doing an experiment in refrigeration.

Bacon is best known for his use of the modern experimental method in scientific reasoning as well as for his belief in the collecting and arranging of scientific data. His philosophy, in general, was practical and scientific in nature. His major philosophical works include *The Advancement of Learning* (1605) and *Novum Organum* (1620). In *The New Atlantis* (1621) Bacon described a scientific utopia. His *Essays* (1597-1625) are well known for the observations they contain about life, as well as for their elegant style.

39. GALILEO GALILEI

Galileo stands on the ramparts of the University of Padua. The year is 1632. He is looking at the heavens through his telescope, which he had assembled in 1609. Through it, the world has been changed. For the first time an enlarged view of the heavens, the stars, and the planets is possible. Because his observations seem to confirm the Copernican view of the universe, which has been officially declared a heresy, he has been forbidden to uphold the view publicly.

"Dogma," Galileo shouts, "I hate it!"

"What's the point in hating," his assistant says, trying to calm him. "Keep this up and they'll have you killed. The Pope is upset with you. Recant. Tell them nothing moves in the heavens, least of all this earth. Cease this endless quest of yours to find answers to unnecessary questions. The Greeks and the Pope have said everything there is to say."

"Shut up and let me be." Galileo walks to his study. "You have all the courage of an old cow," he yells and slams the door. He knows beyond a doubt from his observations of the stars and planets that they do move. He realizes that perhaps he can write a satirical dialogue which will appear to condemn his own ideas but at the same time state them accurately. He places the candle on his writing table and begins. . . .

(A) *"Though the difference between man and other animals is enormous, yet one might say reasonably that it is a little less than the differences among men themselves . . . He who looks the higher is the more highly distinguished, and turning over the great book of nature (which is the proper object of philosophy) is the way to elevate one's gaze . . . The constitution of the universe I believe may be set in first place among all others in grandeur by reason of its universal content. It must also stand above them all in nobility as their rule and standard."*

(B) *"How to forbid oneself to elucidate reality—that is the problem, the difficulty. How to restore the wonder to human geometry—that is the crux of the matter. . . . It is not our instruments which fault us, but the flaccid vision. . . . Our science is the barren midwife of matter—can we make her fruitful?"*

(C) *"Some lofty concepts, like space and number, involve truths remote from the category of causation: and here we must be content, as Aristotle says, if the mere facts be known. But natural history deals with ephemeral and accidental, not eternal nor universal things: their causes and effects thrust themselves on our curiosity, and become the ultimate relations to which our contemplation ends."*

Answer (A): CORRECT! From Galileo Galilei's *Dialogues Concerning the Two Chief World Systems.*

(Answer (B): From Lawrence Durrell's *Tunc.* Durrell (1912-   ) is a contemporary English novelist who seeks to mix fiction and science.

Answer (C): From D'Arcy Thompson's *On Growth and Form.* This analysis of the physical and numerical properties of biological forms by Thompson (1860-1948) supplied the foundations for structural research into the physical nature of living systems.

Galileo Galilei (1564-1642), mathematician, physicist, and astronomer, was born in Pisa. He began to study medicine but switched to mathematics and physics. From 1589 to 1592, Galileo was a professor at the University of Pisa, during which time he established the law of falling bodies. However, Galileo did not perform the experiment from the Leaning Tower credited to him by legend. (A man named Simon Stevin did the experiment several years before Galileo proved his law.)

Beginning in 1592, and for the next eighteen years, Galileo taught mathematics at the University of Padua. During that time he constructed the first complete astronomical telescope, which he used to discover that the Milky Way is made up of separate stars and that the moon has a rough mountainous surface. He studied the phases of Venus and observed sunspots. In 1610 he discovered Jupiter's four largest moons.

Galileo believed Copernicus' theory of the solar system but did not dare publicly declare his beliefs. The Copernican system was denounced by the church in 1616, and Galileo was forbidden to teach it or support it. In 1632 he published *Dialogues Concerning the Two Chief World Systems,* a work upholding the Copernican system, and a year later he was called to Rome and tried by the Inquisition. He was forced to retract all his statements.

Galileo was sentenced to live at Siena, although he was later allowed to move to Arcetri, near Florence. Despite progressive dimunition of sight, he continued his work, until his death in 1642.

Galileo was one of the founders of modern science. His *Dialogues Concerning Two New Sciences,* published in 1638, was his last work and contains most of the discoveries he made in his lifetime.

40. WILLIAM SHAKESPEARE

"Sometimes I love men the same way as women," he says. He lies next to Britches, a tall thin lad who had made his play for him at the London rehearsal hall that morning. Now, they are entwined in each other's arms. The midday sun shines on their naked bodies.

"Turn over, Shakespeare," Britches whispers. Soon the young lad and William are involved in the frenzied motions of passion and pleasure. Yet, even in this exquisite moment, Shakespeare cannot shed the yoke of his alienation. "I feel alone, isolated, deprived of real contact," he thinks to himself. "I create characters, kings and beggars, to meet the world, make the world real for themselves, something I can never do for myself."

Britches is not aware of these thoughts. The youth is exhilarated at his good luck in bedding the Bard, the most successful playwright of seventeenth-century England, a man whose plays bring in more money than the most successful banker could hope to make.

Later in the evening, Shakespeare sheepishly returns home to Anne Hathaway, his wife and mother of their three children. She senses that he is in one of his fits of despair, and greatly in need of comforting.

"You are a genius, Will. Yet you complain of a poor spirit. You want what others seem to have and lack."

"And what is that?" Shakespeare inquires.

"They seem to be who they are. They seem to have made peace with themselves. They stroll through life unencumbered by the vision you see."

"Perhaps you are right. I find my eyes penetrate so deeply into people that I come through the other side and find them vacant, like air."

Shakespeare sits down. He looks at his wife, wanting to confess, knowing that she knows, wanting to say it in a comforting way, knowing that he is something else again, wanting someone else to speak the words to her. He remembers the words of one of his early sonnets as he says . . .

(A) "Farewell, love, and all thy laws for
          ever
      Thy baited hooks shall tangle me no
          more;
      Seneca and Plato call me from thy lore
      To perfect wealth, my wit for to
          endeavor:
      In blind error when I did persevere
      Thy sharp repulse that pricketh eye so
          sore
      Hath taught me to set in trifles no
          store,
      And scape for, since liberty is lever.
      Therefore, farewell! Go trouble
          younger hearts,
      And in me claim no more authority:
      With idle youth go use thy property,
      And thereon spend thy many brittle
          darts.
      For hitherto though I have lost all
          my time,
      Me lusteth no longer rotten boughs to
          climb."

(B) "As an imperfect actor on the stage
      Who with fear is put beside his part,
      Or some fierce thing replete with too
          much rage,
      Whose strength's abundance weakens
          his
          own heart,
      So I, for fear of trust, forget to say
      The perfect ceremony of love's rite,
      And in mine own love's strength seem
          to decay,
      O'ercharged with burden of mine own
          love's might.
      O let my books be then the eloquence
      And dumb presagers of my speaking
          recompense
      More than that tongue and more hath
          more expressed.
      O, learn to read what silent love hath
          writ:
      To hear with eyes belongs to love's
          fine wit."

(C) "To seek thee did I often rove
      Through woods and on the green
      And thou wert still a hope, a love:
      Still longed for, never seen.

      "And I can listen to thee yet:
      Can lie upon the plain
      And listen, till I do beget
      That golden time again."

Answer (A): From Sir Thomas Wyatt's "A Renouncing of Love," in his *Seven Penitential Psalms*. Wyatt (c. 1503-1542), a Tudor poet, brought the Italian influence to English poetry.

Answer (B): CORRECT! From William Shakespeare's "Sonnet 23."

Answer (C): From William Wordsworth's "To the Cuckoo." Wordworth (1770-1850), the foremost English poet of his time, brought the worship of nature out of the pastoral tradition into the more romantic and lyrical mode.

William Shakespeare (1564-1616), considered the greatest playwright in history, was born in Stratford-on-Avon. His father was a businessman. As a boy Shakespeare probably attended school in Stratford. He never completed his education, however, dropping out of school to help his father, whose business had begun to fail. At eighteen Shakespeare married Anne Hathaway, twenty-six and pregnant. They had three children.

Shakespeare's life before 1593 is obscure. He probably went to London as an apprentice in the theatre. By 1593 he had secured the patronage of the Earl of Southampton and was a recognized playwright. In 1594 Shakespeare joined the Lord Chamberlain's Men, a stage company that later became the King's Men under James I. He remained with this company until retirement. During his career Shakespeare became part owner of the Globe and Black Friar's theatres. Through this and other investments he acquired enough money to be able to live comfortably all his life. He retired to the Place, his estate in Stratford-on-Avon, in 1613, and died there three years later.

Beginning in 1590 Shakespeare began writing plays steadily, producing about two each year. There are thirty-eight plays which scholars generally accept as Shakespeare's work, although two are probably collaborations. Shakespeare wrote histories (*Henry VI*, Parts I, II, and III; *Richard II*, etc.), comedies (*Much Ado About Nothing, A Midsummer Night's Dream*), and tragedies (*Hamlet, Macbeth*, etc.). He also wrote sonnets, most of which were composed in the 1590s when the theatres were closed due to the plague. Shakespeare's influence on our culture is immeasurable.

41. THOMAS HOBBES

Soon after setting out from London, the carriage had been attacked by a band of beggars. The lone occupant of the coach, Thomas Hobbes, lying back after the skirmish, notices blood seeping through his coat. The blow, he recalls, felt like a punch. The coach gains speed as the horses are driven through the countryside under the whip. The assailants are left behind. "How ironic," Hobbes thinks, sinking into unconsciousness. "I flee to France for my personal safety, only to come under attack from these despicable creatures." The year is 1640.

Hobbes awakens the following day on the boat bound for France. He is wracked by fever. A sailor attends his wounds. "You see," he says to the sailor, "These people have no right at all to have weapons. If we had a ruler who could, by the strength, power, and financial might of his position, subdue the people, this kind of thing would never happen. Decent people would be safe on the streets at night. Not only were those beggars allowed to assault me, but they seemed to believe that they were in the right. It is the height of absurdity that anyone dare to attack his betters."

Hobbes has gradually worked himself into a heated frenzy as he speaks. He believes in the absolute right of the leaders of society to protect humans from their own worst nature and to restrict those who cannot control themselves. He knows that without such control, no dignity or privilege will be available in the world, privileges that he very much enjoys.

The sailor starts to leave the cabin. His face betrays the anger he feels toward this wounded man. He believes that Hobbes considers him an inferior being.

"Where are you going, my man?" Hobbes asks thinly.

"To perform my lowly service, sir," replies the sailor sarcastically as he makes his exit, slamming the door.

"Typical," thinks Hobbes, struggling to sit up in his bunk. Unable to write, he begins, nevertheless, to make mental notes for a new text on political philosophy, one that he believes will be extremely influential. . . .

(A) "Political parties, however much they may be founded upon narrow class interests and however evidently they may work against the interests of the majority, love to identify themselves with the universe, or at least to present themselves as cooperating with all the citizens of the state, and to proclaim that they are fighting in the name of all and for the good of all. But they always tone down this assertion by adding that in ultimate analysis the interests of the party coincide with the interests of the people."

(B) "To be sure, mere passion, however genuinely felt, is not enough. It does not make a politician, unless passion as devotion to a cause also makes responsibility to this cause the guiding star of action. And for this a sense of proportion is needed. This is the decisive psychological quality of the politician: his ability to let realities work upon him with inner concentration and calmness."

(C) "Again, men have no pleasure, but on the contrary a great deal of grief, in keeping company, where there is no power able to over-awe them all. For every man looketh that his companion should value him, at the same rate he sets upon himself: and upon all signs of contempt, or undervaluing, naturally endeavors, as far as he dares (which amongst them that have no common power to keep them in quiet, is far enough to make them destroy each other), to extort a greater value from his condemners, by damage; and from others, by example."

Answer (A):   From Robert Michaels' *Political Parties.* Michaels, a contemporary political scientist, writes here about politics and the oligarchical nature of democracy today.

Answer (B):   From Max Weber's *Politics as a Vocation.* Weber (1864-1920) was a German sociologist whose work influenced the development of sociology in the United States.

Answer (C):   CORRECT! From Thomas Hobbes *Leviathan.*

Thomas Hobbes (1588-1679), English philosopher, was born in Westport, England, the son of an uneducated local vicar. A rich uncle took an interest in him, paid for his education, and left him some money. At fifteen Hobbes went to Oxford University. After graduating in 1608 he became tutor to an influential British family, the Cavendishes.

By 1640 Hobbes' political writings, royalist in persuasion, had made him extremely unpopular in England, so he went to France, where he mixed with European intellectuals and scientists as well as English royalist refugees. However, after the publication of his *Leviathan* in 1651, his philosophy so antagonized the Roman Catholic Church and the English group in France that Hobbes was forced to flee secretly to London. He returned to the Cavendish household, where he studied and wrote until his death.

Although he dabbled in science and math, Hobbes is chiefly known for his political philosophy, set forth in *Leviathan.* Hobbes believed that the natural state of the human race was anarchy, and that, for the purpose of self-preservation, human beings formed a social contract, or "covenant," essentially an agreement among themselves to submit to a chosen sovereign. Their political power ended once this sovereign was chosen, for his power is unlimited. Hobbes also believed that the power of the state is absolutely superior to the power of the church.

42. RENÉ DESCARTES

René Descartes tosses fitfully in his sleep. He is having one of the disturbed drunken dreams that reflect his agonizing bohemian life in seventeenth-century France.

A cold, refreshing wind suddenly chills the fever of his dream. As if bathed in mountain air, his body is relieved of pain, the poisons leave his mind. His lips taste the beginning of a new life. His ears hear the steady sounds of change. His arms and hands are free of their shaking. He wants to reach out and touch this new life, a white cloud passing by a mountaintop.

Awaking with a start, Descartes realizes with sudden clarity that he, and he alone, is the center, the creator of his own experience, and that this revelation will carry him through any confusion. This one idea is a remarkable advance in human thought. People in seventeenth-century France were restricted by their belief that their existence was created by God and demonstrated by nature.

Descartes gets up and goes to his writing table. He recalls the details of the dream. In it, he stood alone on a river bank, watching the decay of the world float by like a heavily laden barge. Scrawled on the walls of buildings across the river were the words that would occupy his thinking in the future. He read those words in silence, realizing that they were the basis of a new philosophy, a new belief. In them he recognized the perfection of experience, the basis of all truth, and the ability to conceive dramatic new scientific realizations.

He now can write the words that will enable humans to understand that their being is the rationale for the universe. By being the creator of their own world, humans become the thinker's of thought and the proof of God's will.

Descartes picks up his quill, dips it into the inkwell, and, in the early light of morning, begins to write the words that will serve as the basis of his new thinking. . . .

(A) *"At first I know I exist because I can think. I know that perfection exists in the mind. I know that physical things exist in the world which I can touch. I know that these thoughts are the basis for a system that can unify all of man's thought into one glorious whole."*

(B) *"We shall have nothing more to lose and nothing to win. Our deepest instincts and our most secret passions will be analyzed, published and exploited. We shall be rewarded with everything our hearts ever desired. And the supreme luxury of the society of technical necessity will be to grant the bonus of useless revolt and of an acquiescent smile."*

(C) *"We punish facts rather than faults. Injury to the soul we do not regard as so much a matter of punishment as injury to others. Our object is to avoid public mischief rather than to correct personal mistakes."*

Answer (A): CORRECT! From René Descartes' *A Discourse on Method*.

Answer (B): From Jacques Ellul's *The Technological Society*. Ellul's text is about the dangers inherent in contemporary technological society.

Answer (C): From Peter Abélard's *Ethics, or Know Thyself*. Abélard (1079-1142) was a major French religious thinker and philosopher.

René Descartes (1596-1650), French philosopher and mathematician, was born in Touraine. His father was a counselor of the parliament of Brittany and a landowner whose estates René later inherited and sold, thereby providing himself with a yearly income from the money he invested.

He attended the Jesuit College of La Flèche, where he studied logic, mathematics, and philosophy. In 1612 he went to Paris. He became bored with life there and went into seclusion to study geometry. He joined the Dutch army in 1617 and was able to continue his studies because there was no war going on at the time. Two years later the Thirty Years War began and Descartes joined the Bavarian army. According to his work, *A Discourse on Method*, during the winter of 1619, he would get up in the morning and get into a stove where he spent the day formulating his philosophy.

In 1628 he again joined an army, this time in the attack against the Huguenots at La Rochelle. He remained in Holland until 1649, when, at the request of Queen Christina, he went to Sweden to give her lessons. The cold climate, and the fact that the queen insisted that Descartes tutor her at five in the morning, caused him to fall ill and die in February 1650.

Most famous for the phrase "Je pense, donc je suis" ("I think therefore I am"), Descartes is often called the father of modern philosophy.

43. JOHN MILTON

The ceremony in the Church of England has ended moments before. The bride is going home with the groom and his four sparkling children. This marks his third marriage; it is her first. She leads her husband by the hand. He is blind. The year is 1663.

John Milton is deeply moved by the idea of liberty. Nevertheless, he constantly entangles himself in situations that make his own personal liberty impossible. Only through his writing is he able to shake the fetters that bind him and be free. In a sense, he considers himself a scribe, translating what is known about justice, liberty, and God's will to humanity.

Elizabeth, his new wife, knows of his need to continue his writing. Now that he is blind, the transcription must be done by secretaries. "John, we live just so long," she says to him on their way home. "Do you not want to feel the freedom of the wind in your face, smell the fragrance of the flowers? It is spring. Let us enjoy our new life together."

"My love," Milton replies, "freedom comes in resisting temptation and dedicating oneself to follow the course written in the soul. I cannot swallow my talent. It would choke me. I cannot jeopardize my gifts and my work, intoxicated by the smell of a few flowers."

"I would, John." She kisses him on his neck and talks close to his ear. Her voice is warm. "I want the loveliness of the marriage we just vowed to have. I want Paradise here, on earth, with you, for what happens after we die is beyond my imagination and my caring."

Milton is disappointed. His wife's pleading brings him to the unwelcome realization that his work describing liberty must focus not only on the everyday trials and tribulations, but also on the greatest battle of all, the eternal duel between God and Satan. Seated in the carriage with Elizabeth, smelling her scent, feeling her skin, the words of a new work begin to formulate behind the darkness of his eyes. . . .

(A) "Of man's first disobedience and the fruit
Of that forbidden tree whose mortal taste
Brought death into the world, and all our woe
With loss of Eden, till one greater Man
Restore us, and regain the blissful seat,
Sing heavenly muse."

(B) "Guiltless I gazed: heaven listened while you sung:
and truths divine came mended from that tongue.
From lips like those what precept failed to move?
Too soon they taught me 'twas no sin to love:
Back through the paths of pleasing sense I ran,
Nor wished an Angel whom I loved a man.
Dim and remote the joys of saints I see:
Nor envy them that heaven I lose for thee."

(C) "Gather together from your happy spring
Fruits that are sweet, before time ravages
With angry snow the beauty of your head.
The rose will wither as the cold wind rages
And age come gently to change everything
Lest our desire should change old age instead."

Answer (A): CORRECT! From John Milton's *Paradise Lost.*

Answer (B): From Alexander Pope's "Eloise to Abelard." Pope (1688-1744) was one of the wittiest and most interesting of the eighteenth-century English poets.

Answer (C): From Garcilaso de les Vega's "En Tanta que Rose y Azucena," in *Obras.* Garcilaso (c. 1539-1616) was a Spanish poet who brought Italian renaissance poetry to Spain.

John Milton (1608-1674), English poet, was born in London, the son of a scrivener. He attended St. Paul's school and Christ's College, Cambridge, receiving his Masters in 1632. Although he wrote poetry in college, he intended to become a minister. He became disillusioned with the church, however, and decided to be a poet. In 1638 the death of his friend, Edward King, inspired him to write one of his most famous poems, "Lycidas." In 1643 Milton married Mary Powell, his first of three wives. She left him that same year, returning to him two years later to bear him three daughters before she died.

Largely the result of his pamphlet "The Tenure of Kings and Magistrates," Milton was made Latin secretary for foreign affairs in Cromwell's government. Milton, who believed that a bad king could rightfully be killed by the people, supported Cromwell and the Commonwealth. During this period, his eyesight, which had been weak since birth, failed him completely. Totally blind, Milton could only work with the aid of secretaries (one of whom was the poet Andrew Marvell).

In 1656 he married Catherine Woodcock; she died two years later. At the age of fifty-five, he married Elizabeth Minshull, who outlived him.

After the Restoration, Milton was forced into hiding but was finally granted amnesty. *Paradise Lost,* his epic poem in blank verse, was published in 1667. This poem, considered one of the greatest in the English language, is about evil. It tells the story of Satan's fall from grace and Adam and Eve in the Garden of Eden. *Paradise Regained* (1671) describes how Christ overcame temptation by Satan.

44. BLAISE PASCAL

Three scientists engage in a heated argument in a house in Port Royal. The year is 1654. They have been adding columns for six hours and disputing the results.

"I tell you, Blaise," says Pierre, "the total is 6,-908,746. I don't care what you say the answer is."

Henri, who sits across the table, throws his pen on the floor in disgust. "Idiots!" he exclaims. "The answer is 6,908,678. I do not want to know how you arrived at your results, nor do I care whether or not you used my method. You must agree with me."

Blaise Pascal holds his tongue, feeling somehow that he is wrong, although he has done the calculations correctly. This feeling of being wrong is not unpleasurable to Pascal. As a matter of fact, his greatest pleasure is in hating himself, an activity he believes to be the only true virtue. Watching as Pierre once again adds the column of figures, he knows that there is no more than what there is before him: all rational, all neat and clear. This has been his whole life.

"Blaise, what do you have for your answer?" asks Pierre. Pascal announces a total of 6,908,675, a figure different from both the others. "I know I am wrong," he says, enjoying the situation. "But which one of you is also wrong?"

The scientists study and compare the numbers carefully. They are adding numbers of people in a statistical project. "I see!" Blaise pronounces. "Pierre has refused to add half-numbers thinking that there are no half-people. Henri has added them. In my case, the problem is a simple calculating error." Pascal becomes animated as he explains the significance of what has just occurred. . . .

(A) *"The universal of pure being represents the limiting case of the abstractive process. Now even if all science is abstractive, it does not follow that science will still be possible when abstraction has been taken to the limiting case. Abstraction means taking out. But science investigates not what is taken out but what is left in. To push abstraction to the limiting case is to take out everything: and when everything is taken out there is nothing for science to investigate. You may call this nothing by what name you like—pure being, or God, or anything else—but it remains nothing, and contains no peculiarities for science to examine."*

(B) *"We know the truth not only through our reason but also through our heart. It is through the latter that we know first principles, and reason, which has nothing to do with it, tries in vain to refute them. The sceptics have no other object than that, and they work at it to no purpose. We know that we are not dreaming, but, however unable we may be to prove it rationally, our inability proves nothing but the weakness of our reason, and not the uncertainty of all our knowledge, as they maintain.*

(C) *"The fixing of a gulf between God and man was not fatal to religion so long as some measure of original participation remained. To a participating consciousness, apprehending the world and the word as image, many nouns are the names of the Creator and the noun GOD is merely one of them. To a non-participating consciousness, apprehending the world as object, most nouns are the names of idols and the noun GOD can be no exception."*

Answer (A):   From R. J. Collingwood's *Essays on Metaphysics.* Collingwood (1889-1943) was a historian and philosopher of science who raised some of the central questions of contemporary philosophy.

Answer (B):   CORRECT! From Blaise Pascal's *Pensées.*

Answer (C):   From Owen Barfield's *Saving the Appearances.* Barfield (1898-   ) is an English scholar who is also a lawyer and writes profusely about the relation between science and religion.

    Blaise Pascal (1623-1662), French philosopher and scientist, was born in Clermont, Auvergne, the son of a civil servant. Although a sickly child, Pascal was a prodigy, showing an exceptional aptitude for mathematics and science. At nineteen he invented a calculating machine that could add and substract, which he patented. His experiments with fluids resulted in his discovery of what became Pascal's Law. He was also interested in the atmosphere and conducted experiments, with the help of his brother-in-law, using barometers containing mercury.

    In 1654, a narrow escape from death in a runaway carriage caused Pascal to give up entirely his scientific pursuits and associate himself with the Jansenists at Port Royal, a Catholic sect that was anti-Jesuit. He spent the remainder of his life composing religious writings, especially his *Pensées.* His philosophy underwent a radical turnabout. Reason, no longer a sufficient means of understanding the universe and humanity, was replaced by faith as the necessary ingredient for solving problems. Pascal's *Pensées* remains a religious and philosophical classic.

45. BARUCH SPINOZA

The glass is very clear and hard as the lens grinder looks through it and works to adjust its properties. "The light of the room will pass through this glass," he thinks. "The light of the world and the thoughts of the world are one. God is in everything."

"Spinoza. Spinoza!" The lens grinder looks up. A man has walked into the shop, abruptly ending his daydream. "Spinoza," the old Jew demands, "is there immortality?"

Spinoza looks up from his lenses. His family came to Amsterdam, fleeing the Spanish Inquisition, and Spinoza took up lens grinding. He does not want to teach, or to explain his philosophy, or to be distracted by questions from pursuing his ideas and visions. The old man persists. "Spinoza, answer me this: Is there life after death?"

Spinoza is hardly interested in this stranger or his problem. Yet he wonders if these questions can be answered in a word or two, or if they involve fundamental searching, a test of his own ability to perceive and conceive, to express himself. "Why is this man unable to see that eternity is always visible?" Spinoza thinks.

He puts down the polished lens, and replies to the man's question in a way which demonstrates the quality of the question as well as the nature of Spinoza's answer. . . .

(A) *"There is no fear since all comes from God. Nothing finite is self-sufficient, nothing is separable. Everything is a manifestation of God. There is no chance, no free will, since our place is determined in the cosmic, not in the local small patterns of existence. One participates in the infinite plan, not in life and death. No, there is no immortality, nor mortality my friend. None at all."*

(B) *"Think of a great sea bird who comes once every thousand years and takes one grain of sand and flies and drops it on another pile. The seabird comes again and again until all the sand on all the beaches has been moved and after those countless eons eternity has not yet begun."*

(C) *"Faith in the Divinity is never out of mind, and constitutes the ground of all dogma. Body cannot teach wisdom, God only. In the same mind he confirms that virtue cannot be taught: that it is not a science, but an inspiration. The greatest goods are produced to us through mania and are assigned to us by a divine gift."*

Answer (A): CORRECT! From Spinoza's *Ethics* in *The Chief Works of Benedict Spinoza*, 2 vol.

Answer (B): From James Joyce's *The Portrait of an Artist as a Young Man*. Joyce (1882-1941), an Irish novelist, is most famous for his modern classic, *Ulysses* (see selection 84 for further information about Joyce).

Answer (C): From an essay by Ralph Waldo Emerson entitled "Plato, or the Philosophers." Emerson (1803-1882), an American essayist and poet, was a founder of the transcendentalist movement in literature (see selection 62).

Baruch Spinoza (1632-1677), Dutch philosopher, was born in Amsterdam. His family were Jews from Portugal or Spain who had immigrated to Amsterdam to escape the Inquisition.

Educated in the traditional orthodox Jewish manner, Spinoza soon realized that he could not accept the philosophy and interpretation of his religion. When he began to voice his doubts, he was bribed to keep silent. When he refused, he was officially cursed and an assassination attempt was made on his life. Finally, in 1656, at twenty-four, Spinoza was excommunicated and excluded from the Jewish community.

He changed his name from Baruch to Benedict, and in 1660 went to live at The Hague. A skillful lens grinder, Spinoza lived a simple, modest life, devoting a large amount of his time to developing his philosophy. In 1673, he was offered the chair of philosophy at Heidelberg but refused it. Leibniz and other contemporary philosophers visited him, and he carried on a wide correspondence.

He died of tuberculosis, a condition that was probably worsened by the glass dust from lens grinding.

The *Ethics Demonstrated According to Geometrical Order* is his most important work. It presents a metaphysical system, the starting point of which was Spinoza's belief in only one infinite substance, God.

46. ISAAC NEWTON

The members of the Royal Society have been knocking at his door for several minutes. They know he is inside. They want to give him an award and congratulate him on the publication of his *Principia Mathematica*, which they believe will be considered one of the greatest of all human achievements, and the intellectual landmark of late seventeenth-century English culture.

Isaac Newton will not answer his door. He has spent the day at the mint. Money is one of his great interests. Although he gives it away freely, he knows that he has to be rich to be heard. Newton is a strange character. He realizes the importance of his work but will not tolerate public awareness of it, lest someone argue with him. He cannot stand controversy. He considers his life to be a secret: the discoveries he has made belong solely to him. He wants recognition for the brilliance of his thinking without the public display. The tension between those two desires creates an unsettled state among the people who have to deal with him.

"What is wrong with this man?" one of the Society members complains. "He entertains young students but keeps members of the Royal Society standing outside in the cold. Why is he so unwilling to discuss his ideas with us?"

Newton is listening, his ear to the door. Eventually, the disgruntled members depart, after tacking something to the door. As soon as he is sure they are some distance away, Newton removes the paper. He reads it and scoffs. It is a declaration which states that Newton is the greatest mind of his era and that his ideas of force and motion, of optics and of mathematics are incomparable. And all day, Newton has been immersed in his work with alchemy, wanting only to be left in peace and privacy for fear of discovering that someone disagrees with him. Newton has laughed in public only once in his life. He regrets it.

Leaning against the door, the declaration in hand, he thinks about what he has done in his life. He is weary of philosophy since it promises so much and delivers so little. He goes to his desk and begins to write a letter to a friend. . . .

(A) *"Science, if it survives the impending darkness, will next take up the consideration of linguistic principles and divest itself of the illusory linguistic necessities, too long held to be the substance of reason itself."*

(B) *"I do not know what I may appear to the world: but to myself I seem to have been only like a boy, playing on the seashore, and diverting myself in now and then finding a smoother pebble, or a prettier shell than ordinary, while the great ocean of truth lay all undiscovered before me."*

(C) *"The real thing, if you are interested, is total negation of everything man has put together about reality, his philosophies, his gods, his rituals, his beliefs, his behaviour, everything denied totally, denied because you see its absurdity, because it is irrational, it is insane, it is idiotic."*

Answer (A):   From Benjamin Whorf's *Language, Thought and Reality*. Whorf (1897-1941) has changed ideas about language and suggests that language depicts our understanding of the environment.

Answer (B):   CORRECT! From *Sir Isaac Newton,* by E. N. da C. Andrade.

Answer (C):   From an interview with Krishnamurti. Krishnamurti (1897-   ) is a contemporary guru who advocates a life style of simplicity and negation.

Isaac Newton (1642-1727), English mathematician and physicist, was born in Woolsthorpe, Lincolnshire, the year Galileo died, and was left by his mother in the care of his grandparents. He was an ordinary child, slow in school until his teens. In 1660, at the urging of an uncle who was a member of Trinity College, Newton was sent to Cambridge, from which he graduated in 1665. The plague struck a year later, and Newton went to his mother's farm for safety. During that year Newton began developing the calculus, conducting optical experiments with prisms, and thinking about the force that makes apples fall and holds the moon in the sky.

He returned to Cambridge in 1667 and became the Lucasian professor of mathematics in 1669. This position allowed him to continue his research. In 1668 he invented a reflecting telescope, which was a tremendous advance over the refracting telescope. He presented it to the Royal Society, of which he became a member.

In the 1680s Newton began his major work, one of the greatest scientific works ever written, *Philosophiae Naturalis Principia Mathematica (Mathematical Principles of Natural Philosophy)*. It includes his three laws of motion as well as the law of universal gravitation. Written in Latin, the work did not appear in English for forty-two years. The astronomer Edmund Halley, who was Newton's friend, paid for the publishing expenses of the book.

Newton was elected a member of Parliament in 1689. He later became warden of the mint in charge of coinage, resigning his professorship. He was elected president of the Royal Society and was knighted in 1705. He is buried in Westminster Abbey.

47. GOTTFRIED WILHELM VON LEIBNIZ

"He said what?" the Princess of Wales stammers, color rising to her pale cheeks. The valet stands at attention in her drawing room. "Your Highness," he answers, "I distinctly overheard Leibniz talking to himself as he wrote a letter to his friend Arnauld. He said that all is determined, there is no free will, and the example of this is the uselessness of women whom we all try to please although we know what we really want them for."

"This Leibniz is obviously a liar and a fraud," the Princess exclaims. "And to think that I have listened to his fine phrases about this being the best of all possible worlds, about the power of God and the ability of the human will to manifest that power, and about there being only ideas without a physical existence. He deserves to be drawn and quartered the moment he sets foot on English soil!"

The valet, knowing the monetary value of such information, quickly goes to Leibniz. "What does someone who smells like you want?" Leibniz asks, barely opening the door. The valet explains that the Princess will have him killed in the event he goes to England with George I. Leibniz does not accept the valet's words until he explains what he said about Leibniz to the Princess.

"It is because of Newton that this is happening. Everyone is on his side. They actually believe I stole the calculus from him. No one cares that I published my version in 1684, three full years before Newton developed his own system. My philosophy is sound." He continues, "It is because of its rightness, its substance, that no one understands it. At least Arnauld knows what I am talking about. I will write to him my real views. Let them all be condemned on that stupid little island."

Leibniz pays the valet for his information and orders him away. He sits and begins his letter to Arnauld. . . .

(A) *"Anxiety and conscience are a powerful pair of dynamos. Between them they have ensured that I shall work hard, but they cannot ensure that one shall work at anything worthwhile. They are blind forces, which drive but do not direct. Fortunately I have also been moved by a third motive: the wish to see and understand."*

(B) *"In consulting the notion which I have of every true proposition, I find that every predicate, necessary or contingent, past, present, or future, is comprised in the notion of the subject, and I ask no more."*

(C) *"It is not said that life and our knowledge of it are the same. The map of human association shows us many well tried and relatively safe paths. They keep clear of the water, where the familiar melts into mystery. But the mystery exists and challenges."*

Answer (A): From Arnold Toynbee's "Why and How I Work." Toynbee (1889-1976) was a great and admired British historian and philosopher.

Answer (B): CORRECT! From Leibniz's "Letters to Arnauld."

Answer (C): From Idris Parry's *Animals of Silence*. Parry (1922-   ) is a Welsh essayist, critic, and philosopher.

Gottfried Wilhelm von Leibniz (1646-1716), German philosopher and mathematician, called the "Aristotle of the seventeenth century," was born in Leipzig, Saxony. His father, a philosophy professor, died when Leibniz was six years old. By the time he was fourteen, Leibniz had taught himself Latin and Greek, and at nineteen he had a law degree.

From 1666 to 1673 Leibniz served in the diplomatic service of the elector of Mainz. In 1671 he invented a calculating machine that could add, subtract, multiply, and divide, and two years later he was elected to the Royal Society. His system of calculus, called the infinitesimal calculus, was published prior to Newton's work in the field. Although Newton later was to accuse him of plagiarism, Leibniz's system was universally adopted. In 1700 Leibniz became the first president of the Academy of Sciences in Berlin, which he had persuaded the King of Prussia to found.

His major philosophical work, *Nouveaux Essais sur L'endement Humain*, was completed in 1704. Basically, Leibniz believed that the world was the result of a divine plan and was therefore "the best of all possible worlds." The universe was composed of basic elements, called monads, which are indestructible and evolve according to their own specific laws.

48. JONATHAN SWIFT

Jonathan Swift sits cross-legged on his bed in a Dublin hospital ward. The sickness of his mind has spread to his body. It is early in the eighteenth century. Beside his bed sits Stella, his lifetime love and companion. "Christianity obviously must be abolished," he is saying. "We must do away with all forms of love and liking and see if the church will be able to function with everybody simply tolerating each other. For you see, Stella," he smiles, "if love is eliminated, then you and I, who are in love, can be together, since it is really love that keeps us apart."

A group of nurses has gathered around his bed. They are often amused by the wit and satire of the vicar of Laracor. Swift greatly appreciates his pretty young audience, and continues: "If the old timers, the ancients, will give up their prestige and be judged with the moderns on equal footing, then the moderns will win and we can eliminate history. Of course, this will have to be done every few years so that the moderns do not become the ancients!" The nurses laugh at this. "Another task, young things, is to construct a world in which we are giants, and then a world in which we are midgets. That way we can learn to live with a variety of perspectives."

The nurses love the words and stories of this patient. Often he answers their questions in the most comic and tragic ways. Sometimes he is silent and then suddenly breaks into peals of laughter. They treat him with deference and gentleness. First, out of respect. Second, because his health is failing.

One of the nurses has a question. She steps closer to the bed, looking first at Stella and then at Swift. "How should we live our lives, dear Swift?" Swift answers her as though the words lay waiting on the tip of his tongue. . . .

(A) *"You can readily see that any illness imposes certain, should we say, obligations, certain necessities of a prophylactic nature on the authorities concerned with public health, such necessities to be imposed, needless to say, with a minimum of inconvenience and hardship to the unfortunate individual who has, through no fault of his own, become infected."*

(B) *"The people who are so willing to be victims are those who've given up being cannibals themselves, they're not tough enough or ruthless for the golden road to maturity and the ever so wise shrug. They know they've given up. What they are really saying is: I've given up, but I'll be happy to contribute my flesh and blood to you."*

(C) *"If we take an Examination of what is generally understood by Happiness, as it has respect, either to the Understanding or the Senses, we shall find all its properties and Adjuncts will herd under this short definition: That, it is the perpetual Possession of being well deceived."*

Answer (A): From William Burroughs' *Naked Lunch*. Burroughs (1914-   )
is a contemporary writer of experimental fiction.

Answer (B): From Doris Lessing's *The Golden Notebook*. Lessing (1919-   )
is a writer of contemporary fiction.

Answer (C): CORRECT! From Jonathan Swift's "A Tale of a Tub."

Jonathan Swift (1667-1745), Irish writer, was born in Dublin. His father died shortly after Swift's birth and his mother abandoned him. Swift was raised by his uncles, who were responsible for his education. In 1686 Swift received a Bachelor's degree from Trinity College, and in 1692 he graduated from Hart Hall, Oxford, with a Master's. During this time, Swift was secretary to Sir William Temple, a retired diplomat who was writing his memoirs. It was in Temple's employ that Swift met Esther Johnson, the "Stella" in *Journal to Stella*, who was the daughter of one of Temple's servants. They became companions until her death. Also during this time Swift first began suffering from Menières disease, an illness that would continue until his death.

Swift returned to Dublin after the death of Temple. In 1701 he got a Doctor of Divinity degree from Trinity College and became vicar of Laracor. Although at first a Whig, in 1710 Swift came to the realization that the Whigs are uninterested in the welfare of Ireland, and he switched his allegiance to the Tory party, becoming one of its leading spokesmen. When the Tory party collapsed in 1714, Swift, who had been making trips back and forth to London, returned to Ireland for good, as the dean of St. Patrick's Church, Dublin. This period of his life is recorded in his *Journal to Stella*.

Swift became one of the strongest voices in Ireland against British exploitation and abuse. "A Modest Proposal," which describes infants being killed and prepared for the dinners of the English, is one of his tracts against such abuse. *Gulliver's Travels*, his most famous work, a social and political satire, was anonymously published in 1726.

Toward the end of his life, Swift's health began to deteriorate to the point where he was declared legally insane. He died in Dublin. His last words: "I am a fool."

49. GIAMBATTISTA VICO

Giambattista Vico has been sitting all day on a bench outside a church in Naples. The year is 1712. The philosopher is gaining renown as a brilliant professor of rhetoric at the University of Naples.

Today, however, he is not thinking about rhetoric. He is watching his fellow human beings as they gravitate around the church. First, a morning mass. At noon, a funeral. At sundown, a marriage. Vico is pondering the notion that such things are the foundations of society, not just things that happen. "The need for God, law, marriage, and burial of the dead," he reasons, "are fundamental aspects of a culture because they go against the instincts of men. The mythic, inbred desires of lust, abandonment, and murder are contrasted by these institutions. Where they exist, culture exists. Without them, there is no culture."

After a day filled with the headiness of major insights, Vico returns home and is greeted by the reality and turmoil of his daily life. His son has run away, his daughter is ill, and his wife is possessed by venomous anger at a comment made by a neighbor concerning her husband. Vico abandons all hope of continuing his line of thought and escapes out the back door. "Perhaps I will visit one of my mistresses and forget to go to mass tomorrow morning."

All his feelings of the day throb within him as he slowly gets drunk at a local tavern. "We first learn to fear God and then we love him. We then start to create government and then we hate and destroy it. Everything we do is to control our vile and mythic purposes which, in the long run, only destroy us, giving us room to rebuild and rethink."

"Shut up you old preacher," another man says and throws a bottle at him. It misses, and Vico rises to fight the man. Suddenly, in his alcoholic stupor, he realizes yet another insight and begins to write it on the table with a piece of graphite. . . .

(A) "It is true that men have themselves made this world of nations but this world without doubt has issued from a mind often diverse, at times quite contrary, and always superior to the particular ends that men had proposed to themselves: which narrow ends, made means to serve wider ends, it has always employed to preserve the human race upon earth . . . That which did all this was mind, for men did it with intelligence: it was not fate, for they did it by choice: not change, for the results of their always so acting are perpetually the same."

(B) "History is therefore a process of interaction between the historian and the past of which he is writing. The facts help to mould the mind of the historian. . . . History is a dialogue between past and present, not between dead past and living present, but between living present and a past which the historian makes live again by establishing its continuity with the present."

(C) "A more reasonable attitude would be for Man to 'serve nature' in order to serve himself, rather than to serve himself without regard for, or at the expense of, Nature and others. By recognizing and respecting the natural hierarchies of purpose, Man would be better able to gauge his latitude to select and pursue his own chosen purposes without coming in conflict with the purpose of nature which appears to be the continuation of life as long as conditions on the planet permit."

Answer (A): CORRECT! From Giambattista Vico's *New Science.*

Answer (B): From E. H. Carr's *The New Society.* Carr (1906-   ), in this work, makes a dramatic statement of the fascistic tendencies of contemporary democracy.

Answer (C): Jonas Salk's "Survival of the Wisest". Salk (1914-   ) is a biologist who discovered a vaccine against polio.

Giambattista Vico (1668-1744), Italian philosopher and historian, was born in Naples. In 1699 he was made a professor of rhetoric at the University of Naples, and in 1734 he was appointed historiographer to the King of Naples.

Vico developed his major historical theories in his *New Science* (1725). He devised a systematic method of historical research and a theory of history. According to Vico, history is an account of human societies, their conception and development. Each period in history has distinct characteristics, and each period repeats itself in a regular sequence.

The work of Vico did not become well known until the nineteenth century.

50. GEORGE BERKELEY

A man and woman walk in the woods outside Dublin. The year is 1715. They are giggling, laughing, seemingly having a wonderful time together as they arrive at a deep gorge which separates them from their destination.

"We can jump it," George Berkeley says.

"Are you joking?" replies Katherine. "We'll kill ourselves, or at least I will kill myself. No thank you, George."

"Katherine," Berkeley asks, "do you really believe that you can see death?"

"I see the possibility of it happening."

Berkeley lies down in the grass and closes his eyes and meditates for a few minutes. He beckons Katherine to sit down next to him. They have been close companions the past few years. He considers her adequate for long philosophical discussions. In fact, it was with Katherine that Berkeley conceived the idea that matter does not exist as such, but only exists as it is perceived. It is only in the mind that sensible objects become real. Yet, Katherine has always fought this idea, so central to his philosophy, almost as though her integrity depended upon it. This flaw in her character, as he sees it, has always bothered Berkeley. Now he discerns a way to make her relent and consider pure ideas.

"Katherine," he instructs, "close your eyes and lie back." As she obeys, Berkeley says, "Now, Katherine, who is this coming? Why, it is that handsome young man from the ale house where we stopped. The one who looked at you with such longing. Oh, what a fine young man he is. Ah, Katherine, he is coming closer. He is just now sitting down close by you."

Berkeley leans over, holds the pale young woman in his arms, and kisses her with passion and warmth. "Now he has kissed you," he says. "He is getting up and moving away. He is gone. Katherine, open your eyes," Berkeley says.

"George," she exclaims, "I think that it was you who kissed me! My mind tells me that it was you!"

Berkeley smiles. He looks closely into her eyes and repeats the words of his latest work. . . .

(A) *"Give me the body. I believe the life of the body is a greater reality than the life of the mind: when the body is really wakened to life."*

(B) *"The brain, being a sensible thing, exists only in the mind."*

(C) *"There are no 'basic emotions,' instincts or personality, outside of the relationships a person has within one or another social context."*

Answer (A): From D. H. Lawrence's *Lady Chatterly's Lover*. Lawrence (1885-1930) was one of the experimental writers of the first half of this century, reknowned for his moral portraits of men and women.

Answer (B): CORRECT! From George Berkeley's *The Dialogues of Hylas and Philonous*.

Answer (C): From R. D. Laing's *The Politics of Experience*. Laing (1927-   ) is a radical therapist in the contemporary psychiatric world.

George Berkeley (1685-1753), Irish philosopher, was born in County Kilkenny. He attended Trinity College, Dublin, where he became a Fellow at the age of twenty-two.

Berkeley accomplished most of his important philosophical work before the age of thirty. His major works include *A New Theory of Vision* (1709), *The Principles of Human Knowledge* (1710), and *The Dialogues of Hylas and Philonus* (1713). Berkeley's famous phrase "*esse est percipe* ("to be is to be perceived") constitutes a denial of the existence of matter except through the mind's perception of it. He explained the continuing apparent existence of objects as the work of God's observing mind.

Later in his life Berkeley attempted to found a college in the Bermudas for the purpose of educating and training American Indians for the ministry. He spent several years in Rhode Island trying to find support for this project, unsuccessfully, and returned to England. In 1734 he became the Bishop of Cloynes, Ireland. Ten years later, he published *A Chain of Philosophical Reflections and Inquiries Concerning the Virtues of Tar Water, and diverse other Subjects connected together and arising from one another.* This was his last work. He died in Oxford at the age of sixty-eight.

51. BARON DE MONTESQUIEU

The Devil, Eve, Jesus, Erebus, and Aristotle are gathered in a corner watching the evening's events. A young woman has been whipped by six old hags, a grotesque fashion show of fat women in tight clothes has just concluded, a brother and sister have been married, and to top it off, the cooks have served a feast of the sexual parts of three sheep and two cows.

The year is 1748. Montesquieu's costume ball will be the talk of Paris for months to come. He has arranged the evening to present his most important ideas and criticisms of society. Everyone has been asked to wear a bizarre costume. The entire political and cultural society of Paris has been invited. They have all come to be astonished and entertained.

Montesquieu is pleased. He wants to revolt these people, to reveal their lack of moral strength and inability to discern. He wants to give them a taste of what they really want in a society, what they actually secretly allow to happen. As the events conclude, a final act is performed. An old actor, dressed as a scholar, walks pensively and silently among the assembled guests. Still desiring entertainment, they begin to berate the old man. A guest hits him with his cane, and the crowd bursts into uproarious laughter and cheers.

Montesquieu is satisfied. He has revealed the spirit of the ruling class for what it is. Suddenly, at his signal, from the four corners of his huge hall, servants run through the room, passing out copies of the host's new work. Montesquieu announces that there will be no further entertainment during the evening. One by one, the guests open up their books and begin to read. . . .

(A) *"The principle of despotic government is subject to continual corruption, because it is even in its nature corrupt. Other governments are destroyed by particular accidents, which do violence to the principles of each constitution; this is ruined by its own intrinsic imperfections, when some accidental causes do not prevent the corruption of its principles. It maintains itself, therefore, only when circumstances, drawn from the climate, religion, situation, or genius of the people, oblige it to conform to order, and to admit of some rule. By these things its nature is forced without being changed; its ferocity remains; and it is made tame and tractable only for a time."*

(B) *"The old society maintains itself also through theories and ideologies that establish its hegemony over the minds of men who therefore do not merely bite their tongues but submit to it willingly. It will be impossible either to emancipate men from the old society or build a humane new one, without beginning, here and now, the construction of a total counter culture, including new social theories: and it is impossible to do this without a critique of the social theories dominant today."*

(C) *"When an individual finds persons in his presence acting improperly or appearing out of place, he can read this as evidence that although the peculiarity itself may not be a threat to him, still, those who are peculiar in one regard may well be peculiar in other ways, too, some of which may be threatening. For the individual, then, impropriety on the part of others may function as an alarming sign. Thus, the minor civilities of everyday life can function as an early warning system, conventional courtesies are seen as mere convention but nonperformance can cause alarm."*

Answer (A):   CORRECT! From Montesquieu's *The Spirit of Laws.*

Answer (B):   From Alvin Gouldner's *The Coming Crisis in Western Sociology.* A critic of the sociology of Talcott Parsons, Gouldner (1920-   ) is becoming one of the major sociologists in America.

Answer (C):   From Erving Goffman's *Relations in Public*, Goffman (1922-   ) is a sociologist concerned with the formulation of understanding of everyday behavior and its meaning.

Charles Louis de Secondat Baron de la Brède et de Montesquieu (1689-1755), French political philosopher, was born near Bordeaux of a family of lawyers and nobility. He attended Oratorian Collège de Jully, and studied law in Bordeaux and Paris. In 1714 he became a counselor of the French parlement. He succeeded his uncle as president of that body in 1716. In 1721 Monestquieu became known with the publication of *Persian Letters*, a satire of French society and French institutions.

His most important work, *The Spirit of Laws* (1748), had a significant influence on the American Constitution. In it, Montesquieu compares and contrasts three types of government—a republic, a monarchy, and a despotism. Montesquieu held that climate and circumstance determine and influence the government of a country. He believed in governmental separation of powers in order to ensure freedom for the individual. Montesquieu spent the last part of his life defending his ideas as set forth in this work, censored by the Roman Catholic Church. He died in Paris.

52. FRANCOIS AROUET DE VOLTAIRE

"If God did not exist, man would have to invent him." Voltaire sits on the veranda of his chalet, overlooking Lake Geneva. A group of young political activists have come to question him on the nature of politics and religion. Voltaire's ideas on these subjects have often caused him trouble and have kept him on the move, from France to England to Germany and now, in 1754, to Geneva.

"Voltaire," asks Maponche, "what is the meaning of inventing God since, if we could invent him, he would surely already exist?" Voltaire smiles, remembering his provocative phrase of a few years ago, "Crush the infamous."

"Maponche," he replies, "often what one says is a reflection of the person to whom one is speaking and is not intended to be a real thought for all history." This answer causes the group of men to laugh, although they take his statement quite seriously.

"How do you feel about arbitrary punishment, now that you live in a peaceful situation?" Forple questions.

"Arbitrary justice comes from arbitrary power which is put in the hands of the fat and greasy without regard for the implications, just as I could give you another piece of cake despite the fact that you have already eaten enough to make your stomach swell."

By and by, the men depart, leaving Voltaire by the peaceful lakeside. "What is the meaning of all this, my life," he wonders aloud. "I surely do not know. I am certain of the unity of the universe and the contingency of its parts. Yet, if I were to die tomorrow, I hardly know what I would say." Voltaire stares across the lake. Some appropriate words to be said at his death come into his mind. . . .

(A) *"Rose, Oh the pure contradiction, delight of being no one's sleep under so many lids."*

(B) *"I died adoring God, loving my friends, not hating my enemies, and detesting persecution."*

(C) *"Thou shalt know each hidden cause And see the future time: Try what depth the center draws And then to heaven climb."*

Answer (A): From Rainer Maria Rilke's "Tombstone Elegy" in *Poems 1926-1926*. Rilke (1880-1926) was a German expressionist poet, most famous for his *Duino Elegies*.

Answer (B): CORRECT! From *Philosophical Dictionary* in *Writings of Voltaire*.

Answer (C): From Andrew Marvell's "A Dialogue between the Resolved Soul and Created Pleasure." Marvell (1621-1678) was a court poet, most famous for his love poems.

François Marie Arouet de Voltaire (1694-1778), French philosopher and author, was born in Paris, the son of a notary. He attended the Jesuit College of Louis-le-Grand. In 1718 he spent eleven months in the Bastille, wrongly accused of insulting the regent, Philippe II d'Orleans. During his imprisonment, he took the name "Voltaire" and wrote *Oedipus*, a tragedy, which earned him a pension from the regent. Eight years later he was again imprisoned but released on the condition that he go to England.

Voltaire's *Philosophical Letters*, the result of his two years in England, were banned and burned in France. At this time, he moved in with Madame du Chalet, his mistress, at her husband's estate near Cirey, where they lived together (husband included) until her death in 1749. At Cirey, Voltaire began writing plays and corresponding with Frederick the Great of Prussia.

After his mistress' death, Madame de Pompadour helped Voltaire win back his favor at Versailles. He became royal historiographer and gentleman of the bedchamber to King Louis XV. From 1750 to 1753 he was at the court of Frederick the Great, until the two men quarreled and Voltaire departed for Geneva.

In Geneva, Voltaire got into trouble over an article he wrote for Diderot's *Encyclopedia*. As a result he moved over the border to Ferney, France. He lived there until his death, writing and being visited by the important people of Europe.

During this period Voltaire was a spokesman for civil rights, and involved with the problems of the lower classes. He built factories for unemployed watchmen and weavers on his estate. He advocated the town meeting. He spoke out against religious persecution. And he wrote the most popular of his many works, *Candide* (1759).

Voltaire died in Paris at eighty-four, four months after his return to the city for a performance of his play, *Irene*.

53. SAMUEL JOHNSON

What a rowdy dinner party! Just what to expect on an evening in London in honor of Samuel Johnson's newly published edition of Shakespeare. Besides old Sam, there is his sidekick Boswell, Mr. and Mrs. Thrale, Joseph Love, and others. Numerous children stand and crouch in the wings, all ears, awaiting tidbits of Dr. Johnson's brilliant conversation. The year is 1765.

"My friends, no man is a hypocrite in his pleasures." Dr. Johnson says to Mr. Love, who nods, his mouth full of delicious cake.

"Right you are, Samuel," says Thrale. "But some of our pleasures are earned through hard work. I remember learning at school about the wicked smoke which I so fully enjoy now but found so distasteful then."

"Ah, yes, learning is wonderful," Johnson sighs. "But times change. For instance, there is less flogging in our great schools than when I was a lad, but less is learned. Thus, what the boys get at one end they lose at another." The whole table erupts in laughter at Dr. Johnson's wit.

"Yes, Sam, don't you feel any sorrow about the situation?" Thrale's wife asks.

"No, my dear. Grief is a species of idleness. I am never idle. It matters not how a man dies, but how he lives."

The dinner guests are silent. Dr. Johnson is becoming more serious. He seems to be reflecting on his quips and their flippancy. Perhaps he is feeling mellow about a lifetime of major contributions to the culture and to society. He stares across the table at Boswell for a moment before speaking. . . .

(A) "Fame cannot spread wide or endure long that is not rooted in nature, and matured by art. That which long hopes to resist the blast of malignity, and stand firm against the attacks of time must contain in itself some original principle of growth. The reputation which arises from the detail or transposition of borrowed sentiments, may spread awhile, like ivy on the rind of antiquity, but it will be torn away by accident or contempt and suffered to rot unheeded on the ground."

(B) "All works of art are founded on a certain distance from the lived reality which is represented. This "distance" is by definition inhuman or impersonal to a certain degree, for in order to appear to us as art, the work must restrict sentimental intervention and emotional participation, which are functions of 'closeness.'"

(C) "Of all the causes which conspire to blind
Man's erring judgment, and misguide the mind,
What the weak head with the strongest bias rules,
Is pride, the never failing vice of fools.
Whatever nature has in worth denied,
She gives in large recruits of needful pride."

Answer (A):   CORRECT! From "Number 154", an essay by Johnson from the *Rambler.*"

Answer (B):   From Susan Sontag's *Against Interpretation*. Sontag is a well-respected cultural critic, most famous for her essay on "camp."

Answer (C):   From Alexander Pope's "Essay on Criticism." Pope (1688-1744) was a famous and renowned English critic and poet.

Samuel Johnson (1709-1784), English author, critic, and essayist, was born in Lichfield, Staffordshire. His father was a poor bookseller. Johnson contracted tuberculosis as a baby, which left him blind in one eye. He attended Lichfield Grammar School and Pembroke College, Oxford, for a year, but was forced to quit due to lack of money.

In 1735 Johnson married Elieabeth Porter, a widow, and started a school which failed. He then went to London and began writing for the *Gentleman's Magazine*. The publication of his poem, "London", earned him praise from Alexander Pope. During this time Johnson wrote hundreds of essays for periodicals, especially the *Rambler*.

The Dictionary of the English Language, one of Johnson's most significant works, containing over 40,000 words and definitions, was published in 1755. It was a precursor of all later English dictionaries.

Until 1762 Johnson was always on the verge of total poverty and wrote to keep food on the table. He wrote the novel *Rasselas* to pay for his mother's funeral. In 1762 he was granted a royal pension which provided him with some security. He then met James Boswell and helped found "The Club," a literary group which included Oliver Goldsmith, Joshua Reynolds, Edward Gibbon, Edmund Burke, and Boswell. In 1765 Johnson's edition of Shakespeare was published with his critique.

Lives of the Poets was his last major work. The book, a ten-volume compendium of fifty-two English poets from 1660 to 1760, with introductions, is the first example of literary biography in English history.

54. JEAN JACQUES ROUSSEAU

Jean Jacques Rousseau gazes out of a small window in his cold, damp attic in Paris. The year is 1762. He hates the society in which he lives. His mind is wandering: "If only I had lived a free life. If I had made other decisions, I would be healthy and happy. They are out to get me. They are scheming and devising ways to persecute me, torture me. They send germs to infect me, steal my money, open my mail. They are watching me all the time. I have no privacy, and because of their eyes I am impotent. I am the greatest victim the world has ever known. I must do something, say something to place all this in its proper perspective. But first, revenge!"

Rousseau goes downstairs and out into the street, where his five children are playing in front of the house. He has never enjoyed their presence. Nor did he enjoy the foul rutting that resulted in their conception, for that matter. "If only I had married another woman. What a horribly wrong decision!" he mutters grimly, looking down the street for signs of the officials from the orphanage whom he has summoned to take his children away. "I can no longer deal with them. This is my revenge for all the terrible ways in which they have treated me. Diderot, Hume, and the rest of them. They'll be sorry. The children will be abandoned. Yes, this is the right way, the only way. I should have made love with a decent woman instead of that slut from whose womb these runts have come. The children must be sent away, and then I will work. I will execute a political treatise to advocate a return to the pure state, the natural state, with pure races, and leadership by the mighty. I will advocate the demise of the social contract. Man will live in harmony, the same harmony that existed before civilization. Equality is essential, even if it means a loss of liberty."

Later that night, the house in Paris is dark and silent, except for a single candle which burns in the attic room, and the sound of Rousseau's quill as he writes. . . . .

(A) "Man is born free: and everywhere he is in chains . . . . Each man who gives himself to all, gives himself to nobody. The Sovereign, however, merely by virtue of what it is, is always what it should be. Our will is always for our own good: but we do not always see what that is . . . As soon as any man says of the affairs of state, What does it matter, the state must be given up for lost."

(B) "Man has not nature—no simple or homogeneous being. He is a strange mixture of being and nonbeing. His place is between these two opposite poles. There is, therefore, only one approach to the secret of human nature: that of religion."

(C) "Capitalism places every man in competition with his fellow for a share of the available wealth. A few people accumulate big piles, but most do not. The sense of community falls victim to this struggle. Increased abundance and prosperity are tied to growing productivity. A hierarchy of functionaries interposes itself between the people and the leadership. The good of the private corporation is seen as prior to the public good."

Answer (A):   CORRECT! From Jean Jacques Rousseau's *Social Contract.*

Answer (B):   From Ernst Cassirer's *An Essay on Man.* Cassirer (1874–1945) wrote mainly on the relation of philosophy to science in the modern world.

Answer (C):   From Donald Barthelme's *Sadness.* Barthelme (1931–   ) is a writer of fiction whose uses the absurd as a basic context.

Jean Jacques Rousseau (1712–1778), French writer, philosopher, and father of Romanticism, was born in Geneva, the son of a watchmaker. After leaving home at sixteen, he met Louise de Warens, who became his patroness. She sent him to Turin where he converted to Catholicism and worked as a footman, before returning to her in Chambery, Savoy, where he spent the next twelve years as her lover.

In 1742 Rousseau returned to Paris and became good friends with Diderot and his intellectual circle. There he took up with Therese le Vasseur, an illiterate servant girl who bore him five children, whom he eventually had placed in a foundling home.

In 1749 the Academy of Dijon ran a contest asking the question, "Has the progress of the arts and sciences improved or corrupted human conduct?" Rousseau entered and won with his essay in which he stated that man, who was basically good, had been corrupted by civilization. As a result of this contest, Rousseau became both famous and infamous.

In 1754 his *Discourse on the Origin and Foundation of Inequality Among Men* was published. From this point on Rousseau was on the move, driven by circumstance and his paranoias. He left Paris, accusing Diderot and others of plotting against him, and was taken in by the Duc de Luxembourg. During his stay there, he wrote *Julie,* or *La Nouvelle Héloise (1761),* the *Social Contract,* and *Émile* (both 1762). The last-named work so offended church authorities in Geneva and Paris that it was burned in both places. Rousseau escaped to Neuchatel, and then to Bern. In 1765 he was expelled from Bern and went to England to the home of David Hume. He quarreled with Hume and returned to Paris in 1770, moving into an attic where he copied music. He wandered from salon to salon reading his *Confessions* aloud.

55. IMMANUEL KANT

A saddle maker's son arrives at the great house of a Prussian prince to make a delivery. He knows that the prince is a kindly gentleman, yet one taken by mysticism, a prevalent diversion in early eighteenth-century Germany. As Immanuel Kant carries the new saddle to the door, he hears the rumblings of a séance taking place inside. He creeps to the window. Inside, he views a scene which drives him to dark despair. "While the Prince and his friends can afford the luxury of such occult interests," he thinks, "the common people, my mother and father among them, are driven to ruin by such worthless pursuits." He walks to the door, knocks, places the saddle before it, and departs. He is never to forget this event. It is crucial to the formulation of his later thought and work.

As an adult Kant is widely known as a scholar and tutor. His services are cherished for the sons of noble and common men alike. One day, Kant is invited to tutor the grandson of the prince to whom he had delivered the saddle many years before. Although he has come to believe in the uselessness of such people, he agrees to be the young man's tutor. He arrives at the house thinking about the nature of people that defend power and justice with force. He is asked to wait in the library. Looking at the bookshelves, he sees only texts dealing with rational discourse, descriptions of revelations, and mysticism. Moments later, the young man enters the room and finds the great philosopher in a mad frenzy, smashing bookshelves and ripping apart texts. The boy stands very still. Kant, finally taking notice of him, stops. "There can be no learning in this house," he says, "as long as questioning remains within the constrictions of rational nondynamic thinking. These books must go. We need a critique of pure reason, a critique of mysticism and of practical reason."

Kant calms down. He is a born teacher and wants to help instruct the young man, despite these influences. He wants to help him perceive the universe as a changing phenomenon. "Well," challenges Kant, facing him across the debris, "what do you think is important?"

"Copernicus' world view in which the earth circles the sun," the boy immediately responds.

Kant is shocked. This is a brilliant reply. He beckons the young man to sit down next to him, and expounding on his answer, begins to describe the essence of thought . . . .

(A) "Let me ask: When do you know that? Always, day and night? Or only when you are actually thinking of it? Do you know it, that is, in the same way as you know the alphabet and the multiplication table? Or is what you call knowledge a state of consciousness or a process—say a thought of something, or the like?"

(B) "Knowing is centered in the perceiving *mind, not in the object under observation. The mind is the center of experience and not the objects that the mind perceives.*

(C) "*The passions, therefore, not the reason of the human being should sit in judgment. But reason alone should rule in the affairs between men. Passions should be controlled by the construct of culture and not only by the individual.*"

Answer (A): From Ludwig Wittgenstein's *Philosophical Investigations*. Wittgenstein (1889–1951) was an Austrian philosopher (see selection 91 for further details on his life).

Answer (B): CORRECT! From Immanuel Kant's *Critique of Pure Reason*.

Answer (C): From *The Federalist Papers*. This particular section was written by James Madison (1751-1836), who became fourth President of the United States.

Immanuel Kant (1724–1804), German metaphysician, and moral philosopher, was born in Koenigsberg and spent his entire life in East Prussia, in or near his home town. He was a tutor and lectured in science and philosophy at the University of Koenigsberg. In 1770 he became a professor of logic and metaphysics. He never married and his outward life was so strictly regulated that it is said that the townspeople could set their watches by his appearance for his daily constitutional.

In his early writings Kant was more interested in science than philosophy. He wrote about earthquakes, and why whe west wind in Europe was moist.

His first important philosophical work was the *Critique of Pure Reason* (1781), which began the period of his major writings. In 1793 he published *Religion Within the Limits of Reason Alone*, which caused the government to order him to cease further publications on religion. Kant retired in 1797 and went into severe mental decline. He died seven years after his retirement at the age of eighty.

Kant's work influenced the development of Gestalt psychology and the scientific agnosticism of William James and John Dewey. The greatest reaction against Kant came in the works of his successor G. W. F. Hegel.

56. THOMAS JEFFERSON

Thomas Jefferson is faced with a difficult decision as he stands in front of his new home in Virginia. He began building the house after his wife perished in a fire in their old home. During the many years of its construction, Jefferson has worked to incorporate all his wisdom into the placement and construction of the materials. He does not accept one idea in architecture as being sacred, just as he refuses to recognize any such sacred idea in law, science, government, or philosophy. His mind never ceases to question. It is this very quality that has made his name a legend in America at the close of the eighteenth century.

Jefferson's decision concerns whether to place a window facing north, from which the entire valley could be seen from inside the house, or to place the window facing east, from which the view would be limited but efficiency and economy would be preserved. "Art over life," he muses.

"Where shall the window be placed, sir?" one of the carpenters asks Jefferson.

After a pause, Jefferson decides. "Place the window facing east. Then build a special, small window facing north. Construct this window with two layers of glass separated by two inches of air."

Jefferson is pleased with his decision. He has met both circumstances well and, as a result, will have both what he needs and what he wants. At that moment, a messenger rides up with a letter from James Madison, who is drafting the U.S. Constitution. In his note, Madison wants to know if Jefferson will respond as a federalist, in support of the idea of a strong central government, or as an antifederalist, supporting the rights of the individual. Jefferson realizes that this question cannot be answered simply. He decides that his reply to Madison must stem from his own experience. He wants to include every aspect that needs to be addressed, just as he did in considering the placement of the window. He sits down and writes . . .

(A) "The truth is that men cannot achieve wisdom by their own efforts nor goodness. Only a great event can change men—an event in their personal life, or their collective life.

"However, there still seems to be some cosmic demand that we should exercise our best judgment, reason, etc."

(B) "I have never had an opinion in politics or religion which I was afraid to own. A costive reserve on these subjects might have procured me more esteem from some people, but less from myself. My great wish is to go on in a strict but silent performance of my duty: to avoid attracting notice and to keep my name out of newspapers, because I find the pain of a little censure, even when it is unfounded, is more acute than the pleasure of much praise."

(C) "Right and wrong exist by convention not by nature."

Answer (A):   From Henry Luce's letter to Matthews. Henry Luce (1898–1967) was the director and founder of Time/Life, Inc.

Answer (B):   CORRECT! From Thomas Jefferson's letter to Frances Hopkinson.

Answer (C):   From fragments by Archelaus. Archelaus (4th century B.C.) was a Greek philosopher and the teacher of Socrates.

Thomas Jefferson (1743–1826), third President of the United States and author of the Declaration of Independence, was born in Shadwell, Virginia, the son of a prosperous planter. He attended William and Mary College, where he studied law.

In 1775 Jefferson, a delegate to the Second Continental Congress, was responsible for drafting the Declaration of Independence. After serving as a member of the Virginia legislature, and helping to institute such reforms as the abolition of primogeniture and entail, he was elected governor of Virginia (1779–1781). In 1785 he succeeded Benjamin Franklin as minister to France, and in 1790 he became Secretary of State.

His clash with Alexander Hamilton's conservative views led Jefferson to eventually form a group of anti-Federalists, who called themsevles Republicans. This political party gradually gained enough support to have Jefferson elected Vice President in 1796, and the party grew under his leadership. In the presidential election of 1800 Jefferson and Aaron Burr were tied in the electoral vote. The House of Representative gave the office to Jefferson, and he became the first President to be inaugurated in Washington, a city he had helped plan.

Philosophically, Jefferson believed that state and local governments should assume responsibility for their own affairs, while the federal government concentrated on foreign affairs. Jefferson was an idealist who believed in human perfectability. He held that if free education was made available to everyone, it would provide the people with the means to govern themselves well.

In 1809 Jefferson retired to Monticello, a home he designed. Also to his credit were his founding of the University of Virginia, and his leadership of the American Philosophical Society from 1797 to 1815. Thomas Jefferson died on July 4, 1826, the fiftieth anniversary of the nation's founding.

57. JEREMY BENTHAM

The young radical sits in a dark corner of a tavern in London. He is addressing an old man whose back is to the rest of the customers. The subject of their discussion is the world. The year is 1810.

The old man, Jeremy Bentham, is constantly looking around. He is worried that someone may overhear their conversation. Bentham is so shy that only after he has known someone for years will he venture to say anything at all to him. Yet, at home, he will write for days on end. He has written so much that it is inconceivable that all of it could be published.

Bentham listens as the younger man advocates the need for equality and abundance in society. Bentham, in turn, tries to explain the concept of association of ideas. "If society has a minimum amount for each person," Bentham says, "enough to live, abundance so that everyone can desire more, security from theft, murder, or any other violence, and a feeling of equality, then the society will survive."

A barmaid hovers close by. Bentham stops. As soon as she departs, he turns to the young man and continues. "But there is a definite need for these ideas to be presented in association, one with another, so that everyone learns that there is one set of ideas."

The young man considers these words. He knows that it is important not to answer Bentham right away, to give him pleasure in having spoken. He then beings slowly. "I think, however, that no one will abide by this unless punishment is threatened to those who do not agree."

Bentham nods vigorously at this. The question of motivation is crucial to him. "Everyone acts for one reason, and one reason only," he says, his own words inspiring him. He feels he has given the young man a clear description of his philosophy. He continues . . . .

(A) *"It is the mark of a mean capacity to spend much time on the things which concern the body, such as much exercise, much eating, much drinking, much easing of the body, much copulation. But these should be done as subordinate things: and let all care be directed to the mind."*

(B) *"The circumstances of modern life are so complicated, the problems to be dealt with are so difficult, the need for prompt action is often so great that we may easily be led to take up schemes of reform which promise some immediate improvement on the present state of things, but which are not really in the line of advance towards a genuine Collectivism."*

(C) *"The business of government is to promote the happiness of the society, by punishing and rewarding. That part of its business which consists in punishing is more particularly the subject of penal law. In proportion as an act tends to disturb that happiness, in proportion as the tendency of it is pernicious, will be the demand it creates for punishment. What happiness consists of we have already seen; enjoyment of pleasures, security from pains."*

Answer (A): From Epictetus' *Enchiridion*. Epictetus (c. 60–120), along with Lucretius (c. 97–54 B.C.), was the father of Stoicism.

Answer (B): From Sidney Webb's *Socialism, True or False*. Webb (1859–1947) was an English Fabian socialist and historian. Fabian socialism was the political philosophy of many well-known people in early twentieth-century England, including George Bernard Shaw.

Answer (C): CORRECT! From Jeremy Bentham's *An Introduction to the Principles of Morals and Legislation*.

Jeremy Bentham (1748–1832), English philosopher and founder of utilitarianism, was born in London, the son of a lawyer. He went to Oxford at the age of twelve, and after graduating in 1763, he attended law school and was admitted to the bar. Bentham never practiced law, however. Instead he devoted his time to analyzing and criticizing English institutions, laws, and morals. His most important work, *An Introduction to the Principles of Morals and Legislation* (1789), gained him a wide reputation in the Western world.

Bentham's philosophy of utilitarianism held that the basic principle of morality as well as the goal of the state should be the greatest happiness for the greatest number of people. Happiness, for Bentham, meant pleasure.

Bentham was one of the founders of the first journal of utilitarianism, *The Westminster Review*, and he helped found the University College, London. He never married.

58. JOHANN WOLFGANG VON GOETHE

On the evening of his fifty-fifth birthday, Goethe sits alone in his residence in Rome. The year is 1804. As is his birthday custom, he is meditating on the past. His mind flashes back to a lovers' tryst with Frau von Stein many years before.

"I am giving birth to a monster, my love," Goethe recalls saying, "for that is what writing is. I truly expect that this writing will torture me, and the readers, into submission."

"Love is the death of us all," she had replied, "and yet, it is also our birth. Without love we are not continued. With love, we are ended."

Thirty long years later those words still live in Goethe's mind. During these years he has studied optics and science, served as minister to the king, written poetry and plays, and continually fallen in love with beautiful women. Yet, tonight he is reflective. He ponders the meaning of his writing, of loving, and dying. He feels the arrogance of the learned, as well as the mystery of existence. He feels that his monster's career is almost at an end, and yet he recognizes that it is as if it has a life of its own, a life which entered him, possessed him, became him. Goethe genuinely fears the power of the feelings he has had to excite in order to create works to ennoble people's lives. He is troubled.

As he looks at the blank page before him, he feels a hand around his throat. "Has death come to take me before my muse can die on this page before me?"

"Johann," a voice whispers, enticingly.

"Oh, Christiane, it is you. You startled me."

His wife leans down and kisses him. "Come to bed, Johann. I want you."

Goethe is tempted. Christiane is lovely. The glow in her eyes deepens as he slips his hand beneath her skirts and slowly moves it up along her warm thigh. The sensation of his hand on her flesh ignites his mind. The words he has been searching for come to him. With his free hand, he dips his pen into the inkwell and begins to write . . . .

(A)   "Who, if I cried, would hear me among
           the angelic
    order? And even if one of them
           suddenly
    pressed me against his heart, I should
           fade in the strength of his
    stronger existence. For Beauty's
           nothing
    but the beginning of terror we're still
           just able to bear,
    and why we adore it so is because it
           serenely
    disdains to destroy us."

(B)   "Now do I see, no perfect thing is
           given
    To poor mankind. The bliss you have
           bestowed
    To bear me nearer to the gods
    Binds this companion to me:
           doomed I am
    To need the help of him whose
           impudence
    Ensures the cheap abasement of myself
    In his own sight, so much his subtle
           word
    Can sour and stifle all your gift
           of joy."

(C)   "What I have to say does not concern
           that world and
    such a way of life: their way and
           mine diverge sharply.
    I have another world in mind which
           together in one heart
    bears its bitter sweet, its dear
           sorrow, its heart's
    joy, its love's pain, its dear life,
           its sorrowful death,
    its dear death, its sorrowful life.
           To this life let
    my life be given, of this world let
           me be
    part, to be damned or saved with it."

Answer (A):   From Rainer Maria Rilke's *Duino Elegies*. Rilke (1875–1926) wrote this, his most famous work, as an exploration of the relationship between the poet and his world.

Answer (B):   CORRECT! From *Faust*, Part I.

Answer (C):   From Gottfried von Strassburg's *Tristan*. The Tristan story has been told many times, in many different languages, but Gottfried's is generally considered the classic version, written in the thirteenth century.

Johann Wolfgang von Goethe (1749–1832), dramatist, poet, novelist, and scientist, was born in Frankfurt, the son of a lawyer. After a happy childhood, he studied law, music, and art at Leipzig University and completed his law course at Strasbourg.

In 1774, at the age of twenty-five, Goethe made a name for himself with the publication of *The Sorrows of Young Werther*, which he wrote while suffering the pangs of unrequited love. A year later Duke Charles Augustus invited him to his court. Goethe was to spend most of the rest of his life there, serving as chief minister of state for a decade.

Goethe spent the years 1776–1789 in Italy, where he came under the influence of the classical ideal. The result of these two years was *Egmont* (1788), an historical drama; *Torquato Tasso* (1789), a psychological drama, and *Iphigenia at Taurus* (1787). Returning home, he set up house with Christiane Vulpius. She had five children by him, but only one, a son, survived.

Goethe spent the rest of his life on two major works: *The Apprenticeship of Wilhelm Meisters*, a novel, and, *Faust*, a dramatic poem, the work for which he is best known. The latter was published in two parts, the first in 1808, and the second after Goethe's death.

Goethe is buried next to his close friend J. C. F. von Schiller, the poet and dramatist, at Weimar.

59. WILLIAM BLAKE

The black surface waits on the wooden table. A quiet and unassuming man lifts a sharp, pointed tool and adjusts the lamp. His hand is dry and steady as he presses into and through the surface, creating gleaming copper incisions in it. He works hour after hour, transforming the surface into a myriad of lines and shades. As the image of an angel sitting in a tree comes forth, the copper seems to project the lines out into the room. The magic of it makes him sigh deeply and finally cry with relief as he sees the face of God move through his own eyes onto the glossy black surface. William Blake turns the light down, leaves his workroom, and goes to bed.

The next morning, Blake is up early and back at his work table. As he works, he thinks how strange it is that now, in 1789, all of London considers him weird, eccentric, even mad. Yet, at thirty two, he has learned that nothing, including fame and release from a lifetime of poverty, can turn him away from his mystic visions.

Blake works with acid and cloth. He etches the surface. It is all copper and yet the lines have eaten deeply into the surface. He fills the lines with ink, thinking of the irony of the fact that he has to remove the void in order to reintroduce it. He puts the plate on the etching press and watches as an image appears on paper: his muse, the angel, his love, the mystery of the universe sitting in a tree.

As he stares hard at the image, thoughts crowd in on him about the innocence of the mind, the gentleness of love, and the wild and insane nature of life. Blake is a man obsessed with retrieving his mind's phantasies and making them intelligible and beautiful to see. He wants to illustrate the nature of the universe, describe the wondrous mystery that lies just on the other side of conventional observation.

On a writing table across the room, Blake has been making notes about his vision of the world. He gazes down at the pages of words and reads . . .

(A) *"Tell all the truth but tell it slant*
Success in circuit lies
Too bright for our infirm delight
The truth's superb surprise;
As lightning to the children eased
With explanation kind
The truth must dazzle gradually
Or every man be blind."

(B) *"Possibly to be gained (such as*
    gazing in the end
On a cool and God planned paradise
Where the sun shines whitely) by a
    wiser device?
Or would they claim to have found it
    as they bend
To infinity their way? See in this
    surmise
That each coldly reflects the other,
    reflects
The other, to a point where identity
    conflicts
With invisibility and the total of
    hopeful eyes."

(C) *"To see the World in a grain of sand,*
And Heaven in a wild flower:
Hold infinity in the palm of your hand
And eternity in an hour."

Answer (A): From Emily Dickinson's "Tell All the Truth But Tell It Slant". Dickinson (1830–1886) was one of America's first tragic woman poets.

Answer (B): From Emma Swan's "Identical Mirrors Placed Opposite Each Other In A Hall" in *Poems of Emma Swan*. Swan (1914–   ) is a poet of merit whose work has not been widely recognized.

Answer (C): CORRECT! From William Blake's "Auguries of Innocence."

William Blake (1757–1827), English poet and artist, was born in London, the son of a successful hosier. Although Blake never received a formal education, his father, recognizing the boy's talent, sent him to drawing school at the age of ten. At fourteen Blake was apprenticed to an engraver. Later, he attended the Royal Academy but dropped out, unable to tolerate the atmosphere of the institution. In 1782 Blake married Catherine Boucher, the woman who would be his constant companion and adviser for life and whom he taught to read, write, and draw.

During his life Blake had no success with his poetry, which he published himself, or his artwork. He was always on the verge of destitution and was considered an eccentric man. He died in London, the city in which he had spent most of his life.

Blake was a mystic and visionary. He believed in love and liberty and was repulsed by the injustice and cruelty he witnessed all around him, which, he felt, was man's own fault. His major works include *Songs of Innocence* (1789) and *Songs of Experience* (1794). He also wrote prophetic books, including *The Book of Thel*, *The Marriage of Heaven and Hell*, *The French Revolution*, *America*, *Europe*, *The Book of Urizon*, *Milton*, and *Jerusalem*.

60. SAMUEL TAYLOR COLERIDGE

It is late afternoon, tea time in the summer of 1808 in the lake district of England. The river flows nearby as three men and their wives and companions talk and wander through the groves of their minds. William Wordsworth is a confidant of Samuel Taylor Coleridge. Charles Lamb is also a close friend. All are enjoying the intellectual excitement of the ideas expressed that seem to have more life than the birds that glide and fly overhead.

"Nature thrills me," Wordsworth is saying, "with its infinite changeability, with the range of emotions that emerge from the softest stone and the fiercest cloud." He nibbles at a piece of rich chocolate cake, then continues. "I drape myself in the sunlight and wonder what will become of my imagination in such throbbing company."

"Nonsense," interrupts Coleridge, sipping tea. "Nature is just what happens. The beauty of it is the beauty in it, is the beauty beside it and through it. I would rather talk about the words you use to describe nature than what you call nature itself."

Sarah, Coleridge's wife, senses that Samuel has entered one of his "states." A few moments before, he had excused himself and walked off into the woods. When he returned she noticed that he had that odd look in his eyes. "He has taken laudanum again. I can tell," she thinks nervously. "How ironic is his talk of the untouched metaphor of mind when he has just filled his own with nature's chemicals."

Sarah is brought back to the conversation by the sound of her husband's voice. Samuel is resolute about his idea that things created are created in the mind. He stops arguing with Lamb and turns to Wordsworth. His eyes are tracking badly. The assembled company notices that the cadence of his speech is slightly off . . . .

(A) *"The next creative act may bring man to a new dignity. Man's search for the sources of dignity changes with the pattern of his times. In periods during which man saw himself in the image of God, the creation of works to the greater glory of God could provide a sufficient rationale for the dignity of the artist, the artisan, the creative man. But in an age whose dominant value is a pragmatic one and whose massive achievement is an intricate technological order, it is not sufficient to be merely useful."*

(B) *"The history of the evolution of life, incomplete as it is, already reveals to us how the intellect has been formed, by an uninterrupted process, along a line which ascends through the vertebrate series up to man. It shows us in the faculty of understanding as appendage of the faculty of acting, a more and more precise, more and more complex and supple adaptation of the consciousness of living beings to the conditions of existence that are made for them."*

(C) *"The primary imagination I hold to be the living power and the prime agent of all human perception, and as a repetition in the finite mind of the eternal act of creation in the infinite I AM. The secondary I consider as an echo of the former, coexisting with the conscious will, yet still as identical with the primary in the kind of its agency and differing only in degree and in the manner of its operation. It dissolves, diffuses, and dissipates in order to recreate: or, where this process is rendered impossible, yet still, at all events, it struggles to idealize and to unify. It is essentially vital even as all objects (as objects) are essentially fixed and dead."*

Answer (A):   From Jerome Bruner's *On Knowing*. Bruner (1915–   ) is one of the foremost educational theorists in America.

Answer (B):   From Henri Bergson's "Creative Evolution." Bergson (1859–1941) was a major French philosopher of science and literature.

Answer (C):   CORRECT! From Samuel Taylor Coleridge's *Biographia Lieraria*.

Samuel Taylor Coleridge (1772–1834), English Romantic poet and essayist, was born in Devonshire at his father's vicarage. He attended Christ's Hospital School in London and Cambridge University, from which he graduated after brief service with the dragoons. At twenty-two, Coleridge met the poet Robert Southey. Together, they planned a communist utopia called a "pantisocracy" to be established on the Susquehanna River in the United States. Their plan was never realized, however, because it was too impractical.

In 1795 Coleridge married Sarah Fricker, the sister of Southey's wife. The marriage was not a happy one, although four children resulted.

In 1794 Coleridge met Wordsworth who moved next door to his home in Nether Stowey. The two poets jointly published *Lyrical Ballads,* a volume of their work which included Coleridge's "The Rime of the Ancient Mariner." Wordsworth's influence on Coleridge was important and can be seen in his best known works: "Kubla Khan," "Christabel," as well as "Rime."

Coleridge's poor health eventually led him into an addiction, opium in the form of laudanum, which was legal at the time. In 1800, after spending some time in Germany with Wordsworth, Coleridge moved to Keswick. His addiction had increased and his health deteriorated. "Dejection: An Ode" was written there. In 1808 he left his family, and from 1816 until his death, he lived with Dr. James Gillman in London.

In 1817 *Biographia Literaria*, his most important prose work, was published. It is composed of essays on philosophers and writers, as well as a statement of his theory of creative imagination.

61. ARTHUR SCHOPENHAUER

"The world is a terrible place in which to live," declares the thirty-year-old man, turning to his mother. The woman, an elegant, accomplished lady, listens to her son as she sips her cognac. "Fear, greed, murder, and general insensitivity make it impossible ever to create a situation where one's expectations can be met," he moans.

"Don't be so gloomy," she laughs and pats his knee.

"But mother, how can my expectations for life ever be satisfied if you have different and contradictory ones for me?"

"Arthur, my dear, I just want you to be happy. Danzig is very gay. Go visit your friends, cultivate a woman, start to live a little, and you will get over this pessimism."

Her son, infuriated by her total lack of understanding, leaves the room in a rage, bounding up the stairs of the early nineteenth-century palatial house. At the top of the stairs, he opens the door into a small attic. Bare and cold, it contains nothing but a cot, a writing table, and a straight-backed chair. He locks the door and bolsters the chair against it. "I will never speak to that woman again," he vows to the grey walls.

He takes off all his clothes and lies naked on the bed. "Pleasure is merely the absence of pain," he thinks. He runs his hands sensuously over his lean body. "One must renounce all desire and all action." Even as he thinks these thoughts, his hand touches himself and begins to move rhythmically. Despite the cool autumn breeze flowing through the window, his body is becoming warm, much warmer.

Later, Arthur Schopenhauer is exhausted. He is totally disgusted with himself, with the world. After some time, he rises from the bed, walks across the room to the writing table, and scribbles down a short statement which will enable people to understand how to live together in a world of conflicting wants. He slips the parchment under the door. Arthur is comforted in knowing that his mother will soon read his words when she brings him supper.

That night, his mother carries a tray of warm food up the long flight to the attic room. As she sets it down outside the door, she discovers the parchment. In the dim light of the hallway, she reads . . .

(A) *"The most intelligent and the most stupid cannot be changed. Those who ruin themselves and cast themselves away cannot be changed. Yet, willing to learn, all can be changed."*

(B) *"Whether truth be said to have, or whether it be understood not to have, beginning or end, truth can be limited by no beginning or end."*

(C) *"Withdrawal from people, especially women, and sympathy for them is the only way. No wife, no friends, and no company with other people and small amounts of any feelings are all that is possible."*

Answer (A):   From Ch'eng I's *The Philosophy of Human Nature*. Ch'eng I (1033–1107) was a classical Chinese scholar most famous for his commentaries on Confucious.

Answer (B):   From Saint Anselm's *The Dialogues on Truth*. Anselm (1033–1109) was a scholastic theologian and philosopher best known for his ontological proof for the existence of God.

Answer (C):   CORRECT! From Arthur Schopenhauer's "Wisdom of Life".

Arthur Schopenhauer, (1788–1860), German philosopher of pessimism, was born in Danzig, into a prominent commercial family. In 1803 he was sent to a boarding school in England, which he detested. He later became a clerk in a commercial house at his father's behest.

Schopenhauer entered the University of Göttingen in 1809 to study medicine. In his second year there, he switched to philosophy.

He went to Berlin in 1811 to hear the lectures of philosophers Johann Fichte and Friedrich Schleiermacher. In 1813 he was awarded a doctorate for *On the Fourfold Root of the Principle of Sufficient Reason*, which won Goethe's praise. From 1814 to 1818, he wrote his main philosophical work, *The World as Will and Idea*. Schopenhauer thought it to be of grand importance and said that portions of it had been dictated by the Holy Ghost. It was a terrible failure commercially, although some philosophers took notice of it.

After 1831 Schopenhauer lived in Frankfurt-am-Main. He was a misogynist, although occasionally engaging in inconsequential love affairs.

Schopenhauer considered himself to be the successor to Immanuel Kant. He believed in pessimism and that humans would always be in a state of conflict because of their competitive wants. He also believed that the will was superior to knowledge.

62. RALPH WALDO EMERSON

The lecturer stands in the wings of a small theatre in Evanston, Illinois. The year is 1868. He has been touring the United States, talking to audiences about transcendentalism and his ideas about solitude. On stage the master of ceremonies introduces him as a philosopher and statesman. He tells of the guest speaker's work on the *Dial* as well as other magazines and of his friendship with Samuel Taylor Coleridge and William Wordsworth. The lecturer listens to the introduction, and asks himself, "Can this be me?" The words seem to describe another person. As he walks onstage, greeted by the enthusiastic applause, Ralph Waldo Emerson is suffering from an extreme case of mental, spiritual, and physical malaise.

Emerson clears his throat and picks up his notes. The applause continues. "What a paradox," he muses, "I am about to speak of the glory of solitude from a podium in Illinois when I really want to walk silently through the woods, contemplating the beauty and transcendental nature of experience." The irony of the situation is almost amusing. "I am lecturing about solitude, yet I do it in front of an audience. I give people autographs, and yet I tell them to avoid the kind of event for which we are gathered tonight. Perhaps I will tell them what a fraud I am! They don't realize that when they listen to me, they don't listen to themselves," Emerson thinks, sighing. "How fruitless it seems to make a man great so he can no longer live the existence which allowed him to forge his greatness."

The audience quiets. Emerson senses that they are waiting, but he knows that they are not waiting for him. He begins. Immediately he feels that his voice is not his own, but a transcendent aspect of his being. This being so, he realizes that he can, he will share it with the audience . . . .

(A) *"Our strength grows out of our weakness. The indignation which arms itself with secret forces does not awaken until we are pricked and stung and sorely assailed. A great man is always willing to be little. Whilst he sits on the cushion of advantage he goes to sleep."*

(B) *"One does not succeed by devoting oneself to harsh discipline and austerities, but by devoting oneself to the enjoyment of all desires, one rapidly gains success. Don't move your lips for the eating of food you've begged, nor should you be attached to these offerings. It is by moving your lips in the recitation of prayers that the body becomes whole and confirmed in the enjoyment of all desires."*

(C) *"You cannot be vital unless the organs of the body are possessed of at least a normal degree of strength and are performing their functions harmoniously and satisfactorily. To be vital means that you are full of vim and energy, that you possess that enviable characteristic known as vivacity."*

Answer (A):   CORRECT! From Ralph Waldo Emerson's "Compensation."

Answer (B):   From the *Tantras*. The *Tantras* (ninth century a.d.) express the idea that inner realization is more important than outward prayer or devotion.

Answer (C):   From Bernarr McFadden's *Vitality Supreme*. Exercise is the subject of this interesting and obsessive text.

Ralph Waldo Emerson (1803–1882), the prime figure of the nineteenth-century transcendental movement in America, was born in Boston. His father, who died when Ralph was young, was a Unitarian minister. Ralph was raised by his mother and an aunt, Moody Emerson, who had a great deal of influence on him. He attended Boston Latin School and Harvard, where he began to keep his journals, graduating in 1821. In 1829, after Harvard Divinity School, he became pastor of the Second Church of Boston. The same year he married Ellen Tucker, who died two years later. Her death and Emerson's personal conflicts over certain religious sacraments forced him to resign from the church in 1832.

That year, Emerson went to Europe, and his interest in transcendentalism bloomed. He met William Wordsworth, Samuel Taylor Coleridge, and Thomas Carlyle, with whom he later carried on a regular correspondence.

When Emerson returned to Boston, he began to lecture from his *Journals*. In 1835 he remarried and moved to Concord, Massachusetts. "Nature," an essay stating his transcendentalist philosophy, was anonymously published in 1836. In 1840 Emerson and other transcendentalists published the *Dial*, a magazine. From 1841 to 1843, his disciple and contributor to the magazine, Henry David Thoreau, lived in the Emerson household.

In 1841 and 1844, two collections of his *Essays* were published, which including such pieces as "Self-Reliance" and "The Oversoul." After another trip to Europe, he went on a lecture tour of the United States. These lectures were later published as *English Traits*.

In the late 1860s, Emerson began to show signs of a decline in mental faculties, and he eventually slipped into a "blank state." He died at the age of seventy-nine.

63. CHARLES DARWIN

Publication day. Darwin slumps in his chair in Downs, England, as if overcome by a humid wind. He has not moved for hours. It is 1859. His major work, the study he has labored over for fourteen years, is being published today. The publisher has arranged for printing of 1250 copies of *The Origin of Species by Means of Natural Selection, or the Preservation of Favoured Races in the Struggle for Life.*

Over twenty years have passed since his famous voyage on the *Beagle* to the Galapagos Islands. Since then, many have thought that Darwin has been avoiding work. Yet he has always kept at it, although he is fully aware of the damage that is done to people in his position who advocate an unpopular idea.

Darwin's idea is that all species on earth change and adapt through the course of time from the pressure of the environment. Random physical mutations act to produce species which will survive and adapt better to the environment in which they live. For the religious, this theory is heretical since it does not assume that all species have been here from the beginning. What is even more threatening is Darwin's suggestion that apes preceded the human species. Many prominent men believe these ideas. Darwin's advantage lies in being a superb naturalist, in having empirical data to back his argument.

A knock on the door brings Darwin slowly to his feet. A young neighbor stands outside. He traveled all the way to London to purchase a copy of Darwin's book only to find the edition sold out within hours after the printer opened his doors. Darwin is cheered by this news. He gives the lad one of his own copies of the work and sends him on his way. As the young man walks home, he opens the book and begins to read . . . .

(A) *"Nothing that has a beginning and an end is either infinite or eternal.*
"If it were not one, it would be bounded by something else."

(B) *"As the ideas men's words stand for are of different sorts, so the way of making known the ideas they stand for, when there is occasion, is also different.*
"For were there a monkey, or any other creature, to be found that had the use of reason to such a degree, as to be able to understand general signs, and to deduce consequences of general ideas, he would no doubt be subject to law, and in that sense would be a man, how much soever he differed in shape from others of that name."

(C) *"Nothing can be effected, unless favorable variations occur, and variation itself is apparently always a very slow process. Man can act only on external and visible characters: nature cares nothing for appearances, except in so far as they may be useful to any being."*

Answer (A): From fragments of Melissus of Samos. Melissus (fourth century B.C.) was a pupil of Parmenides and a philosopher and statesman.

Answer (B): From John Locke's *Essay Concerning Human Understanding.* Locke (1632–1794) was the first philosopher of the industrial world.

Answer (C): CORRECT! From Charles Darwin's *The Origin of Species.*

Charles Darwin (1809–1882), English naturalist, was born in Shrewsbury, Shropshire. His father was a noted doctor. Following in his father's footsteps, Darwin began studying medicine. He then switched to the church but had no talent for preaching. He finally decided to take his hobby, natural history, more seriously. At the age of twenty-two Darwin set out on the *Beagle,* as the ship's naturalist, for a five-year trip around the world.

When he returned to England in 1836, he summarized and published the observations he had made in *A Naturalist's Voyage on the Beagle* (1839). This work was successful and made him famous.

From 1838 to 1844, Darwin was secretary to the Geological Society of London, which resulted in his forming a close friendship with the geologist, Sir Charles Lyell. In 1844, after collecting and classifying his data and research, Darwin began writing a book about his notion of natural selection. He worked on the project for fourteen years. Ironically, in 1858 Alfred Russel Wallace, another English naturalist, published a paper stating a similar theory to Darwin's, and sent Darwin a copy for his comments. After contemplating dropping his own publication plans, Darwin was persuaded to press them. In 1859 *The Origin of Species* appeared.

Darwin's theory of evolution created a great deal of controversy in religious circles, a controversy that still continues. However, by the time of his death, Darwin's theory was triumphant. He was buried at Westminster Abbey, the only honor ever bestowed upon him by his country.

64. SØREN KIERKEGAARD

An attractive young nurse sits across the room from a crippled man in a wheelchair. They both gaze out the window at the stark Danish seashore. The nurse imagines that Søren Kierkegaard must be pondering the structure of the universe or some obscure metaphysical system. In fact, he is wondering just how this woman would describe the scene before them.

Kierkegaard is a melancholy man, a lonely man. In 1837, when he was twenty-four, he was happily engaged to a lovely child of fourteen. The marriage never occurred. Now he sits, swaddled in a blanket, his hands folded across his feeble legs, a broken man.

He asks the woman to describe the seashore. "It is rocky and jagged," she begins, hesitantly, "lashed with rough water. The wind is blowing the sprays into a fine mist and the sun peers through the clouds and makes shadows in the mist. The water looks inviting and yet dangerous. I can imagine being the rocks, being the water, feeling the tension and energy."

Kierkegaard has listened carefully. "Thank you," he replies. "I will now describe the same setting with regard to the following ideas: First, that thought and things are not the same. Second, that one cannot imagine existence. Third, that perfect isolation is the basis of all ethical human experience. Thus, my description will differ somewhat from yours." He continues . . .

(A) *"The waves knock against the rocks to reach pain and suffering and the rocks build a cathedral of understanding of the nature of pain and suffering and so become more conscious and ever more questioning under the constant tension between the waves and the sun and the air. And there is no relief without the faint whisper during the calm that there is a greater force than this tension which makes the learning possible."*

(B) *"The salt water that towers above your head as the waves go by you heed not, nor the wind's voice: you press your bright face to the red blanket. If this danger were danger to you, your small ear would attend my words."*

(C) *"No exit from the sea breakers. Here are sharp rocks off shore and the sea a smother rushing around them. Rock faces rising sheer from straight deep water. Nowhere to stand and fight free of the tumult of surf, or rock, or wind. Out beyond here the message is carried on the wine dark sea."*

Answer (A): CORRECT! From Søren Kierkegaard's *Either/Or*.

Answer (B): From the lyrics of Simonides of Creos. Simonides was a Greek poet of the fifth century B.C.

Answer (C): From Homer's *Odyssey*. The Poem, written 700 years before Christ, is one of the greatest epics in literature (for further information on Homer, see selection 5).

Søren Kierkegaard (1813–1855), Danish philosopher, was born in Copenhagen, the last of seven children. His father had made his fortune early in life and retired to study religion and philosophy. Søren was brought up in a religious atmosphere and was deeply affected by his father's melancholic belief that he and his family were cursed by God.

Søren attended the University of Copenhagen, where he studied literature, philosophy, and history. During this period, he was estranged from his father and from religion, which he scorned with a deep and bitter cynicism.

When his father died, Søren experienced a religious conversion. He resumed his abandoned religious practices and, in 1840, passed his exams in theology. He had been engaged to Regina Olsen, a fourteen-year-old girl, with whom he was apparently very much in love, but he broke it off.

From 1843 to 1846 his aesthetic works were published, all under pseudonyms, although the identity of the author was generally known. These works, which set forth his dialectic of existentialism, include *Either/Or*, *Philosophical Fragments*, and *Stages on Life's Way*, among others. After 1846, he published his religious works, including *Fear and Trembling*, which were inspired, according to his *Journal*, by a religious experience which had transformed him. In 1854 he engaged in an attack of the Danish church which he felt was preaching a weak, emasculated Christianity. He died at the age of forty-two while writing a defense of his ideas.

65. HOPI

The professor is nervous. It is a brillilant, clear morning in 1860, and yet he feels as if he were back in much earlier times. He sits on a dry, split mesa in the western part of North America, a notebook under his arm. He is observing the pueblo life below him, realizing that his words and descriptions will never capture the gentleness and beauty that he has come to know through watching the Hopi for the past few months.

The Hopi know he is there. Perhaps they know what he is doing. He feels their awareness, but he believes that his words and thoughts are an invasion that may destroy their very existence. He is afraid of the power that his European education will bring to them. It is incredible that he has been reading Ralph Waldo Emerson, Plato, and Blaise Pascal, while watching men and women live a life which is completely isolated from what he knows as culture. At times he has wondered if they think about anything. Then he becomes angry with himself, for he knows from examining their art objects and watching their rituals that the Hopi are deeply religious and profound.

Today he is going to approach the pueblo in order to listen to an old man tell stories. He has watched the Indian hold forth from the same spot every day and has figured out a place where he will be able to hear what is being said without being noticed. The professor looks at his hands, the pencil, and note pad. He sadly reflects that he is writing the Hopi's epitaph rather than pursuing a study of their life patterns. Nevertheless, he goes down to his spot and waits.

The old man arrives. He sits beneath a pine tree. Three young children sit before him. He tells a tale which fills the professor with admiration for its sensitivity and naíveté . . . .

(A) *"On top of the plateau is the entrance to that other world. And there stands a skin that separates the two worlds; dead men go through it without a noise, but we have to break it with an outcry. The wind gathers strength, the same unruly wind that blows on the plateau. When the wind has gathered enough force, the man has to yell and the wind will push him through. Here his will has to be inflexible, too, so that he can fight the wind. All he needs is a gentle shove: he does not need to be blown to the ends of the other world."*

(B) *"When a jar is planted on a high mountain or in a sandy desert or near a village where there is no water, the materials in the jar will draw water from the distant ocean to supply you without end. The time will come when the villages you establish during your migration will fall into ruins. Other people will wonder why they were built in such inhospitable regions where there is no water for miles around. They will not know of the magic water jar, because they will not know of the power and prayer behind it."*

(C) *"The revolutionaries use disbelief in spirits. If you say there are spirits, you can pretend to be spirits yourselves, practice magic, and mislead simple rustic fools. This is the value of teaching people to believe in spirits. If you say there are no spirits, the uses of it are even greater. First, if there are no spirits, then you don't need to respect your ancestors: this is the prime source of revolution in the family. If you say there are no spirits, then there is no retribution from Hell, no punishment from Heaven, and you can act in any way, defying heaven's laws, and so arouse the unholy joy of dissolute youths."*

Answer (A): From Carlos Castaneda's *The Teachings of Don Juan.* Castaneda (1931–   ) has developed a style and set of ideas which allow the inner workings of the mind to be mapped by external objects.

Answer (B): CORRECT! From *The Book of the Hopi.*

Answer (C): From Liu T'ieh-yun's *The Travels of Lao Ts'an,* a classic novel of China at the turn of the century.

The Hopi, located in northeastern Arizona, are a group of Pueblo Indians that lives as farmers, growing corn, squash, and beans, and raising cotton and wheat.

The Hopi divide their villages into clans. Each village has a chief who is their spiritual leader. Each clan has certain religious or political duties to perform.

Historically, the isolated location of the Hopi prevented the European influence that affected other Indians from reaching them. In 1629 the Spanish set up missions at several Hopi pueblos. In 1860 the missions were destroyed in a revolt by the Indians, who left their villages and moved into the mountains. In the nineteenth century, many Hopi villages were taken over by the Navajo Indians. In 1882 a Hopi reservation was established, but since 1943 the Navajos have taken over a large part of it.

66. HENRY DAVID THOREAU

Henry and Ralph are talking in Ralph's bedroom. A crackling fire warms them on this cold, wintry New England night. It is midway through the nineteenth century.

Ralph is in bed under quilted covers. Henry, dressed in Ralph's robe and slippers, paces back and forth in front of the fireplace. The two men have often carried on these dense metaphysical dialogues while Henry has lived in Ralph's house. The topics are invariably concerned with questions of righteousness and sensuality. Henry is always advocating a life that does not intrude on others and that allows a person to express the nature of his or her being. The argumentative nature of both men makes the discussion lively and a wonderful source of mutual pleasure.

On this particular evening, Henry David Thoreau is considering leaving the home of Ralph Waldo Emerson. He wants to live on his own at a nearby pond. He plans to build a cabin in the woods and live a frugal life.

"But Henry," Ralph says, "why not take some money out of your father's pencil factory and use it to travel and see the world?"

"My world," Henry replies, "is in my mind and I cannot travel without stepping on other's property and rights."

"Think it over carefully, my dear Henry. You are no monk. We live in a climate of survival and destruction."

Thoreau is silent. Emerson smiles at him, a generous, gentle smile. "My conscious activity will make me travel farther than any train or horse," Thoreau explains, smiling back at his friend. He continues, "Just give me the old familiar world with my own mind which cannot be worn out with slow treading."

Emerson laughs at Henry's naíveté. "Why don't you forget your woods and your pond and just stay here with me and do some more writing?"

Thoreau watches the dancing flames devouring the wood. He walks across the room and sits down on the edge of the bed. From the look in Henry's eyes, Emerson knows that his young friend has already made up his mind to leave. Thoreau says . . . .

(A) *"One perceives by one's own nature. Because your own nature is essentially pure and utterly still, its immaterial and motionless substance is capable of perception."*

(B) *"Let me say to you and to myself in one breath, cultivate the tree which you have found to bear fruit in your soil."*

(C) *"A creature in its prime doing harm to the old is known as going against the way. That which goes against the way will come to an early end."*

Answer (A): From Hui Hai's *On Sudden Illumination*. Hui Hai was a Zen Buddhist who studied at the Great Cloud Monastery in China in A.D. 780.

Answer (B): CORRECT! From Henry David Thoreau's *Walden*.

Answer (C): From Lao-tzu's *Tao Te Ching*. Lao-tzu is credited with having written this basic Taoist text in the sixth century B.C. (see selection 6).

Henry David Thoreau (1817–1862), American naturalist and author, was born in Concord, Massachusetts, the son of a pencilmaker, and grew up in his native town. He went to Harvard, during which time he was first introduced to the work of Ralph Waldo Emerson, the transcendentalist.

After college Thoreau taught grammar school and worked in his father's factory. In 1841 Emerson, who had befriended the younger Thoreau, invited him to live in his house. Thoreau helped Emerson edit the *Dial*, a transcendentalist magazine, and wrote prose and poetry for it, as well as serving as handyman around the house.

From 1845 on, for a period of two or more years, Thoreau lived alone on Walden Pond in a cabin he built himself. He grew his own food and earned enough money to survive by doing odd jobs around the nearby town. He read, observed nature, and kept a journal which later became *Walden* (1854).

In 1846 Thoreau refused to pay a poll tax because it supported the Mexican War which he opposed and was sentenced to spend a night in jail. "Civil Disobedience," one of his most important essays, was the outcome of this experience. In it he champions civil disobedience as a means by which individuals can protest government actions they feel unjust.

In 1906 Thoreau's complete works were published posthumously, in twenty volumes.

67. KARL MARX

Marx dozes off in the library of the British Museum. He dreams of that last year in Paris in 1848. He is arguing with and hollering at his lifelong collaborator and friend, Friedrich Engels. The possibilities of life have just occurred to these young men for the first time. Before their recent intellectual breakthroughs, they had never imagined that all men could share the good life or that feasible steps could actually be taken in that direction. They are obsessed with the thought that they are on the threshold of explaining the economic basis of inequality. When they arrive at a solution of this problem, they believe, they can then make and design a world where people of unequal birth can, without problems, move into a society in which they can be fishermen in the morning, manufacturers in the afternoon, and poets in the evening.

"It's so easy!" exclaims thirty-year-old Marx. "You organize the society so that you take from each person according to his ability and you give back what he needs. It is so obvious."

"Wait a minute," Engels interrupts. "It won't work. We must first convince people that their needs are real and that their abilities can be changed."

"My friend, you are a fool," Karl counters. "We will organize the leaders from the groups that are now the most exploited. They will always honor the rights of their class."

"But for how long?" Friedrich questions. "How long will the son listen to the father?"

"He will listen if there is no need not to," Karl states with finality. He realizes that this day's discussion has opened up new areas of philosophy and political ideology. "I am going to go home and set this down in writing before I lose the thread of my thoughts."

"I'll come with you," says Friedrich, and the two friends walk out of the Parisian café.

The sound of footsteps abruptly awakens Marx from his dream. The librarian is standing over him announcing that the museum is closing. As he begins to shut the books, his eyes fall on a section of *The Communist Manifesto* that he remembers laboring over with Engels long into that night twenty years before. He reads . . . .

(A) "Whoever wants to know a thing has no way of doing so except by coming into contact with it, that is by living in its environment. If you want knowledge, you must take part in the practice of changing reality. If you want to know the taste of a pear, you must change the pear by eating it yourself. If you want to know the theory and methods of revolution, you must take part in revolution. All genuine knowledge originates in direct experience."

(B) "By liberty we mean a power of acting or not according to the determination of the will; that is, if we choose to remain at rest, we may: if we choose to move we also may. Now this hypothetical liberty is universally allowed to belong to everyone who is not a prisoner and in chains. Whatever definition we may give to liberty we should be careful to observe two requisite circumstances: first that it is consistent with plain matters of fact: secondly, that it is consistent with itself."

(C) "The essential condition for existence, and for the sway of the bourgeois class is the formation and augmentation of capital: the condition for capital is wage labor. Wage labor rests exclusively on competition between laborers. The advance of industry, whose involuntary promoter is the bourgeoisie, replaces the isolation of the laborers due to competition, by their revolutionary combination, due to association. The development of modern industry therefore cuts from under its feet the very foundation on which the bourgeoisie produces and appropriates products. What the bourgeoisie therefore produces, above all, is its own gravediggers."

Answer (A): From Mao Tse-tung (1893–1976) *The Quotations from Mao Tse-tung*, a most powerful and widely read book by the former leader of the People's Republic of China.

Answer (B): From David Hume's *An Inquiry Concerning Human Understanding*. Hume (1711–1776) was one of the great philosophers of the English Enlightenment.

Answer (C): CORRECT! From Karl Marx and Friedrich Engels' *The Communist Manifesto*.

Karl Marx (1818–1883), German social philosopher and chief theorist of modern socialism, was born in Treves. His father was a Jewish jurist who converted to Christianity when Marx was a child. Marx studied law at Bonn and Berlin before turning to philosophy, receiving a doctorate from the University of Jena in 1842. After publishing a liberal newspaper which was suppressed by the authorities, he went to Paris, where he met Engels, a factory manager from Manchester, England. In 1848 they collaborated on and published *The Communist Manifesto*, which laid the foundation for Marx's later work, *Das Kapital*. That same year, Marx took part in French and German uprisings and for this reason was forced to leave the continent. He chose to settle in England, where he remained for the rest of his life, a poor man, doing research in the British Museum and writing about economics.

Marx was influenced by the German philosophers G. W. F. Hegel and Ludwig Feuerbach. His fundamental theory is that the history of all existing societies is concerned with class struggle and every social order based on class division contains the seeds of its own destruction. His monumental work, *Das Kapital* (1867) has been compared in its influence to the *Bible*, the *Koran*, and Newton's *Principia Mathematica*.

68. WALT WHITMAN

They roll in the grass in a New York park, kissing each other, thoroughly enjoying a lovely, mild Sunday. The year is 1861. They are carefree in their attitude, oblivious of the crowd that is angrily gathering.

Their reverie ends when a growling dog tears at the young man's coat. They hurriedly get to their feet when they notice the group of people around them. Jack, the young man, brushes himself off. Walt Whitman puts his arms around him, protectively, and they begin walking away.

"You should be ashamed of yourselves," an old woman shouts after them.

"I am fine, woman," Whitman retorts. "My only problem is that you are disturbing me."

Later that night, at a tavern frequented by artists, Jack expounds on Whitman's talents. "His face is a picture of openness and love," he pronounces. "He wants to make the world totally democratic, with no prejudice and no war." The other young men look unimpressed as they continue their drinking and laughing.

Whitman arrives at the tavern. He is greeted by a hushed silence. "And what are my lovelies doing here tonight? Are you making plans to open the rivers to the fresh wishes of young men?"

"Oh, Walt," Jack says angrily. "I have been trying to make them understand you, your beauty, the range of your concerns."

Whitman reaches into his pocket and pulls out a well-worn copy of his poems, *Leaves of Grass*. He searches through the pages. The young men wait, full of curiosity. Soon the poet of love and democracy begins to read, the tone of his voice tinged with anger and dismay . . . .

(A) "Nothing could seem too rich to
clothe the sun,
Much less those joys which tramp
on his head.

"As flames do work and win, when
they ascend
So did I weave my self into the
sense,
But while I bustled, I might hear
a friend
Whisper, How idle is all this long
pretence!
There is in love a sweetness ready
penned:
Copy out only that, and save
expense."

(B) "I resist anything better than my
own diversity,
Breathe the air but leave plenty
behind me,
And am not stuck up, and am in my
place.

"Failing to fetch me at first keep
encouraged
Missing me one place search another
I stop somewhere waiting for you."

(C) "Whether on earth in air or main,
Sure everything alive is vain.
Does not the hawk all fowls survey
As destined only for his prey?
And do not tyrants, prouder things,
Think men were born for slaves to
kings?

"Be humble, learn thyself to scan:
'Know pride was never made for man."

Answer (A): From George Herbert's "Jordan II." Herbert (1593–1633) was one of the great religious and metaphysical English poets of his age.

Answer (B): CORRECT! From Walt Whitman's "Song of Myself."

Answer (C): From John Gay's "Fables." Gay (1685–1732) was an English poet and playwright, most famous for his satires and parodies of pastoral poetry.

Walt Whitman (1819–1892), American poet, was born in West Hills, Long Island, and grew up in Brooklyn. His father was a housebuilder. After quitting school in 1830, he got a job as a printer's devil and compositor. Later, he taught school on Long Island and edited a newspaper. He became editor of the Brooklyn *Daily Eagle* in 1846 but was fired from this job two years later because he advocated abolitionism and "free soil." He then traveled to New Orleans before returning to Brooklyn.

In 1855 Whitman published *Leaves of Grass*, a collection of twelve poems, at his own expense. There were to be nine expanded and revised versions of this book published during his lifetime. The first edition was a commercial failure but earned Whitman a name and the praise of Ralph Waldo Emerson.

From 1862 to 1865, he worked as a volunteer nurse in Washington during the Civil War. A volume of poetry, *Drum Taps* (1865), came out of this experience, and then a sequel, which contains "When Lilacs Last in the Dooryard Bloomed," one of his best-known poems.

After the war, Whitman went to work as a government clerk. He was fired because *Leaves of Grass* was considered immoral. He suffered a paralytic stroke in 1873, and lived the rest of his life as a semi-invalid. He died in Camden, New Jersey, at the age of seventy-three.

Whitman was one of America's greatest poets. His poetry praises the individual, freedom, democracy, the body, nature, the cosmos, and the spirit of America.

69. FEODOR DOSTOEVSKY

The pale light of morning illuminates the Nevsky River in St. Petersburg. A man stands on a bridge, overlooking the military compound situated on the river bank. The year is 1878.

Feodor is recalling a day twenty-nine years before when he and several comrades were tied to posts, their chests bared, awaiting imminent death by firing squad. Their offense: operating a printing press. As he stood there at dawn, Feodor had felt the blows that killed his father, he had heard the insults the critics flung at his work like so many stones, he had recoiled at his rejection by beautiful women, he had sensed the agony of searching for the right word to express the anguish that the world served him. He had known then that every death was absurd and that this one, execution as punishment for printing poetry, was as ridiculous as any. Still, his body had shaken uncontrollably. When the messenger came from Nicholas I informing the captain that the sentence was commuted to exile in Siberia, he had wept.

For ten long years Dostoevsky was not allowed to return to St. Petersburg. When he finally did come home, no one remembered him, or his work. He began again from scratch. In the years that followed, he stumbled around and finally began writing one work after another. Eventually he regained his form and turned out amazing work that he believed would change the nature of fiction.

As he stands on the bridge, his mind full of his past, Dostoevsky laughs at the irony of it all. He now looks at freedom as a tragic idea that lingers in the diseased mind of Western man. He also thinks about a passage from his current work, *The Brothers Karamazov*, which contains a statement that he believes provides insight into the nature of his own soul . . . .

(A) *"But how can he believe in its reality up there? Insects whine, the sun is almost warm, he can gaze off at the red earth and millions of blowing stalks, and fall nearly in a light trance: in shirt sleeves, with his bony knees pointing up, the grey suit jacket wrinkled years beyond last pressing bundled under his ass to soak up the dew."*

(B) *"For the secret of man's being is not only to live but to have something to live for. Without a firm conception of the object of life, man would not consent to go on living, and would rather destroy himself than remain on earth, though he had bread in abundance. That is true. But what happened? Instead of taking men's freedom from them, you make it greater than ever. Did you forget that man prefers peace, even death, to freedom of choice in the knowledge of good and evil?"*

(C) *"My mind was absorbed in romances, and I had no well placed relatives from whom I could learn distinguished manners or court customs. Apart from the romances, I could not know them. I had always been in the shadow of my antiquated parents, and had been accustomed not to go out except to see the moon and flowers. So when I left home, I felt as if I were not I nor was it the real world to which I was going."*

Answer (A): From Thomas Pynchon's *Gravity's Rainbow*. In addition to this epic novel of extraordinary proportions, Pynchon (1937–   ) is also well known for his experimental novel, *V*.

Answer (B): CORRECT! From Feodor Dostoevsky's "The Grand Inquisitor," in *The Brothers Karamazov*.

Answer (C): From the Daughter of Takasue's *The Sarashina Diary*. Daughter of Takasue was one of the writers of pillow books in eleventh-century Japan.

Feodor Mikhailovich Dostoevsky (1821–1881), Russian novelist, was born in the charity hospital in Moscow, where his father, an alcoholic, served as resident physician. His family was poor, of low nobility, and Russian Orthodox. Dostoevsky's mother died when he was sixteen, in the same year he was forced to enter the School of Military Engineers at St. Petersburg to study draftsmanship. Two years later his father was brutally murdered by his own serfs.

After graduating, Dostoevsky spent a brief period in a government job before quitting to devote his time to writing. He published his first novel, *Poor Folk*, in 1846, to great acclaim. During the late 1840s he was involved with a group of utopian socialists who were operating an illegal printing press. The discovery of the press by the police led to the groups's arrest. After he was sentenced to death, Dostoevsky's penalty was commuted to hard labor in a Siberian penal colony.

He served four years at hard labor, during which time he developed epilepsy. After that, he was sent to serve in a battalion in Asia. When he finally returned to St. Petersburg in 1859, he brought with him a woman he had met and married while in Siberia, and her son.

Dostevsky edited *Time*, a magazine, with his brother and made frequent trips to western Europe. Because of his passion for women and gambling, he was constantly in debt and wrote to pay off his creditors. His wife died in 1864, and his brother a year later.

In 1867 Dostoevsky married his young secretary, a woman who gave him the support and security which allowed him to produce the finest works of his career, and several of the most important and influential works in the history of literature. His most noted works are *Notes from Underground* (1864), *Crime and Punishment* 1865–1866), *The Idiot* (1867), *The Possessed* (1871–1872), and *The Brothers Karamazov* (1879–1880).

70. GREGOR MENDEL

For hours he has been going up and down the rows of plants, noting the characteristics of each in turn. His colleagues at the monastery in Bruno watch these daily activities. They are always amused and puzzled by his continuing interest and focus.

Gregor Mendel has several notebooks in hand. He notes the characteristics of each plant. He has so many books that he carries them in a wheelbarrow. As he works, he is often heard muttering praise for Francis Bacon and Charles Darwin. The monks notice that the flowers change color every year. First they were red and white, then pink ones were interspersed, and now the pink ones have become more prevalent. Years have passed since Mendel published his second and last paper in 1869. Still, no acknowledgment has come to him. The monks believe that although he is kind and gentle, he is, nonetheless, an idiot whose only interest is peaplants.

Each day Mendel leaves the monastery to teach at the local high school. He is as absorbed with the growing minds of his students as he is with his flowers. He also enjoys involving them in his experiments. Today, he explains to them that by mixing red and white flowers in certain proportions, the result will be pink flowers.

A student challenges him by asking to see the plants change. "You cannot see them change," answers Mendel. "The change takes years before it is fully realized."

"Then, it is not a change. It is only chance," the student retorts. "What's more, you have lied to us!"

Mendel is disturbed and saddened by this outburst. It is difficult for him to be clearly understood, either by his peers or by his students. That evening, back in his room, he writes a letter to a trusted friend about the nature of his work with plants . . . .

(A) *"Hence the number, the variety, and even the complication of facts contribute ultimately to separate truth from falsehood: and the same causes which, in any case, render the first attempt toward a theory difficult, make the final success of such attempts just so much more probable."*

(B) *"Future methods of observation and communication will enable people to be better orientated in relation to their place in the universe than in the past. They will have a much better understanding of themselves and their relationship to the continuity of life that is our fundamental experience. Exactly how that continuity and communication may be symbolized I do not venture to forecast."*

(C) *"As must be expected, the experiments proceed slowly. In the beginning some patience is required, but later, when several experiments are progressing concurrently, matters are improved. Every day, from spring to fall, one's interest is refreshed daily, and the care which must be given to one's wards is thus amply repaid. In addition, if I should, by my experiments, succeed in hastening the solution of the problem, I should be doubly happy."*

Answer (A): From John Playfair's *The Huttonian Theory of the Earth*. Playfair (1748–1819), renowned mathematician, was a good friend of James Hutton and other geologists and physicists of early nineteenth-century England.

Answer (B): From J. Z. Young's *Doubt and Certainty in Science*. Young (1907–   ) is one of the most brilliant practitioners and theorists of biology and neurophysiology today.

Answer (C): CORRECT! From Gregor Mendel's *The Origins of Genetics*.

Gregor Mendel (1822–1884), botanist and monk, was born in Heinzendorf, Silesia, the son of a peasant. As a child he tended the fruit trees for the manor lord. In 1843 Mendel entered the Augustinian monastery in Bruno. Four years later he was ordained a priest.

Mendel was sent by his order to the University of Vienna in 1851 to study mathematics and science so that he could teach secondary school. He later taught science in Bruno.

Mendel's interest in botany and mathematics resulted in his growing peas in the monastery garden and conducting experiments with them, breeding dwarf-pea and tall-pea plants in various combinations and noting the results. He wrote up his conclusions as a theory of heredity, and in the early 1860's sent his paper to Nageli, a well-known botanist, for his opinion. Nageli returned the paper without really reading it or taking it seriously. Mendel was put off by this reaction. It was difficult for him to get anyone interested in his work or his theories. He published two papers, one in 1865 and one in 1869, and that was the extent of his efforts.

In 1869 Mendel became a prelate, and this new job, plus failing eyesight, gradually brought an end to his garden experiment. He died an obscure man in 1884. His papers were rediscovered in 1900 and his theories, known as Mendelism, became the basis for genetics.

71. SAMUEL CLEMENS

He sits in a field, somewhere in Missouri. The year is 1894. As he reminisces about his early years on the river that now flows before him, Samuel Clemens hears a teacher questioning her pupils in the nearby one-room schoolhouse: "How do you spell Mississippi?" One by one, the hesitant voices of the children spell a word whose roots came not from their native English, but from an Indian tongue that seems to capture a deep understanding of nature. "How beautiful," things Clemens, "that the Indians decided to name the rivers, even though they probably had no idea of their entire length, nor where they emptied." As he dwells on the magic of naming something alive and forceful, he is suddenly saddened to hear the teacher screaming: "No, no, that is incorrect!"

In his haughty yet jocular manner, Clemens gets up and walks to the school and knocks on the door. The teacher, a severe looking young woman, opens the door. "Afternoon, m'am, the district supervisor sent me over to tell the children a story. I am Mark Twain, the famous storyteller. Perhaps you have heard of me?"

The teacher is dazzled. Indeed she has heard of Mark Twain. "Children," she announces, "Mr. Twain has come to tell you a story." The children are pleased. Anything is better than spelling. Sitting back in their seats, sliding on the polished wood, they listen as Twain begins: "Once upon a time there was a young boy who had no family, in his mind, and no real sense of where he was going."

Twain talks on for an hour, weaving the story of Huckleberry Finn. The children have not moved, nor made a sound. He continues, hoping to capture the mystery of the river and the mystery of knowing in general . . . .

(A) "We had the sky up there all speckled with stars, and we used to lay on our backs and look up at them, and discuss about whether they was made or only just happened. Jim he allowed that they was made, but I allowed that they just happened: I judged it would have took too long to make so many. Jim said the moon could a laid them, well, that looked kind of reasonable, so I didn't say nothing against it, because I've seen a frog lay most as many, so of course it could be done."

(B) "Well, who created the world? You? Who made the sky, the stars, the sun, the moon, man, and the animals?" My brother's answer was that everything evolved. He mentioned Darwin. But, my mother wanted to know, how can a creature with eyes, ears, lungs, and a brain evolve from earth and water? My father used to say, you can splatter ink but it won't write a letter by itself. My brother never had an answer for this. As yet none has been found."

(C) "I wonder if the ground has anything to say? I wonder if the ground is listening to what is said? I wonder if the ground would come alive and what is on it? Though I hear what the ground says. The ground says It is the great spirit that put me here."

Answer (A):   CORRECT! From Mark Twain's *Huckleberry Finn.*

Answer (B):   From Isaac Bashevis Singer's "Voices for Life." Singer (1904–   ) is one of the classic writers of Jewish tales and folklore in America.

Answer (C):   From *Touch the Earth,* compiled by T. C. McLuhan. This is a collection of quotations from Indians of America throughout their history of interaction with white men.

Samuel Langhorne Clemens (1835–1910), American author and humorist, was born in Florida, Missouri. His father was a land speculator. When Sam was four, the family moved to Hannibal, Missouri, where he grew up. His father died when Sam was twelve, and he left school to become an apprentice to a printer. Later he became a journeyman printer. In 1857, on his way to South America to get rich, he stopped in New Orleans. He decided to stay in the region as the pilot of a Mississippi River steamboat until the Civil War ended the traffic on the river. After serving as a Confederate volunteer, he went to Carson City, Nevada, with his brother and tried his hand at mining, with no luck.

In 1862 Clemens became a member of the staff of the Virginia City *Territorial Enterprise,* adopted his pseudonym "Mark Twain" (which means two fathoms deep), and began his career as a humorous journalist. In 1865 "The Celebrated Jumping Frog of Calaveras County" was published in the New York *Saturday Press.* The story made Mark Twain famous.

Twain spent a lot of time traveling and lecturing abroad, touring the Holy Land and the Mediterranean. The result of this was *Innocents Abroad* (1869). In 1870 he married Olivia Langdon, an heiress, and settled in Hartford, Connecticut. He became a partner in a publishing company and did some of his best work, including *The Gilded Age* (1873), *The Adventures of Tom Sawyer* (1866), *The Adventures of Huckleberry Finn* (1884), *The Prince and the Pauper* (1882), and *A Connecticut Yankee in King Arthur's Court* (1889).

After investing a great deal of money in a typesetter that failed, he was suddenly broke and in debt. To pay off these debts, he gave a series of lectures worldwide which were later published as *Following the Equator* (1892). Twain died in Redding, Connecticut.

The Adventures of Huckleberry Finn has been called the first American novel. Twain's unique style of writing had a great influence on the American writers who followed him.

72. WILLIAM JAMES

The waves lap at the sides of the boat as it makes its way through the calm water. William James gazes out toward the horizon. The year is 1901. The distinguished professor from Harvard is en route to Edinburgh University to deliver a series of lectures which he calls "Varieties of Religious Experiences." He hopes to be able to spend some time in England to continue to think and write. The water is a good partner for his thoughts.

A fellow passenger arrives on deck wearing a tuxedo. He approaches James at the rail. "Professor," he begins, "I have noticed you throughout this voyage. Not once have you seemed the slightest bit perturbed or distraught. Truly, you are a most remarkable man."

"What makes me happy is what is true," James answers, giving the man a warm smile. "Truth to say, I am not sad because I make what happens into moments to bring me happiness. There is no reason to be sad, and so I am not."

The passenger, a distinguished American industrialist and man of the world, responds, "Doesn't your mind tell you about the situation in India, the approaching wars in the world, the brutal injustices perpetrated in the name of good government?"

"Events such as those you describe are part of the lives of those participating in them. Since my mind, as you call it, does not know anything, but exists solely as a place of relations, I do not, in fact, know of what you speak. Since I don't actually experience it, I do not feel guilty or sad."

"Do you believe in God, Professor James?"

"I believe in what I believe about God. Thus, God is true if the events that I feel about it or him are true and real. Just look out at the ocean, my friend."

The two men stand at the rail, looking out to sea. After many minutes of silence, the upcoming wind turns cold. The American industrialist gets a chill and departs for his cabin. James, however, becomes even more involved and does not feel the cold, transcending the scene. He realizes that he can use these immediate thoughts as a model for his beliefs . . . .

(A) *"If we close our eyes and think of a place where it would be pleasant to spend a vacation, and if there slide across the black eyes, like a setting on the stage, a rock that sparkles, a blue sea that lashes, and hemlocks in which the sun can merely fumble, this inevitably demonstrates, since the rocks and the sea, the wood and the sun are those that have actually been familiar to us, that much of the world of fact is the equivalent of the world of the imagination, because it looks like it."*

(B) *"That is the sting of it, that in the vast driftings of the cosmic weather, though many a jeweled shore appears, and many an enchanted cloud bank floats away, long lingering ere it be dissolved—even as our world now lingers for our joy—yet when these transient products are gone, nothing absolutely nothing remains to represent those particular quantities, those elements of preciousness which they may have enshrined. Dead and gone are they, gone from the very sphere and room of being. Without an echo, without a memory: without an influence on aught that may come after to make it care for similar ideals."*

(C) *"By the infinite plurification of itself equally in every direction light extends matter everywhere equally in the form of a sphere: and it follows of necessity that in this extension the outmost parts of matter are more extended and more rarefied than the inmost parts near the center. And since the outmost parts will have been rarefied to the utmost, the inner parts will still be susceptible of greater rarefication."*

Answer (A): From Wallace Stevens' *The Necessary Angel*. Stevens (1879–1955) was one of America's greatest poets, bringing dignity to the relationship between poet and mind.

Answer (B): CORRECT! From William James' *Pragmatism*.

Answer (C): From Robert Grosseteste's "On Light." Grosseteste (c. 1170–1253) was an English philosopher, scientist, and bishop, present at the signing of the Magna Carta.

William James (1842–1910), American philosopher of pragmatism, was born in New York City. His father was a wealthy philosopher who followed the tenets of Emanuel Swedenborg. His younger brother was Henry James.

James was educated in America and Europe. In 1860 he decided that he was destined to be a great painter. He studied for a year only to discover that he was only average. He then entered Harvard Medical School, although he had no intention of becoming a doctor. In 1865–1866, he went on an expedition to Brazil with the great naturalist Louis Agassiz. On this trip he contracted smallpox and eye trouble, which marked the beginning of a plague of physical problems. He graduated from Harvard with a medical degree in 1869, and in 1872 began teaching there, lecturing on anatomy and physiology. He married Alice Howe Gibbons in 1878.

In 1890 *Principles of Psychology* was published. In this work lies the basis of James' philosophy of pragmatism, more fully developed later in *Pragmatism: A New Name for Some Old Ways of Thinking* (1907). In 1901 a series of lectures which James delivered at Edinburgh University was published as *Varieties of Religious Experience*. Some of his other works are *The Meaning of Truth* (1909), *A Pluralistic Universe* (1909), and *Essays in Radical Empiricism* (1912).

James invented a doctrine he called "radical empiricism," which he first explicated in the essay "Does 'Consciousness' Exist?" In that essay James denied the dualism of subject and object, or mind and matter, saying that it involved a false distinction. Consciousness is not a thing, and the prime element of the world is "pure experience."

James was also a proponent of pragmatism, which holds that an idea is "true" as long as it is profitable to life. That idea would influence much of later philosophy, particular the work of John Dewey.

73. FRIEDRICH NIETZSCHE

Some university students laugh and run down the street after a festive dinner washed down with many steins of beer. Basel in the late nineteenth century is a lovely, friendly town, and these young men are enjoying their student days to the limit.

As they round a corner, pushing and shoving each other in playful intoxication, one of the boys slips and falls next to a barred window. "Careful, Heinrich," shouts a comrade, "or we will commit you to the funny farm." Heinrich rises and brushes himself off. He peers through the window. The scene within causes the blood to drain from his face.

A dirty, disheveled man vainly struggles against the belts of a straitjacket. He screams, falls down, picks himself up, and falls again, rolling on the foor in utter agony and frustration. The mad, wild man locked inside this padded cell in the insane asylum is none other than the brilliant Friedrich Nietzsche, the popular lecturer at the university who dropped mysteriously from sight recently.

"What a freak!" exclaims one of the students.

"That man is Friedrich Nietzsche, the great philosopher," Heinrich whispers.

"Oh, really! Then I am Attila the Hun!" the student crows, and they all laugh loudly, racing off down the street, leaving Heinrich behind.

Heinrich remembers when he attended Nietzsche's lectures two years ago. He remembers hearing Nietzsche say that strength and nobility are the only admirable traits in a human being. Nietzsche used to shout tirades against aiding the sick and the weak. And now, before his eyes, is this pitiful creature, Friedrich Nietzsche, sick, weak, and insane.

Heinrich taps on the windowpane. Startled, Nietzsche looks up at him. His eyes are red. They glow. With a tone of irony in his voice, Heinrich yells through the window, "And now, *Übermensch*, do you still believe in strength as the only virtue?"

Nietzsche struggles to get up, and when he does, begins to awkwardly stride back and forth, bellowing at the stranger at the window. . . .

(A) *"The important thing in persuasion is to learn how to play up the aspects that the person you are talking to is proud of, and play down the aspects he is ashamed of. Let him build on your words but pretend that you are unaware that he is doing so and in this way abet his wisdom."*

(B) *"Without a strong organization that in the struggle carries on under all circumstances and in all periods there can be no talk of a systematic plan of activity enlightened by firm principles and unswervingly carried out which is alone in being called a tactic."*

(C) *"We must seek the superman who will represent the instincts of competition and survival and who will not advocate any slave ethic. Observe suffering well and use it as a source of pleasure. Do not ever be ascetic and destroy the infirm so that our experience will always be marked by the evidence of a superman."*

Answer (A):   From *The Basic Writings of Han Fei Tzu.* Han Fei Tzu was a philosopher and legal scholar in China in the third century B.C.

Answer (B):   From V. I. Lenin's *What Is to Be Done?*

Answer (C):   CORRECT! From Friedrich Nietzsche's *The Genealogy of Morals.*

Friedrich Wilhelm Nietzsche (1844–1900), German philosopher, was born in Rocken, Prussia. His father, a pastor in the Lutheran Church, died when Nietzsche was five years old, and he was raised in a totally female household.

He attended Bonn University, and later, before getting his doctorate, was offered the chair of philosophy at Basel, which he accepted.

When the Franco-Prussian War began, Nietzsche joined the German army ambulance corps, until illness forced him to be discharged, and he returned to Basel. During this period in his life, he was a close friend of the composer Richard Wagner and often visited the latter's villa at Lake Lucerne.

In 1879 nervous disorders and eye trouble caused Nietzsche to resign his position at Basel. For the next ten years, he wandered in Italy and Switzerland seeking to improve his failing health. His sanity was deteriorating, and by 1889 he showed definite signs of madness. Never recovering, Nietzsche died on August 24, 1900.

His most important works are *Thus Spake Zarathustra* (1883–1885) *Beyond Good and Evil* (1886), and *The Genealogy of Morals* (1887). Nietzsche was a moralist who violently rejected what he considered to be the inferior bourgeois civilization of the Western world and its religion, Christianity. He believed in a "super man" whose "will to power" would enable him to transcend normal levels of experience and go beyond accepted standards of good and evil.

74. SIGMUND FREUD

A man stops before a lighted window. Inside, a beautiful young woman is taking off her clothes. She slowly turns as she removes each article of clothing, so that her bare breasts and body face his gaze. He is mesmerized by the scene.

Sigmund Freud has been strolling through the streets of Vienna on his early evening walk. The year is 1902. He has been thinking about all the things that bother him, the things that prevent him from being the man he knows he could be. Now, he stares at this naked creature, although at the same time he feels compelled to look away.

Freud abruptly turns and walks away, still excited by the image. He cannot help imagining ways to get up to her room, to force himself on her, to make passionate love to her. A woman he doesn't even know. He is tormented by the many forces pulling at him. What drives him to want her so much? And why since he does not know her, does not want to know who she is? What is the fascination?

Freud finds himself transported back to his childhood. He sees himself, a very young boy, peering into his parents' bedroom at his mother, who is naked. This memory agitates Freud. He becomes suddenly nervous. He reaches for the cigar in his pocket. He bites off the end, and as he puts the cigar in his mouth, he becomes uncontrollably excited.

Later, seated in his drawing room, Freud watches his wife, Martha, walk across the room. She does not excite him. He is disturbed. "Martha," he clears his throat. "Society makes us do things which control our inner instincts against their proper expression. I do not believe that society can resolve this. There will always be a terrible tension. I must try to figure out when these forces which build up in us begin to develop. I must try to understand them."

Martha listens as she continues with her own work about the house. She is accustomed to his ramblings. "That sounds interesting, Sigmund. Why don't you go over to Breuer's and tell him about it."

"Yes, I think I will." Freud sets off for his partner's house, confident that he is on the threshold of something important. On his way he thinks about how he will express his dawning insight to Breuer....

(A) *"I am I, that is the fundamental proposition of our life. My assertion that this proposition in which mankind expresses its egotism is a mistake will not shatter the world as it would do if people actually believed it. But they cannot, and will not believe it. I don't believe it myself, and yet it is true. I am by no means 'I' but a continually changing form in which the It displays itself, and the 'I' feeling is one of its tricks to lead men astray in his self knowledge, to render his self deception easier, to make of him life's pliant tool."*

(B) *"The baby is subjected to these forces of violence, called love, as its mother and father before, and their parents and their parents before them, have been. These forces are mainly concerned with destroying most of its potentialities, and on the whole this enterprise is successful. By the time the new human being is fifteen or so, we are left with a being like ourselves, a half crazed creature more or less adjusted to a mad world. This is normality in our present age. Love and violence, properly speaking, are polar opposites. Love lets the other be, but with affection and concern. Violence attempts to constrain the other's freedom, to force him to act in the way we desire, but with ultimate lack of concern, with indifference to the other's own existence or destiny."*

(C) *"The ambivalence which has allowed repression to come into being by means of reaction-formation also constitute the point at which the repressed succeeds in breaking through again. The vanished effect is transformed, without any diminution, into dread of the community, pangs of conscience, or self reproaches: the rejected idea is replaced by a displacement substitute, often by displacement onto something utterly trivial or indifferent. For the most part, there is an unmistakeable tendency to complete re-establishment of the repressed idea. Failure of repression of the quantitative factor brings into play, by means of various taboos and prohibitions, the same mechanism of flight as we have seen at work in the formation of hysterical phobias. So the final form of the work of repression in the obsessional neurosis is a sterile and neverending struggle."*

Answer (A): From Georg Groddeck's *The Book of the It.* Groddeck (1866–1934) explored the field of psychosomatic illness and psychically generated behavioral conditions.

Answer (B): From R. D. Laing's *The Politics of Experience.* Laing (1927–   ) is a prominent experimental psychoanalyst who has completely reviewed the concept of schizophrenia.

Answer (C): CORRECT! From Sigmund Freud's *General Psychological Theory.*

Sigmund Freud (1856–1939), Austrian psychiatrist and founder of psychoanalysis, was born in Pribor, Czechoslovakia. When he was four his family moved to Vienna. Freud attended the University of Vienna, receiving his medical degree in 1881. During the period of his training he became interested in neurology. In 1885 Freud went to Paris to study with Jean Charcot, a French neurologist, who was interested in the phenomenon of hysteria. Returning to Veinna, Freud began collaborating with Josef Breuer, who was investigating a treatment of hysteria utilizing hypnosis.

In 1893 Freud and Breuer published "On the Psychical Mechanism of Hysterical Phenomena," a paper which was elaborated upon two years later in *Studies in Hysteria.* The medical profession, however, did not appreciate the significance of their work. Freud and Breuer soon parted ways because of certain basic disagreements.

Freud replaced hypnotism with his method of free association in treatment. In 1900 he published his *Interpretation of Dreams,* and in 1905 *Three Contributions to the Sexual Theory,* which contained his theories on infantile sexuality.

During this period, Freud became associated with a group of men, including Alfred Adler and Carl Jung, which became the First International Congress of Psychoanalysis. The association was short-lived. By 1913 all three men had gone their separate ways, forming their own schools of psychoanalysis.

In 1930 Freud received the Goethe prize, and in 1936 he was elected to the Royal Society. When Nazis occupied Vienna in 1938, he departed for London, where he died a year later.

75. JOSEPH CONRAD

A ship steams around the Cape of Good Hope. The year is 1878. The men on board are quiet after a night of rough seas. They tell stories about the past and the future. Some recount events that have just happened as if they took place twenty years ago. On the high seas ideas are nostalgic since there is such a fine line between life and death.

Joseph Conrad lights his pipe and listens to an old salt. In his heart lie stories of adventure and suspense that no evening in the slings can possible equal. Conrad possesses the gift of insight. He knows why people say what they say and tell what they tell. He sees the pain of the collapse of an individual's ideals. He sees the anguish in the discovery that no one guides fate except man himself. He feels the spasmodic crying of the person who suddenly comes face to face with his own mortality and futility.

Conrad looks at the members of the crew. Each one has a repertoire of stories that they tell and retell. The prepositions are always the same: "I was *in* Hong Kong"; "I was *on top of* that wench"; "I was *down to* my last ten pounds." Conrad listens carefully to their tales.

"Did I tell you about the time on the river in Patagonia?" Jenkins says, turning to Conrad. "I looked over the edge of the ship and saw a man's face. It was frozen solid with reality, the reality of being an image for other people." Conrad takes mental notes as Jenkins unfolds his tale. He is already planning how he will write it, starting with the ending and working backward . . . .

(A) *"The greater part of sailors die at sea: and when they find their end approaching, if it does not, as is often the case, come with warning, they cannot, as on shore, send for a clergyman or some religious friend, to speak to them of that hope in a Saviour, which they have neglected, if not despised through life: but if the little hull does not contain such a one within its compass, they must be left without human aid in their great extremity."*

(B) *"The punishment has been severe, observed the sculptor. Even justice might now forgive: how much more a woman's tenderness! Roderick Ellison, whether the serpent was a physical reptile, or whether the morbidness of your nature suggested that symbol to your fancy, the moral of the story is not the less true and strong. A tremendous egotism, manifesting itself in your case in the form of jealousy, is as fearful a fiend as ever stole into the human heart."*

(C) *"It was as though a veil had been rent. I saw on that ivory face the expression of somber pride, of ruthless power, of craven terror—of an intense and hopeless despair. Did he live his life again in every detail of desire, temptation, and surrender during that supreme moment of complete knowledge? He cried in a whisper at some image, at some vision—he cried out twice, a cry that was no more than a breath: The horror, the horror!"*

Answer (A): From Richard Henry Dana's *Two Years Before the Mast*. In this work Dana (1815–1882) documents the hardships of sailors in the early nineteenth century.

Answer (B): From Nathaniel Hawthorne's "Egotism, or the Bosom Serpent." Hawthorne (1804–1864) was an American novelist who never achieved recognition for his greatness during his lifetime.

Answer (C): CORRECT! From Joseph Conrad's *The Heart of Darkness*.

Joseph Conrad (1857–1924), English novelist, was born Joez Teodor Konrad Nalecz Korzeniowski, in the Ukraine. His family escaped from Russia, and in 1869, Conrad was orphaned and taken in by an uncle in Cracow.

Conrad went to sea when he was seventeen, first in the French marine service, and then, in 1878, in the service of an English merchant ship which traveled to the Far East. He got his Master Marine's certificate and became a naturalized British subject. In 1894, after a rough trip up the Congo, Conrad quit the sea permanently to write.

Although his first and second languages were Polish and French, Conrad chose to write his novels in English. In 1894 his first novel, *Almayer's Folly*, was published. Four years later he produced *An Outcast of the Islands*. He married that same year and later had two children, although it is said that he saw little of them because he locked himself up for days at a time to write.

Conrad's wrote numerous popular novels. *The Nigger of the Narcissus* (1898) earned him a reputation early in his career. His other novels include *Lord Jim* (1900), *Typhoon* (1903), *Nostromo* (1904), *Secret Agent* (1907), and *Victory* (1915).

One of the greatest novelists of the twentieth century, Conrad is noted for his profound psychological insights. His works are symbolic in nature, pitting man against his own isolation and against the world.

76. ALFRED NORTH WHITEHEAD

Two men sit on the floor picking up the pieces of the large puzzle they have been working on for months. The year is 1922. Alfred North Whitehead and Bertrand Russell have been talking and laughing, engaged in their usual intellectual jesting late into the night in Russell's London flat.

"Now, since we have picked up all the pieces of the puzzle," Russell says, "would you say that we have picked up the puzzle?"

Whitehead smiles. There is always a certain challenge inherent in their conversation that goes beyond mere joking. "You will pick up the idea of the puzzle and the puzzle in pieces," he answers, "but not the puzzle as it means the puzzle assembled."

Russell is satisfied that Whitehead is still awake. Whitehead, sensing a challenge, says, "When we look at any of the pieces of the puzzle, are we looking at the whole of it, or only one part? If you say only one part, how do you know that? And if you say that we are looking at both the whole and the part, then the parts are really the whole as ideas. The key is the distinction between the physical and the intellectual."

Russell smiles. Whitehead is obviously going to outshine him. The only thing to do is listen and appreciate his extraordinary cogitations.

Whitehead continues: "Reality is simply the organic interplay of the ideas and the physical reality through which these ideas take form. As we think new thoughts, we change what we see, and as we change what we see, what we see changes. So the puzzle is constantly shifting from being a piece of the puzzle in the puzzle, to the puzzle as a whole, and then to being part of the puzzle. We constantly need to assess the factors that are important in describing reality."

"And what are these important factors, Alfred?" inquires Russell in his most solicitous, yet friendly tone.

Whitehead begins to answer with his usual clarity and precision, disregarding Russell's tone . . . .

(A) *"There are two principles inherent in the very nature of things, recurring in some particular embodiments whatever field we explore–the spirit of change, and the spirit of conservation. There can be nothing real without both. Mere change without conservation is a passage from nothing to nothing. Its final integration yields mere transient non-entity. Mere conservation without change cannot conserve. For after all, there is a flux of circumstance, and the freshness of being evaporates under mere repetition. The character of existent reality is composed of organisms enduring through the flux of things."*

(B) *Now as matter may be great or little, yet never shrink by subdivision into nothing: so is it not probable, that motion also may be indefinitely swift or slow, and yet never come to quiescency? And so consequently there can be no rest in nature, more than a vacuity in nature. The following observations seem to make out, that the minute particles of most (if not all) bodies are constantly in some kind of motion, and that motion may be both invisibly and unintelligibly slow, as well as swift, and probably is as unseparable an attribute to bodies as extension is."*

(C) *"Of the infinite there is no beginning, but this seems to be the beginning of the other things and to surround all things and steer all, as all those say who do not postulate other causes, such as mind or love, above and beyond the infinite. And this is the divine: for it is immortal and indestructible."*

Answer (A):   CORRECT! From Alfred North Whitehead's *Science and the Modern World*.

Answer (B):   From Henry Power's *Experimental Philosophy*. Power (1623–1668) was a physician and experimental researcher with the microscope and member of the Royal Society.

Answer (C):   From fragments by Anaximander. Anaximander (c. 611–547 B.C.) was a Greek philosopher who believed that the *apeiron* is the mysterious substance of which all things in the universe are made.

Alfred North Whitehead (1861–1947), English metaphysical philosopher and mathematician, was born at Ramsgate on the Isle of Thanet and spent his childhood in a vicarage on the eastern coast of Kent. He graduated from Trinity College, Cambridge, in 1884, and until 1911, lectured at Cambridge University on mathematics. From 1911 to 1924, Whitehead was at the University of London, both as a lecturer and, later, as a professor of mathematics. During this time he collaborated with Bertrand Russell on their monumental work, *Principia Mathematica* (1910–1913), a study of the logical foundations of mathematics. Whitehead left England for the United States in 1924 to become a professor at Harvard University, where he remained until his death in 1947. He was awarded the Order of Merit in 1945.

Whitehead called his thought the philosophy of organism and he developed a special language to describe his notion of reality. His aim was to show that the universe is an organized system of relationships. Rather than a thing, it is a process which is unified and dynamic; time, space, and matter are all interrelated.

Some of his other works are *The Organization of Thought* (1916), *An Enquiry Concerning the Principles of Natural Knowledge* (1919), *The Concept of Nature* (1920), *The Principle of Relativity* (1922), *Science and the Modern World* (1925), and his masterwork, *Process and Reality* (1929).

77. OGOTEMMELI

The chickens scatter in a whirl of dust and feathers when the French ethnologist enters the village in French West Africa. Professor Marcel Griaule has traveled a great distance to visit the renowned wise man of the Dogons, a tribe of peasant warriors. The year is 1946.

A villager escorts the professor to Ogotemmeli's hut. The smells are overwhelming. There is amazing vitality in the voices of the people and the cloth that they wrap around their bodies. It is intricate and beautiful. They wear it proudly in the midst of the squalor and visual chaos.

Ogotemmeli sits cross-legged on the ground. He is very old. The white wall behind him supports his meager frame. His gauntness is accentuated by the void in his face. Both eyes are missing. Griaule asks him if he may buy a few trinkets. Ogotemmeli knows that the man has come to learn about his culture, not to buy trinkets. He invites him to sit.

"As long as we are trading," Griaule begins, "please tell me about your culture since I love the cloth that comes from it and am fascinated by the myths and legends of your people."

"Everything we do is what we know," Ogotemmeli begins. "Our doing and knowing have not suffered any explosions. When we talk, we include our past. When we make love, we are repeating the history of our culture." He takes a pinch of snuff from his worn leather box and puts it under his tongue. "Tobacco makes for right thinking," he says.

"I understand what you are saying," replies Griaule. "Yet it is hard for a European such as myself to make the distinction between what is important and what is simply habit."

Ogotemmeli is puzzled by the word "important." He takes another pinch of snuff, and is quiet for several moments before answering . . . .

(A) *"Yes, it is dangerous to be a doctor. Some doctors are fool enough to get trickery mixed up in it, but they always have to pay later on. It confuses the doctor's medicine, his damaagomi, which gets wilder and wilder, and in the end he turns against his father and mother the doctor, and destroys him. It is hard to be a doctor. But I weave well. I weave the quail pattern. I weave fishing nets. Nothing pretty."*

(B) *"A man saw a ball of gold in the sky: He climbed for it, and eventually he achieved it—It was clay. Now this is the strange part: When the man went to earth and looked again, lo there was the ball of gold. Now this is the strange part: It was a ball of gold. Ay, by the heavens, it was a ball of gold."*

(C) *"The words that the spirit uttered filled in all the interstices of the stuff; they were woven in the threads and formed part and parcel of the cloth. They were the cloth, and the cloth was the word. That is why woven material is called soy, which means, it is the spoken word."*

Answer (A): From Jaime De Angulo's *Indian Tales*. Angulo has collected and written the Indian stories contained in this volume.

Answer (B): From Stephen Crane's "A Man Saw A Ball of Gold." Crane (1871–1900) was the author of *The Red Badge of Courage*.

Answer (C): CORRECT! From Marcel Griaule's *Conversations with Ogotemmeli*.

Ogotemmeli was a member of the Dogons, a tribe of Lower Ogol, in French West Africa.

From the age of fifteen, Ogotemmeli was taught the mysteries of his people's religion by his grandfather and then his father. He grew up to be a skillful hunter. He was, moreover the father of twenty-one children.

When Ogotemmeli lost his sight in a hunting accident, he took his blindness to be a sign, a warning that he should give up hunting and killing. Suddenly in darkness, he began to think about the years of lessons and information that had been passed on to him by his ancestors. He soon became famous throughout the plateau and hills as a wise man.

In October 1946 Professor Marcel Griaule, a French ethnologist, was granted an audience with Ogotemmeli. For thirty-three successive days of conversation, Ogotemmeli revealed to Griaule the incredibly sophisticated cosmology and religion by which the Dogon live. These conversations are recorded in a book by Griaule, *Conversations with Ogotemmeli*.

78. MOHANDAS GANDHI

His face is composed and quiet. Yet beneath the surface his heart and mind are struggling under the weight of the life he has chosen. The highly personal acts of fasting and nonviolence seem directly opposed to the ideas of politics and control in a country the size of India. Nevertheless, the fragile and brilliant Gandhi is set on a path of nonviolent protest as a means of urging fair treatment for all the people of his country, whether they be Hindus or Muslims.

On this day in 1947, Gandhi is troubled. India is to be divided into two parts. The Muslims will have Pakistan, the Hindus will have India. Gandhi hates this idea, but he has chosen to support the partition to put an end to the continual struggles of two peoples who cannot seem to reconcile their difference. Yet, his heart is pounding and his voice trembles. His doctor and his niece sit by him. He lies on a mat on the floor in a shack in New Delhi. They try to calm him. Gandhi's face suddenly contorts in pain as he clutches at his chest.

"Lie still, Mahatma. Please lie still or you will die," pleads the doctor. As Gandhi rests he resolutely decides to come to grips with the partition of India. Searching his mind and heart, he finds peace. "I will be all right now," he tells his niece, who is gently rubbing his calloused feet.

The doctor checks Gandhi's blood pressure and listens to his heart. "Everything is perfectly normal now, Mahatma," he announces in disbelief. Gandhi winces, this time not from pain, but from the sound of the name "Mahatma," the "wise one," which he dislikes. It is too grand and so out of touch with his own personal aims. "It is amazing," the doctor says, "to have such control, such vision."

After a brief nap, Gandhi reflects on the doctor's final words. He is perfectly aware of why he has such control. He reaches for a pencil stub and, on the back of a scrap of paper, writes . . .

(A) "To see the universal and all pervading spirit of truth face to face one must be able to love the meanest of creatures as oneself. And a man who aspires after that cannot afford to keep out of any field of life. That is why my devotion to truth has drawn me into the field of politics; and I can say without the slightest hesitation, and yet in all humility, that those who say that religion has nothing to do with politics do not know what religion means."

(B) "Where we desire to be informed it is good to contest with men above ourselves; but to confirm and establish our opinions, it is best to argue with judgments below our own, that the frequent spoils and victories over their reasons may settle in ourselves an esteem and confirmed opinion of our own. Every man is not a proper champion for truth, nor fit to take up the gauntlet in the cause of verity."

(C) "But alas it is both common and lamentable, to behold simplicity entrapped by subtility, and those that have the most might, to be infected with the most malice. The spider weaveth a fine web to hang the fly, the wolf weareth a fair face to devour the lamb, the merlin striketh at the partridge, the eagle often snappeth at the fly. Men are always laying baits for women, which are the weaker vessels: but as yet I could never hear man by such snares entrap man: For true it is that men themselves have by use observed, that it must be a hard winter, when one wolf eateth another."

Answer (A): CORRECT! From Mohandas K. Gandhi's *An Autobiography.*

Answer (B): From Sir Thomas Browne's *Religio Medici.* Browne (1605–1682) was a scholarly doctor and literary figure.

Answer (C): From John Lyly's *Euphues: The Anatomy of Wit.* Lyly (c. 1554–1606) was a courtier and literary wit of the Elizabethan court.

Mohandas Karamchand Gandhi (1869–1948), Indian spiritual leader and politician, was born in Porbandar, India, and educated both at home and in England. He became a member of the English bar in 1889 and practiced law, rather unsuccessfully.

In 1893 Gandhi went, with his wife and children, to South Africa where he began a new law practice and supported the rights of Indians against discrimination. In 1905, after several crucial years of thinking and reading, Gandhi changed his life style entirely. He gave up Western habits of living and dressing, and replaced them with a Hindu mode of life. Dressed in a loincloth and shawl, he practiced celibacy and asceticism.

In 1907 Gandhi organized his first *satyagraha* (holding to the truth), a nonviolent demonstration against certain laws he felt to be unfair. In 1914 the South African government agreed to correct certain anti-Indian policies. When Gandhi returned to India in 1915, he was a famous man and was held in high esteem. In 1919 thousands of Indian nationalists were massacred by the British in Amritsan. Gandhi held more *satyagrahas* in protest, but he was forced to halt this practice when violence broke out.

Gandhi's dream was of a united, free India. He wanted small industries revived. He wanted to abolish the caste of untouchables. Many supported his ideas; at the same time, many Indians were opposed to his radical reforms.

After his famous 200-mile march to the sea, Gandhi was imprisoned. He was released in 1931 so that he could attend the London Round Table Conference as the representative of the Indian National Congress. He was jailed again in 1942 for starting the Quit India Movement. He lived to see Indian independence, as well as the creation of Muslim Pakistan.

On January 30, 1948, during a prayer meeting in New Delhi, Gandhi was assassinated by a Hindu who was angry at Gandhi's tolerance of the Muslims.

79. MARCEL PROUST

"They think I am up here writing everyday, but I am not. As soon as I wake up in the morning I immediately go to my desk and work for several hours to clear my head of the dreams that have obsessed me throughout the night. Then, at midday, I disguise myself and go for a stroll. I always look quite handsome. I walk in the park, along the fashionable streets, and without fail, I encounter a charming young woman with whom I strike up a conversation. No one realizes that they are talking to Marcel Proust. They believe the rumor that I spend all day in bed, writing in a corklined room, wearing mufflers, sweaters, gloves, a nightcap. Yet, I am actually up and about, talking to a young woman, impressing her with the seriousness of my writing and how I find it necessary to take breaks. She is sympathetic. We begin walking in the direction of my flat, stopping at my favorite café. The waiter brings us tea and madeleines. We drink to our health. I recall all that I have written that morning and begin to focus on this new woman who has entered my life. She is not always beautiful, but she is always interesting. Her eyes dart back and forth as she tries to get a good look at me without my noticing. My stare disconcerts her. She invariably asks me to tell her more about my book. I use her features to describe my aunt. I look deep into my cup and tell her how the tea has stimulated me to recall a vast treasure which I could not have come to without it. I tell her that I recall things through my sense experiences of events, which, when they occurred, I hardly noticed. She is fascinated, usually. We go to my rooms where we talk. Sometimes she spends the night. Sometimes she stays for weeks on end. Inevitably, she feels trapped in the repetition of my daily routine, although when we are out together, we stroll and talk and I do not look for other women. She usually will cry and depart forever. I cannot help this. I cannot help myself. Today I will write a few pages and go out. . .

(A) "This was untrue. I am not even faintly like a rose. She was only extemporizing, but a stirring warmth flowed from her, as if her heart was trying to come out to you concealed in one of those breathless, thrilling words. Then suddenly she threw her napkin on the table and excused herself and went into the house."

(B) "But when from a long distant past nothing subsists, after the people are dead, after the things are broken and scattered, still, alone, more fragile, but with more vitality, more unsubstantial, more persistent, more faithful, the smell and taste of things remain poised for a long time, like souls, ready to remind us, waiting and hoping for their moment, amid the ruins of all the rest: and bear unfaltering, in the tiny and almost unpalpable drop of their essence, the vast structure of recollection."

(C) " 'And that is why the feeling that you have deliberately caused injury to someone upsets you so much, and why you are so reluctant to admit the fact. Pardon me if I have been impertinent, but the psychology, it is the most important fact in the case.' "

"Linnet said slowly, 'Even supposing what you say were true—and I don't admit it, mind—what can be done about it now? One can't alter the past: one must deal with things as they are.' "

Answer (A):   From F. Scott Fitzgerald's *The Great Gatsby*. Fitzgerald (1896–1940) has received wide acclaim for this, one of the best novels of the 1920s.

Answer (B):   CORRECT! From Marcel Proust's *Swann's Way*.

Answer (C):   From Agatha Christie's *Death on the Nile*. Christie (1891–1976) was noted for her popular Poirot mysteries, including this one.

Marcel Proust (1871–1922), French novelist, was born in Paris. His father was a physician and his mother a Jewish heiress. Proust was raised as a Roman Catholic. At the age of nine, he suffered his first attack of the asthma that would become chronic and debilitating. Although a sickly child, he attended the Lycée Condorçet for a few years, received a diploma from the University of Paris, and served briefly in the army.

Proust spent most of his youth in the fashionable world of Paris society, in the drawing rooms of his high-born friends, from which he would later draw the characters about whom he wrote.

During the last thirteen years of his life, he withdrew gradually from high society, spending days in bed, writing in a cork-lined room in his family's apartment on the Boulevard Haussman. He died at the age of fifty-one.

Proust's life work was his semiautobiographical novel, *À la Récherche du Temps Perdu (Remembrance of Things Past)*, published in seven sections. The first section, *Du Côté Swann (Swann's Way)*, was published in 1913 and received little attention. *A L'ombre des Jeunes Filles en Fleurs (Within a Budding Grove)*, the second section published in 1919, received the Prix Goncourt.

Remembrance is essentially the story of the hero's life from childhood, and the story of the village of Combray. Proust was an observer of humanity which he looked at "through a telescope."

80. GERTRUDE STEIN

The salon is packed with great artists and intellectuals of the day—Pablo Picasso, Juan Gris, Ernest Hemingway, Sherwood Anderson, Ralph Vaughan Williams, Ezra Pound, and many more. The conversation is completely dominated by a masculine, robust woman with a crew cut who sits like a Buddha on a chair on one side of the room while everyone else sits on the other. Paris in the 1920s is the most vital art community in the world. Gertrude Stein is the *grande dame* of that community. Going to her house is like stepping into the future, for these minds will shape the world in the next half-century.

"All art is irritation," Gertrude pronounces to Alice B. Toklas, her lover. Alice listens, smiling, and continues to knit.

Picasso leaps to his feet, grabs a rose from the vase, and puts it between his teeth. "And what do you think of roses that do not irritate, ma chère?"

The guests are amused, Gertrude included, since they are all familiar with her famous phrase, "A rose is a rose is a rose is a rose."

Gertrude nonchalantly asks Hemingway, "Ernest, why is it that your prose is so concerned with the past?"

Hemingway is stunned. She has been so supportive. This comment suggests that she does not approve of his work. "But you . . ."

"Never mind, Ernest," she interrupts, "you are still my favorite pupil." Everyone laughs. Gertrude disappears, going up to her room to write. She wants prose to be in the present. She wants to make it happen. She sits down at her desk and begins to write. . . .

(A) "What do we mean by reading? Do we mean the reading of words as words, the recognition of the structure, the interpretation of the references—in brief the explication, as we put it, of the text? Or do we mean the reading of the substance of the words, what the words in their combination and their structure, their sounds and their significance, are about?"

(B) *"A noun is the name of anything. There is no hope of their pleasure. It is very nice to change your mind about roses. Please have it with all without it. It is very strange but it is true that they did say it because however alike they found it. There is no doubt that I like the thing they have for use for me. It is an hour after they came. May be with them."*

(C) *"So they decided against me. Now I will have to go through the door after all—like all those others. They'll draw the curtains for me, too. Into that other room—then back across the passage—saying goodbye as I go, like those others. I will not be here anymore."*

Answer (A): From Archibald MacLeish's "What Is English?" MacLeish (1892–   ) is a poet and critic.

Answer (B): CORRECT! From Gertrude Stein's *How to Write*.

Answer (C): From Theodore Dreiser's *An American Tragedy*. A newspaper reporter and novelist of the 1920s, Dreiser (1871–1945) became famous for this novel.

Gertrude Stein (1874–1946), American author, was born in Allegheny, Pennsylvania. Shortly afterwards her parents moved to Europe. When they returned they settled in California, where Gertrude Stein grew up.

She attended Radcliffe College from 1893 to 1897, studying under William James. In 1897 she went to Johns Hopkins University in Baltimore to study medicine. She left before graduating to join her brother, Leo, in Florence, where he had been living for a number of years.

By 1903 Stein was firmly established in Paris. She and her brother began collecting paintings of hitherto unknown artists: Paul Cézanne, Henri Matisse, Pablo Picasso, and the like. In 1907 she met Alice B. Toklas, the woman who became her secretary and lifetime companion.

For the remainder of her life, Stein traveled in Europe and occasionally lectured in the United States. She died in Paris at the age of seventy-two.

Gerturde Stein had wide influence. Her apartment became a meeting place for the artists and writers living in Paris after the First World War. The effect of her criticism on the development of subjective realism in art was significant. Her friendships with Picasso and Juan Gris are legendary. She also influenced the literary world. In her own works, her objective was to create a new kind of writing, one which used words and phrases to express the immediate present. Among her most important works were *Three Lives* (1909), *Tender Buttons* (1914), *The Making of Americans* (1925), and *The Autobiography of Alice B. Toklas* (1933).

81. CARL JUNG

"Ideas, Sigmund, ideas. You are obsessed with concepts." Carl Jung and Sigmund Freud are sitting in Jung's drawing room in Vienna. The year is 1912. Freud is complaining that Jung has gone off the deep end, dragging psychoanalysis into disrepute.

"I realize that mysterious events are interesting, Carl. However, they are not as important as the basic backdrop of the mind. Sexual conflict is more important than the 'life force.' It is obvious that archetypes are not really essential for the analysis of neurotics."

"You are a difficult and stubborn man, Sigmund. You refuse to see that there are archetypal patterns that affect us. Even as you smoke that cigar, you are fulfilling the old custom of smoke and safety. Certainly you understand the relationship between myth and character construction?"

Before Freud can form an answer, Jung's secretary enters the room. The two men, both married and fully analyzed, look longingly at the young, attractive woman. Their conversation ceases.

Jung, catching Freud staring at her, breaks the silence. "You should be ashamed, Sigmund. She is young enough to be your daughter. You know what this means."

Freud looks hurt at this admonishment from his protegé. He rises from his chair, walks over to the woman, and gives her a light kiss on the cheek. Seated again, he says to Jung in a tone thick with sarcasm, "She loves the attention and is flattered that someone as intellectual as I am can be overcome by mythic patterns."

Jung resents this attitude. He has had enough of the great teacher. He wants to walk his own path. He bids Freud goodnight and goes to his study, where he begins to formulate his thoughts regarding the conversation. . . .

(A) "When common purposes do not exist the answer is to manufacture them. The most important inherent difficulty in the operation of cooperative systems is the necessity for indoctrinating those at lower levels with general purposes. This may actually involve deception. We say then that as long as the participants do not recognize that, there are serious divergencies of their understanding of that purpose as the object of cooperation. Hence, an objective purpose that can serve as a basis for a cooperative system is one that is believed by the contributors to be the determined purpose."

(B) "This is where those perilous aberrations begin, the first of which is to dominate everything by the intellect . . . . Experience is stripped of its substance, and instead mere names are substituted, which are henceforth put in the place of reality. No one has any obligations to concepts. That is what is so agreeable about conceptuality—it promises protection from experience. The spirit does not dwell in concepts, but in deeds and facts. Words butter no parsnips: nevertheless this futile procedure is repeated ad infinitum."

(C) "Many attempts have been made toward fitting the concept of freedom into the confines of an organized structure. Compromisers propose that the secret lies in not over-organizing but striking the optimal ratio of unhindered action on the parts of both players. Contract theorists point to an exchange of rights on the part of the citizen for protection and general welfare furnished by the state. Others claim that knowledge rather than will is the important consideration. An ass is a slave so long as it does not recognize the necessity of the load and chafes under it rather than willingly shouldering it."

Answer (A): From Charles Perrow's *Complex Organizations*. Perrow writes here about the nature and problems of complex organizations.

Answer (B): CORRECT! From C. G. Jung's *Memories, Dreams, Reflections*.

Answer (C): From R. G. H. Siu's *The Tao of Science*. This particular text discusses the relation of Eastern wisdom and Western knowledge.

Carl Gustav Jung (1875–1961), Swiss psychiatrist and founder of analytical psychology, was born in Kesswil, near Basel. Jung's father was a clergyman. As a youth, Jung read philosophy and was influenced by Immanuel Kant and Arthur Schopenhauer. The works of J. W. Goethe and Friedrich Nietzsche also played an important part in his early thinking.

At first indecisive about what studies he wanted to pursue, Jung finally decided to take up medicine. His father, being poor, applied to the University of Basel for a stipend for his son. Jung was ashamed of this, and even more ashamed when he received it. He entered the university in 1895. In 1900 he took up a post as assistant at Burgholzli Mental Hospital in Zurich, studying with Eugen Bleuler. He received his medical degree in 1902, and in 1905 he became a lecturer in psychology at the University of Zurich and the senior physician at the psychology clinic.

Jung met Freud after sending him a paper entitled "The Psychology of Dementia Praecox," which Freud found interesting. They traveled together to the United States in 1909, a seven-week trip during which they were constantly together, analyzing each other's dreams. In 1911 Jung was named president of the International Psychoanalytic Society. His theory of the collective unconscious was beginning to develop, and Freud was gradually losing his authority over the younger man. In 1912, with the publication of *The Psychology of the Unconscious*, Jung's break with Freud was more or less official. Two years later Jung founded his own school of analytical psychology.

Jung's work is important for his formulation of several unique approaches to human psychology and the human psyche. He is most noted for his idea of the collective unconscious, which is symbolized in archetypal images that Jung believed to be primordial.

82. MARTIN BUBER

A small man sits in a temple in Jerusalem. The year is 1950. He is attending the Kol Nidre service during Yom Kippur, the Day of Atonement. During the prayers he meditates on the nature of the human relationships that so often and so quickly become a process of negation. In his precise and focused view of the world, he sees the tragedy of the human condition. Deep in communication, he listens as the rabbi leads the solemn service, which concerns itself with prayers for the dead. "How can I perceive the death of a human being whom, in life, I have never known or even heard of?" he ponders.

After the service, the man wanders the streets lost in thought. At midnight, he finds himself at the house of a friend. Is it too late to knock? No.

From the second floor, his friend, barely awake, peers through the curtains at the figure below who is knocking at the door. "Oy vay, it's him again," he mutters. "Buber?" his wife groans from the bed, reaching to turn on the light. They look at each other, both thinking the same thought: no matter what the circumstances, they cannot refuse entry to this sincere and wise man, despite his reputation of involving people in discussions that are compelling but beyond their scope.

The front door opens and Buber is welcomed. The wife goes to make tea. Buber makes himself at home in the modest living room. "I have just had one of my most intense conversations, but no one was there. I worried that perhaps my thoughts about the need for concrete and direct communication with people is a mere idea." He relates his earlier thoughts on death to his friend.

"Martin, we talk with the dead in the same way that we talk with the living. You talk with those who have died in the same way that you talk with me, since the responsibility is always within you. You have taught me that."

"Yes, yes, my friend. You have graciously received me tonight. You are here for me. I am grateful. Yet, the import of my question on death has been to consider you merely as an idea. I am sorry for that."

The wife serves tea. Buber delicately sips from the cup and further explains his ideas. . . .

(A) "The experience of being the actual medium for a continual process of creation takes one past all depression or persecution or vain glory, past even chaos or emptiness, into the very mystery of that continual flip of nonbeing into being, and can be the occasion of that great liberation when one makes the transition from being afraid of nothing to the realization that there is nothing to fear. Nevertheless, it is very easy to lose one's way at any stage, and especially when one is nearest."

(B) "The relation to you is unmediated. Nothing conceptual intervenes between you and I: no prior knowledge and no imagination: and memory itself is changed as it plunges from particularity into wholeness. No purpose intervenes between you and I, no greed and no anticipation: and longing itself is changed as it plunges from the dream into appearance. Every means is an obstacle. Only where all means have disintegrated encounters occur."

(C) "One day he looked in the mirror and saw he was an old man whose hair was as white as snow. Suddenly he remembered having climbed through a hole in the coin. What happened sixty years ago seemed like only yesterday. He was strong and full of spirit then, and now he was old and decrepit. Life was like a dream! Had he known that this was all that a man could hope for in life, he would have been able to detach himself from many of the cravings he thought he had to satisfy! Now it was too late. He wondered if he could find the way back to the ladder up which he had climbed so many years ago."

Answer (A): From R. D. Laing's *The Politics of Experience*. Laing (1927–   ) is an experimental psychoanalyst who has become famous for his position on schizophrenia.

Answer (B): CORRECT! From Martin Buber's *I and Thou*.

Answer (C): From Li Ju-chen's *Flowers in the Mirror*. This eighteenth-century Chinese novel of philosophy and love is considered a classic.

Martin Buber (1878–1965), Jewish religious philosopher and existentialist, was born in Vienna. He spent his childhood at his grandfather's home in Lvol, Galicia. His grandfather was a businessman and a scholar of Rabbinic literature.

From 1896 to 1900, Buber studied philosophy and art at the Universities of Vienna, Leipzig, Berlin, and Zurich. Buber was active in the Zionist Movement. In 1901 he became editor of *Die Welt*, a Zionist journal, and in 1916 he founded *Der Jude*, a German Jewish monthly. From 1924 to 1933 Buber was a professor of philosophy of Jewish religion at Frankfurt-am-Main.

In 1920 Buber founded an institute for adult Jewish education with Rosensweig. He remained there, even when the Nazis came to power, concerned with supporting and giving strength to the German Jewish people.

He traveled to Palestine in 1938 and taught sociology at Hebrew University. Buber was the leader of a movement to create an Arab-Jewish state. He died in Jerusalem in 1965.

Buber's most popular work, *I and Thou* (1923), sets forth his philosophy of religion. Buber envisioned the relationship between human beings and God to be one of personal and direct communication. He was greatly influenced by the mysticism of Hassidism and Sören Kierkegaard's existential philosophy. Some of his other works are *Jewish Mysticism and Legends of Baalshem* (1931), *Mamre* and, *Moses* (both 1946), and *The Origin and Meaning of Hassidism* (1960, trans.).

83. ALBERT EINSTEIN

What a sight! The world's most famous man strolling down a sidewalk in Princeton, New Jersey, eating an ice-cream cone. He is dressed in an old sweatshirt and wears his shoes without socks. His tousled white hair frames his head in a chaotic halo. His eyes seem to draw the universe into their depths. The children playing along the street stop their games to watch him pass. His very presence communicates his strange contact with the basic laws of the universe, his true connection with the ultimate, and an idea of the power that he alone can penetrate. The year is 1953. Albert Einstein is returning home from his office at the Institute for Advanced Studies.

One of his students catches up with him, falling into step beside him. "Excuse this question, Professor, but what will be the place of the relativity theory in the scheme of things in fifty years?"

Einstein is slightly annoyed. He does not tolerate too much of this kind of questioning. "The logical resting place of any workable theory is as a subset of a yet greater theory," he answers perfunctorily.

"Ah, yes," the student breathes, somewhat satisfied. He escorts Einstein to the door of the famous scientist's house and then realizes that he is to go no further. Yet, the student wants to ask Einstein another question. Sensing this, Einstein lingers a moment, finishing his ice-cream cone.

"We can't know everything in the world. There are so many strange things. What about the unknowable?"

Einstein is accustomed to such half-formed questions. It is as if most of the questions directed at him are in everyone's mind. He finishes the cone, wiping his mustache with a crumpled handkerchief, and replies . . .

(A) *"The most incomprehensible thing about the universe is that it is at all comprehensible. The fairest thing we can experience is the mysterious. It is the fundamental emotion which stands at the cradle of true art and true science."*

(B) *"General relativity has important consequences for large scale problems, including the structure of the universe. It is likely that in the future some relationship may emerge which links these ideas also with the characteristics of small scale, i.e., atomic problems, but this is as yet unknown."*

(C) *"In the course of its history, physics will have to decide whether the world-picture of the theory of relativity is securely founded theoretically and whether it finds complete experimental verification. Its decision on this, epistemology cannot anticipate: but even now it can thankfully receive the new impetus which this theory has given the general doctrine of the principles of physics."*

Answer (A):   CORRECT! From Albert Einstein's *The World as I See It.*

Answer (B):   From R. E. Peierls' *The Laws of Nature.* Peier's (1907–   ) provides a theoretical study and analysis of the basic ideas of physics.

Answer (C):   From Ernst Cassirer's *Substance and Function and Einstein's Theory of Relativity.* Cassirer (1874-1945) was a philosopher of science.

Albert Einstein (1879–1955), physicist, was born in Ulm, Germany. His family moved to Munich when he was a child, and although Jewish, he was sent to a Catholic grammar school. He was, like Isaac Newton, an unexceptional student.

Einstein attended the Federal Institute of Technology in Zurich, graduating in 1900. From 1902 to 1909 he held a job in the Patent Office in Berne, during which time he also did his own work. In 1905 he received his doctorate. That same year, he had five papers published in the *German Year Book of Physics:* one on photoelectricity; another, an explanation of Brownian motion; and a third, his theory of special relativity, expressed in the famous formula, $E = mc^2$.

In 1909, Einstein became a professor at the University of Zurich, and by 1913 he was world famous. He was invited to Berlin to be a professor of physics at the Kaiser Wilhelm Physical Institute. In 1915 he published his paper on the general theory of relativity, having to do with particle acceleration in a gravitational field.

When World War I broke out, a group of German scientists signed a nationalistic prowar proclamation. Einstein, however, signed a peace proclamation. He was awarded a Nobel Prize in physics in 1921.

From 1930 until his death, Einstein resided in the United States, teaching in California and at Princeton, and eventually becoming an American citizen. During that time he worked on his unified field theory. Einstein refused to accept Werner Heisenberg's principle of indeterminancy, which allows for statistical analysis of phenomena.

84. JAMES JOYCE

His sight has become so dim and feeble that most minor daily operations require the aid of his wife and friends. A secretary has been hired to transcribe his writings. What a tragedy for James Joyce to lose sight of the world he wants so much to encompass! He has taken to creating mysterious paths in his work to compensate for the lack of imagery. The paths often lead to his own idosyncratic life and to the myths and archetypes that resound in his mind from his Irish education. The year is 1938. Joyce is living in Paris where he has many admirers, his work having achieved a high degree of prominence.

One bright afternoon, the painter Augustus John visits Joyce. He wants to do a portrait of him and is pleased that Joyce will allow it. Joyce explains that he has been occupied with creating a novel that will never end, and has been working out new forms for this purpose. In his mind, he envisions each story, each element, spreading like fire in a forest, burning up and down each major tree, one at a time.

John, busy setting up his easel and mixing paints, likes the image. "What does writing mean to you?" he questions.

Joyce's painful eyes strain to see the man from which the question comes, and he directs his answer at the blur of moving light and shadow. "It allows me to construct a universe in which all the parts work together."

John begins sketching. "What are the major strategies an artist should employ in his life?" he asks abruptly.

Joyce is silent. This question is one which has plagued him for many years. The sound of John's sketching fills the room and then fades away as Joyce answers, framing his true mark as a writer. . . .

(A) "And whenever he spoke (which he did almost always), he took care to produce the very finest and longest words of which the vocabulary gave him the use; rightly judging that it was as cheap to employ a handsome, large, and sonorous epithet, as to use a little stingy one."

(B) "You asked me what I would do and what I would not do. I will tell you what I will do and what I will not do. I will not serve that in which I no longer believe whether it call itself my home, my fatherland, or my church: and I will try to express myself in some mode of life or art as freely as I can and as wholly as I can, using for my defense the only arms I allow myself to use—silence, exile and cunning."

(C) "I couldn't even think I nor even think I want to wake up nor remember what was opposite to awake so I could do that I knew something was passing but I couldn't even think of time then all of a sudden I knew that something was it was wind blowing over me from where it was I was not blowing the room."

Answer (A): From W. M. Thackeray's *Vanity Fair*. This work by Thackeray (1811–1863) is considered one of the classic English novels of the nineteenth century.

Answer (B): CORRECT! From James Joyce's *A Portrait of the Artist as a Young Man*.

Answer (C): From William Faulkner's *As I Lay Dying*. The work is considered one of Faulkner's greatest novels. Faulkner (1897–1962) received the Nobel Prize for literature in 1949.

James Joyce (1882–1941), Irish novelist, was born in Dublin, into a family of nine brothers and sisters. He attended a Jesuit school and graduated from the University College, Dublin, in 1902. Although a brilliant student, he resented the constraints of Catholicism and rebelled, leading a rowdy, drunken student life.

In 1904 he went with his girlfriend, Nora Barnacle, to Europe, where he lived with her. He moved about from Paris to Zurich to Trieste for the next twenty-five years.

Dubliners was published in England in 1914 after being published and then burned in Ireland two years earlier because Joyce used real names in the stories. Joyce and Nora and their two children went to Zurich for the duration of World War I. In 1916 *A Portrait of the Artist as a Young man* was published, and a year later Joyce began suffering from glaucoma, which plagued him with near blindness and pain for the rest of his life.

During his publishing career Joyce was aided financially by several patrons, especially Harriet Shaw Weaver, editor of *The Egoist*, a periodical. She published sections of *Ulysses*, which Joyce had a hard time getting published in its entirety because it was considered obscene. Finally, Sylvia Beach, who owned a famous bookstore in Paris, published the book.

From 1922 to 1939, Joyce worked on *Finnegan's Wake*. In 1933 *Ulysses*, banned in the United States until then, was published there. Joyce died in 1941, while undergoing an operation for an ulcer.

Joyce is a major figure of twentieth-century literature, who has had an immeasurable effect on other writers. He was an inventor of literary techniques that freed the novel through his innovative use of lanugage and form. *Ulysses*, his greatest work, is about a day in Dublin in the life of Leopold Bloom. Its grand design is based on Homer's *Odyssey*.

85. VIRGINIA WOOLF

Her determination is ferocious. She encounters anything that interests her with such obsession that sparks fly. Her novels emerge from her intense desire and perhaps even from hatred and defiance of the world which has received them so poorly. Her friends have been the giants of literature and thought in England: John Maynard Keynes, Lytton Strachey, H. G. Wells. They have all encouraged her to write. But she is supremely depressed by the limits that being a woman has imposed upon her existence. She suffers mental anguish for her personal fate, as well as for the fate of other women who suffer inhuman treatment from the world at large. Beyond this, the reality of the Second World War drives her to despair. She wanders aimlessly through the large rooms of her house in Rodmell, beginning to compose yet another work that will bring all the madness inside and outside her into a precise and emotional whole. The year is 1940.

Virginia Woolf walks out to the garden where children run and laugh, playing out fantasies that only they can know. She wants to join them in some way but realizes that she can only do so through her words. "These words are my link to a world that exists only through their presence." She thinks about her father, who had helped her to learn but had not set aside any funds for her education. She misses him. She wants to include his absence in everything she says. "How sad that women do not get to carry on the energy of their fathers but are forced to join with men to help them do it. It is no different than my living through my words."

Leonard, her husband, joins her in the garden. "Virginia, you must come in and take a nap," he begs her.

"Yes, my dear lover, my brother. I will, but you must respect my need to organize my time myself."

Virginia is often on the verge of collapse, and Leonard is always there to help her untangle the webs in her mind. He walks with her to her room and puts her to bed. Sleep comes quickly, and with it, a dream. It is a scene that represents the relationship between the known and the felt, the inside and the outside, the past and the present. . . .

(A) "She had not much of anything to say to her father, for that matter: but he did not antagonize her. She discovered that he interested her, though she realized that he might not interest her for long: and for the first time in her life she felt as if she were thoroughly acquainted with him. He kept her busy serving him and ministering to his wants. It amused her to do so. She would not permit a servant or one of the children to do anything for him which she might do herself. Her husband noticed, and thought it was the expression of a deep filial attachment which he had never suspected."

(B) "She was by that time tired of men—or she imagined that she was: for she was not prepared to be certain, considering the muckers she saw women coming all around her over the most unpresentable individuals. Men, at any rate, never fulfilled expectations. They might, upon acquaintance, turn out more entertaining than they appeared: but almost always, taking up with a man was like reading a book that you had read when you had forgotten that you had read it. You had not been for ten minutes in any sort of intimacy with any man before you said, But I've read all this before. . . . You knew the opening, you were already bored by the middle, and especially you knew the end."

(C) "There is only a thin sheet between me now and the infinite depths. The lumps in the mattress soften beneath me. We stumble up—we stumble on. My path has been up and up, towards some solitary tree with a pool beside it on the very top. I have sliced the waters of beauty in the evening when the hills close themselves like bird's wings folded. I have picked sometimes a red carnation, and wisps of hay. I have sunk alone on the turf and fingered some old bone and thought: When the wind stoops to brush this height, may there be nothing found but a pinch of dust."

Answer (A):   From Kate Chopin's *The Awakening*. Chopin wrote this novel at the turn of the century, although it has only recently become more widely known.

Answer (B):   From Ford Maddox Ford's *No More Parades*. Ford (1873–1939) was a English novelist who collaborated with Joseph Conrad. His most famous novel is *The Good Soldier*.

Answer (C):   CORRECT! From Virginia Woolf's *The Waves*.

Virginia Woolf (1882–1941), English author, was born in London, the youngest of four children. Her father was Sir Leslie Stephen, a man of letters, and Virginia was educated largely at home. Her mother died when she was thirteen, probably precipitating her first nervous breakdown. Her father died in 1904, and Virginia moved with her sister and two brothers to Gordon Square, Bloomsbury. She wrote reviews for the *Times Literary Supplement* during the period. In 1904, after one brother had died and her sister, Vanessa, had married Clive Bell, Virginia and brother Adrian moved to Fitzroy Square. Their house became the meeting place for a group of people, including John Maynard Keynes, Roger Fry, and Lytton Strachey, that became known as the Bloomsbury group.

In 1912 Virginia married Leonard Woolf, a writer and critic. Together, they set up the Hogarth Press. Virginia wrote novels for the next twenty years, being cared for by Leonard while she had her periodic battles with depression. She suffered another complete breakdown when she was thirty-three. In 1941 Woolf drowned herself in the river near her home.

Her first novels were *The Voyage Out* (1915) and *Night and Day* (1919). As she continued to write, her style developed, becoming more distinctive and less traditional. Some of her other works include the novels *Jacob's Room* (1922), *Mrs. Dalloway* (1925), *To The Lighthouse* (1927), and *The Waves* (1931), and a feminist essay, *A Room of One's Own* (1929).

86. FRANZ KAFKA

Max and Franz are sitting in a windowless room in Prague. The year is 1923. They have been trying for years to work together on a novel that will be a story about them and their ideas.

Franz Kafka is not happy. His friend Max Brod likes working in a windowless room to avoid distractions. Kafka, who likes to look out at the street, is sullen. Max, who is writing a paragraph on friendship, looks up. "Franz," he says, "your commitment to friends is so pure. Yet I always get a sense that you are alone. Why?"

Franz looks at the wall in front of him and replies, "Simply because one can never get through the medium of everyday life to discover who someone is. When I look at a woman, for example, I can only see her as a peculiar model of what others expect her to be. She talks to me of things that have to do with fashion, custom, but rarely of the ideas that run through my brain."

"I am not a woman," Max interjects. "Still, you keep me at a distance. I am not concerned with everyday matters, with the commonsensical world. Yet, you separate yourself from me. Why?"

"Perhaps because you are concerned with friendship. Perhaps because you ask me for feelings and expressions of feelings when the evidence of my desire to work with you should suffice."

Max is stunned. "But, Franz, how can you know yourself? With whom can you interact in order to measure yourself, to discover how you have changed?"

"I look inside," Franz replies. "I remember how I felt earlier. I lean close against the wall and remember how my flesh felt when I was a child. Max, we are working together on a novel, and these issues must be part of it. Do not believe others. Trust in your ability to compose."

Max is distressed by his friend's dire position. "How can you enjoy the human condition from such an isolated post?" he asks.

Franz does not answer. He is lost in thought. Writing on a small piece of paper, he expresses how he feels. . . .

(A) "From now on we row farther and farther out to sea. It is for this reason that all these people gathered to see us off. Little by little at every stroke of the oars, the watchers standing by the shore slip away into the distance, just as we, on the boats, grow more and more indistinct to them. On the shore, perhaps, there are things that they would like to say to us. On the boats there are thoughts we wish to convey to them—but to no avail. Even so, though we can expect no reply, we compose this last poem:
"No courier have we, and though with heavy hearts
We leave—perhaps they'll never know we grieved."

(B) "And the man reborn, as men are never reborn out of their dead selves, by life itself. For as there are many faiths and many conceptions of the one paradox by which man exists as transient flesh and enduring spirit, all these faiths stem from one faith, the one wonder and mystery of which we are an inseparable part. Let each man, though bereft of teacher, priest, and preceptor, but depend on this faith and so be reborn by life itself into a greater whole. And see before him at last, through the cycles of his widening perception, the one road which is his to tread with all."

(C) Whoever leads a solitary life and yet now and then wants to attach himself somewhere, whoever, according to changes in the time of day, the weather, the state of his business, and the like, suddenly wishes to see any arm at all to which he might cling—he will not be able to manage for long without a window looking on the street. And if he is in the mood of not desiring anything and only goes to his window sill a tired man, with eyes turning from his public to heaven and back again, not wanting to look out and having thrown his head up a little, even then the horses below will draw him out into their train of wagons and tumult, and so at last into the human harmony."

Answer (A): From Ki no Tsurayuki's *The Tosa Diary*. This is a historical diary written by a governor in Japan in A.D. 936. It is a classic of Japanese literature.

Answer (B): From Frank Water's *The Man Who Killed the Deer*. Water's novel of Pueblo Indian life has become a popular book for understanding the spirit of these Indians.

Answer (C): CORRECT! From Franz Kafka's "The Street Window"

Franz Kafka, (1883–1924), Czech writer, was born in Prague. His parents were prosperous Jews. After studying law and receiving his degree from the German University of Prague in 1906, he took a government job in an insurance office in the city.

At the age of thirty-four, Kafka contracted tuberculosis, which kept him ill until his death at forty-one in a sanitorium in Austria. Kafka was engaged twice during his life, but he never married, leading an extremely solitary life. A slow and meticulous writer, by the time of his death only a few of his stories had been published, among them, "In the Penal Colony" and "Metamorphosis."

Kafka left instructions with his friend Max Brod to destroy all his unpublished writings when he died, which Brod, of course, ignored. Instead, he assembled the manuscripts of *The Trial*, *The Castle*, and *Amerika*.

Kafka's vision was a terrible one, one of futility and the individual's vain search for salvation. The world he created is, in the existentialist tradition, absurd, his characters consumed with guilt, anxiety, and isolated from one another.

87. JOHN MAYNARD KEYNES

John Maynard Keynes is lunching with the prime minister in an elegant London club. Wealthy men sip wine and dine on exquisitely prepared cuisine, oblivious to the economic privations being suffered by people throughout the world. The year is 1931.

Former millionaires sell apples on street corners. Bread lines stretch down the block. The value of money has inflated and deteriorated so rapidly that although the rich who have kept their cash working continue to prosper, the average person's savings has vanished. Many voices cry out asking what should be done. One voice alone offers the most reasonable and attractive alternative to the situation.

Keynes had once been a strict advocate of a free capitalist economy. He had argued against government intervention in economics except for the regulation of the value of currency. The depression has changed all that. Keynes sees that the implementation of massive government work programs will provide the population with jobs and distribute accumulated wealth more quickly among those who have suffered most. The government should involve people in projects which will open up new economic possibilities, projects such as roadbuilding, housing, electrical and water works. These projects should be designed to stimulate the accumulation of capital in the middle classes, thus enabling them to better weather the problems of inflation or depression.

Keynes, draining the wine from his glass, says to Ramsay MacDonald, "If, during the nineteenth century, everyone had decided to live well and not reinvest as they did, the depression would have happened twenty years ago."

MacDonald nods in agreement and asks Keynes what will happen if government becomes so strong that it eventually employs everyone.

"This will not happen since government cannot extend its wealth that far. Besides, an action like that would cause both inflation and stagnation," Keynes explains.

"Well, then, Keynes, what should we do to keep the economy rolling and improve the quality of life for everyone?"

Between mouthfuls of chocolate mousse, Keynes answers . . .

(A) "I say the first object of renascent liberalism is education and I mean that its task is to aid in producing the habits of mind and character, the intellectual and moral patterns, that are somewhere near even with the actual movement of events. It is, I repeat, the split between the latter as they have externally occurred and the ways of desiring, thinking, and of putting emotion and purpose into execution that is the basic cause of the present confusion in mind and paralysis in action."

(B) "Empire calls for discipline, coordination of forces, duty and sacrifice: this explains many aspects of the practical working of the regime and the direction of many of the forces of the state and the necessary severity shown to those who would wish to oppose this spontaneous and destined impulse of governments to oppose it in the name of superseded ideologies."

(C) "The pace at which we can reach our destination of economic bliss will be governed by four things—our power to control population, our determination to avoid wars and civil dissensions, our willingness to entrust to science the direction of those matters which are properly the concern of science, and the rate of accumulation as fixed by the margin between our production and our consumption: of which the last will easily look after itself given the first three."

Answer (A): From John Dewey's *Liberalism and Social Action*. Dewey (1859–1952) formulated the ideas and operating plan for education in America for the second half of the twentieth century.

Answer (B): From Benito Mussolini's *The Doctrine of Fascism*. Mussolini (1883–1945) was head of the fascist state in Italy before and during World War II.

Answer (C): CORRECT! From John Maynard Keynes' *Essays in Persuasion*.

John Maynard Keynes (1883–1946), British economist, was born in Cambridge. He attended Cambridge University and became part of a group of young intellectuals who founded the Bloomsbury group.

After graduating from Cambridge Keynes joined the India office of the civil service where he was involved with Indian currency problems. His reputation as a economist grew, and in 1919 he was one of the principal British Treasury experts at the Versailles Peace Conference. Keynes resigned his position, however, in protest over what he felt were unfeasible economic provisions in the Treaty of Versailles. He wrote *The Economic Consequences of the Peace* (1919) to express his objections to the treaty.

In 1929 Keynes supported a program of government spending in public works to promote employment. During the 1930s Keynes advocated government spending programs to combat deflation and depression and to increase employment. These theories had a tremendous influence on Franklin Roosevelt's formulation of New Deal programs.

During the Second World War Keynes was a consultant to the British Treasury, involved with the first proposals for a world bank. He died shortly after the war's conclusion.

Keynesian economics has influenced the economic policies of most of the democratic governments of the world, especially that of the United States. Keynes' chief work was *The General Theory of Employment, Interest, and Money* (1936).

88. ORTEGA Y GASSET

The streets of Madrid in 1935 are dangerous. The country is torn by civil strife: the republicans against the forces of Franco. Ortega y Gasset, a republican sympathizer, is en route to a lecture date. The essayist and philosopher, a mild man, is frightened by the crowd that engulfs him as he arrives at the hall. The people buffet him back and forth like a puppet. Some support him while others have come to taunt him. As a group of uniformed thugs appear at the edge of the mob, his fright turns to anger.

The scene fills Ortega with the passions of one who is watching a world he loves disappear. Leaders are making decisions not on the basis of truth and the obvious rightness of an idea, but on whether they can get a consensus from the masses. Ortega strongly feels that the masses have no foundation on which to form opinions.

Ortega is ushered into the safety of the lecture hall. The audience loves him, in spite of the fact that so many of them are the "mass-men" he so vehemently deplores. He begins his lecture with an explanation of why the world is as it is: "Western society has elevated everyone to a condition of self-orientation. Everyone cannot bear this. Without a purpose, an external goal, life is meaningless and so other people mean nothing. Good ideas and bad ideas are simply emotional issues without the foundation necessary to make a distinction between them. Why has this come about? Because the cynics who stressed negation lived on the belief that what they said could not come true. Those who rejected the ideas of man could do so only as long as man existed. Without human beings, without culture, these ideas themsevles would find no voice."

Ortega pauses. His mind is distracted by the effects of the mob situation he has just endured. He knows that without men and women devoted to leadership, the masses will return to a more destructive and more alienated world than the one that now exists.

He looks up from his notes at the audience and continues. He must transmit this idea. . . .

(A) *"A creative life implies a regime of strict mental health, of high conduct, of constant stimulus, which keeps active the consciousness of man's dignity. A creative life is energetic life, and this is only possible in one or other of these two situations: either being the one who rules or finding oneself placed in a world which is ruled by someone in whom we recognize full right to such a function: either I rule or I obey. By obedience I do not mean mere submission–this is degradation–but on the contrary, respect for the ruler and acceptance of his leadership, solidarity with him, and enthusiastic enrollment under his banner."*

(B) *"You know perfectly well what is the matter with you. You have known it for years though you have fought against the knowledge. You are mentally deranged. You suffer from a defective memory. You are unable to remember real events, and you persuade yourself that you remember other events that never happened. Fortunately it is curable. You have never cured yourself of it because you chose not to. There was a small effort of the will that you were not ready to make. Even now I am well aware that you are clinging to your disease under the impression that it is virtue."*

(C) *"Everything we admire on this earth today–science and art, technology and inventions–is only the creative product of a few peoples and originally perhaps of one race. On them depends the existence of this whole culture. If they perish, the beauty of this earth will sink into the grave with them. The inner nature of peoples is always determining for the manner in which outward influences will be effective. What leads the one to starvation trains the other to hard work. All culture depends on men and not conversely."*

Answer (A):   CORRECT! From José Ortega y Gasset's *The Revolt of the Masses.*

Answer (B):   From George Orwell's *1984.* In this popular fiction, a satire, Orwell (1893–1950) provided one of the most forceful images in contemporary life.

Answer (C):   From Adolf Hitler's *Mein Kampf.* This book foretold the atrocities that Hitler (1889–1945) would perpetrate on the world.

José Ortega y Gasset (1883–1955), Spanish philosopher, was born in Madrid of an aristocratic family. He was educated by the Jesuits and at the University of Madrid from which he received his doctorate. He went to Germany and was influenced by the philosophy of Immanuel Kant. In 1910 he returned to Spain and became a professor of metaphysics at the University of Madrid.

In 1936, at the outbreak of the civil war, Ortega left Spain, going first to France and then to Argentina. After World War II he returned to Madrid once more and founded the Institute of the Humanities.

Ortega called his philosophy "the metaphysics of vital reason." The work which made him famous, *The Revolt of the Masses* (1929), is an analysis of the effect of the masses on government and the arts. It calls for the control and direction of the masses by a small group of intellectuals.

89. NIELS BOHR

The clock tower strikes midnight. Across the way in a suite in the Hotel Metropole, two men are having an argument. Niels Bohr and Albert Einstein, in Brussels for the 1927 Solvay Conference, have been at each other all evening. Einstein, his hair streaming in all directions; Bohr, the deeply serious and somber man, his hands always working with his pipe.

Bohr and Einstein are arguing about God. This, in itself, is not strange, except for the fact that they are the two most prominent physicists in the world. "Whatever you say," Einstein hollers, "God does not play dice!" He is referring to Bohr's assertion that knowledge about any very small atomic event must be statistical, allowing for a margin of error, rather than exact.

"But, Albert, when you look at these events you look with electrons and photons. Their energy disturbs the phenomena that you are observing. Thus, the phenomenon you see is not what you want. It is just the result of looking. Therefore, we can only assume a range of possible conditions that are present and utilize them to make the assertions and theories that we want to make. There is no reason to fight this, is there?"

Einstein is stubborn. He has always said that he refuses limits to human knowledge, no matter what the form. He understands what his Danish colleague is getting at, he agrees with it in logic, yet in his heart he cannot live with the implications of the theory.

Bohr is frustrated. Without Einstein's acceptance the world will not readily adopt these new thoughts on indeterminacy. He wants Einstein, the most prominent and obviously the most brilliant man in the world, to agree with him. But Einstein will not. Perhaps, he cannot. The new indeterminacy theory throws into question the very basis of Einstein's own personal reason for being, namely, the quest for knowledge.

Bohr has gone out onto the balcony. The street below is dark and quiet. He takes several deep breaths of cold air. He is thinking of one last convincing word to offer Einstein. Finally, he reenters the room, and says . . .

(A) "Being is full and solid, not-being is void and rare. Since the void exists no less that the body, it follows that not-being exists no less than being. The two together are the material causes of existing things. And just as those who make the underlying substance one generate other things by its modifications, and postulate rarefaction and condensation as the origin of such modifications, in the same way these men too say that the differences in atoms are the causes of other things."

(B) "I need hardly stress that the word consciousness presents itself in the description of a behaviour so complicated that its communication implies reference to the individual organism's awareness of itself. Moreover, words like thoughts and sentiments refer to mutually exclusive experiences and have therefore since the origin of human language been used in a typically complementary manner. Of course, in objective physical description no reference is made to the observing subject, while in speaking of conscious experience we say I think or feel. The analogy to the demand of taking all essential features of the experimental arrangement into account in quantum physics is, however, reflected by the different verbs we attach to the pronoun."

(C) "Matter is the general name which has been given that substance which, under an infinite variety of forms, affects our senses. We apply the term matter to everything that occupies space, or that has length, breadth and thickness. It is only through the agency of our five senses that we are enabled to know that any matter exists. A person deprived of all sensation could not be conscious that he had any material existence. A body is a distinct portion of matter existing in space."

Answer (A):   From *Fragments* by Leucippus. Leucippus was a Greek philosopher of the seventh century B.C. who, with Democritus, was the first atomist.

Answer (B):   CORRECT! From Niels Bohr's *Essays 1958–1962 on Atomic Physics and Human Knowledge.*

Answer (C):   From Malcolm Wells' *Natural Philosophy.* Wells' (1818–1870) wrote one of the first textbooks of physics (natural philosophy, as it was called) that was widely used in the United States.

Niels Henrik David Bohr (1885–1962), Danish physicist, was born in Copenhagen. His father was a professor of physiology. In 1911 he received his doctorate from the University of Copenhagen. He went to Cambridge, England, where he did research on the atom under Sir James J. Thompson, and then to Manchester where he worked under Lord Ernest Rutherford. In 1916 he became a professor of theoretical physics at the University of Copenhagen, and in 1920, director of the Institute of Theoretical Physics.

Bohr solved the problem of explaining the stability of the nuclear model of the atom with his theory that electrons circulate around the atom in restricted orbits. He explained how an atom absorbs and emits energy, combining quantum theory with his concept of atomic structure.

In 1922 he received the Nobel Prize in physics. He visited the United States in 1938 and 1939, where he worked with scientists on the theory that the uranium atom could be split into halves. Scientists at Columbia confirmed his theory.

Bohr returned to Denmark but fled during the Nazi occupation, coming back to the United States. There he worked in New Mexico on atomic bomb research.

His major works are *The Theory of Spectra and Atomic Constitution* (1922) and *Atomic Energy and the Description of Nature* (1934).

90. MARCEL DUCHAMP

Marcel Duchamp sits in his New York studio in front of the ever-present chessboard. The year is 1962. He awaits a reporter from an art journal who has made an appointment to interview him. He is prepared to be sarcastic, having little use for reporters, museum curators, and the like. Recently, he was asked to display one of his works in a museum. He refused. "Why do you want to keep all your work in your rooms, or with other individuals?" the curator had asked. "Because they are my friends and the rest does not interest me," Duchamp had replied.

The doorbell rings. To his undisguised pleasure, the reporter is a young, blonde woman, startlingly attractive. Along with art and chess, the appreciation of women is one of Duchamp's favorite pastimes. "Sit, my dear, make yourself comfortable. How good of you to be on time."

In the presence of such a splendid creature, Duchamp eagerly unfolds and begins to explain himself. "I have never worried about money, so I have been free to experiment in a range that few have dared to enter. I consider myself a revolutionary, but in a much more subtle sense than those who have come before me. I painted a urinal and made it art. I have collected a wide variety of objects—a typewriter cover, a bottle, a bicycle wheel—and turned them into art. I noticed that everyone was looking desperately into the museums to perceive art. I decided to stare out my windows into the streets and thus extend the walls of the museum by doing so.

"I have made my works for myself, for my explorations into the mind and into the universe. If they are appreciated, understood, and applauded today, perhaps I have not gone far enough. What happens now does not interest me. I care about what endures. In fifty years my audience will be a sincere one."

The young woman is taking careful notes. She settles in for a long afternoon. Her list of questions concerns such things as the Large Glass, the beard made out of soap suds, the bronze casting of a vagina, and Duchamp's explorations of the limits of art and life.

Duchamp is very cooperative. He envisions his words in print far into the future, and thus answers her questions very precisely, very deliberately. Late in the afternoon, the reporter ends the session with this question: "What does life mean to you?"

Duchamp answers with his usual sense of irony and paradox. . . .

(A) "Things are happening to you, and you feel them happening, but except for this one fact, you have no connection with them, and no key to the cause or meaning of them. The performing animals in a circus go through their programme, I believe, in that same way. Those who have been through such events, in a way, say that they have been through death–a passage outside the range of imagination, but within the range of experience."

(B) "The role of the individual artist, in the business of making unique objects for the purpose of giving pleasure and educating conscience and sensibility, has repeatedly been called into question. Some literary intellectuals and artists have gone so far as to prophesy the ultimate demise of the art-making activity of man. Art, in an automated scientific society, would be unfunctional, useless."

(C) "I believe that art is the only form of activity in which man as man shows himself to be a true individual. Only in art is he capable of going beyond the animal state, because art is an outlet toward regions which are not ruled by time and space. To live is to believe, that's my belief, at any rate."

Answer (A): From Isak Dinesen's *Out of Africa*. This book is an exceptional journal about a woman who lives in and creates a world in Africa and in her mind. Dinesen (1885–1962) was a Dutch author.

Answer (B): From Susan Sontag's *Against Interpretation*. Sontag, a contemporary art critic and philosopher of art, provides a profound look into art and criticism in this work.

Answer (C): CORRECT! From Marcel Duchamp's *The Salt Seller*.

Marcel Duchamp (1887–1968), French painter and father of pop art, was born in Blainville, France. His father was a well-to-do notary. His brother was Jacques Villon, also a painter. Duchamp studied at the Académie Julian in Paris.

In 1911 at the Salon des Indépendents, and in 1913 at the New York Armory show, which was the first modern art exhibit in America, Duchamp's painting, "Nude Descending a Staircase," created a huge controversy. Critics attacked it for its degeneracy, using it as a prime symbol of the state of European art. It has since become one of the most well-known of cubist paintings. Duchamp also created what he called "ready-mades" out of common objects such as a toilet or birdcage.

In 1915, he helped to found the Dada group in New York with Man Ray and François Piccabia. The movement was international, and its themes were nihilistic. In 1920 Duchamp constructed a machine that had no purpose.

He emigrated to the United States in 1942 and married in 1954. He died in France at the age of eighty-one.

91. LUDWIG WITTGENSTEIN

A group of settlers have drawn their covered wagons together in a circle. Surrounding them, a band of Apache Indians move in for the kill. Women and children huddle together as the men fight fiercely against the red savages.

Ludwig Wittgenstein is at the movies. The year is 1930. As often as possible, he leaves his rooms at Trinity College to immerse himself in the imperceptible kinesthetic events that are triggered in his body and mind as shadows of screen people move in their mysterious ways. He always sits in the front row, loving the exposure to the size and scale of the images. He prefers American westerns.

In his lap rests his ever-present notebook. He likes to write down his ideas while he is being bombarded by the flickering light. This afternoon, as he watches, listens, and takes notes, he notices a tough young man in the aisle. Without taking his eyes off the screen, Wittgenstein realizes that the man is about to sit down next to him. Wittgenstein is both terrified and excited. The man's head lolls on the back of the seat, and the faint smell of alcohol fills the air. He realizes that the man is drunk and has probably come into the theatre to sleep it off. He returns his attention to the screen, only to be distracted by words muttered in sleep by the man. "Pass over . . . the case . . . what is the use." Wittgenstein jots the words down. They seem significant. He has been spending his time at Cambridge working on notes about how to think and understand ideas. Gradually, he is leaving behind the ideas developed in his influential *Tractatus Logico-Philosophicus*, published in 1921 when he was thirty-two.

The movie begins to skip, and the sound track becomes garbled. The drunk awakens with a start. "Silence!" he pronounces at the top of his lungs, and falls back to sleep. Wittgenstein laughs, remembering the first and last lines of his *Tractatus.* . . .

(A) *"The influence of particular symbolic formulations on the very data of knowledge led the most influential thinkers of our era Charles Pierce, Sigmund Freud, and Ernst Cassirer, for instance, to contemplate the possible modes of symbolism itself.*

. . .

"To reconstruct in theory what probably or even conceivably happened in actuality is still a large undertaking."

(B) *"A description of the origins and purpose of this book, if it is logical enough to be of any use to the reader, cannot help but distort history."*

. . .

"The system places competition before cooperation, mastery before pleasure, conceptualization before sensation."

(C) *"The world is all that is the case.*

. . .

"What we cannot speak about we must pass over in silence."

Answer (A): From Susanne Langer's *Mind: An Essay on Human Feeling,* Vol. 1. Langer (1895–   ) is one of the principal aesthetic philosophers of our time.

Answer (B): From Phillip Slater's *The Glory of Hera.* Slater, a contemporary thinker, provides here his most interesting and articulate book, and the one most sound in its observations and descriptions of human behavior.

Answer (C): CORRECT! From Ludwig Wittgenstein's *Tractatus Logico-Philosophicus.*

Ludwig Wittgenstein (1889–1951), Austrian philosopher, was born in Vienna. He went to Berlin when he was seventeen to study engineering. In 1908 he traveled to England, where he became a research student in aeronautics at Manchester University, designing a jet-reaction engine and propellor.

After reading *Principia Mathematica* by Bertrand Russell and Alfred North Whitehead, Wittgenstein abandoned engineering and went to Trinity College, where he studied under Russell for a year. Wittgenstein served in the Austrian army during the First World War and was captured and held prisoner in Italy. After the war, he taught in elementary school throughout Austria.

In 1921 Wittgenstein's *Tractatus Logico-Philosophicus* was published in Germany. A year later it appeared in England. This was to be his only full-length work published during his lifetime.

In 1929 Wittgenstein moved permanently to Cambridge. He received his doctorate the same year, having submitted *Tractatus* as his thesis. From 1930 to 1935 he was a fellow at Trinity College. In 1938 he became a naturalized British subject and a year later, a professor of philosophy at Cambridge.

During the Second World War Wittgenstein worked as a porter in a London hospital. After the war he resigned his position at Cambridge. He died of cancer in 1951, at the age of sixty-two. His other major work, *Philosophical Investigations*, was published posthumously in 1953.

Wittgenstein's work influenced the development of linguistic analysis and semantics. His main interest was the examination of the structure and limits of thought.

92. MARTIN HEIDEGGER

"If they could see me!" he chuckles with delight. The year is 1940. Germany is embroiled in a world war. He is fifty-one years old but nevertheless comes up to the attic everyday to play with his dollhouse.

Several characters live in his dollhouse. "Being" is very introspective. "Time" is always present. "Existence" stays in the front room. "Essence" can always be found upstairs. "God" is not there. The famous philosopher moves the doll figures about and creates conversations. He speaks for the narrator, and he speaks for himself, Martin Heidegger, as well.

The man who has succeeded Edmund Husserl to the Chair of Philosophy at Freiburg crouches on his hands and knees. "Today I will have 'Essence' precede 'Existence' into the living room. An absurd situation that is obviously wrong. 'Being' asks to see 'God' who is never allowed in this house. We have a discussion on that point. 'Being' comprehends my point and begins once again to talk to himself. Martin wants to make the house bigger but he cannot figure out how to take it apart and put it back together so that it will be bigger. The small house depresses him. The characters are having a hard time with the limits. Sometimes they consider going beyond, but that is absurd.

"The characters often request to have discussions with me. I refuse, of course. Introspection and subjective analysis are the only legitimate tools of examination. Martin decided long ago not to put the names of the characters on their shirts in case someone spotted them and could recognize them. Martin gets especially upset if anyone forgets about 'Being' and lets him wander away.

"Sometimes Martin joins me. We go downstairs and write a paper, hoping to finally have a book. I look forward to these times since, during them, we become very close. Last night, Martin and I got together and wrote . . .

(A) "Thinking only begins at the point where we have come to know that Reason, glorified for centuries, is the most obstinate adversary of thinking."

(B) "Every step they have made in natural knowledge has tended to extend and rivet in their minds the conception of a definite order of the universe which is embodied in what are called, by an unhappy metaphor, the laws of nature—and to narrow the range and loosen the force of men's belief in spontaneity, or in changes other than such as arise out of that definite order itself."

(C) "From these ingenious views the step is very easy to a farther opinion that it does not much matter what things are in themselves, but only what they are to us: and that the only real truth of them is their appearance to, or effect upon, us."

Answer (A):   CORRECT! From Martin Heidegger's *Being and Time*.

Answer (B):   From Thomas Henry Huxley's *On the Advisableness of Improving Natural Knowledge*. Huxley (1825–1895) biologist, writer, and teacher who helped pave the way for Charles Darwin's work.

Answer (C):   From John Ruskin's *Modern Painters*. Ruskin (1819–1900) was an English poet and art historian.

Martin Heidegger (1889–1976), German philosopher and major existentialist thinker, was born in Baden. He studied at Freiburg, where he was influenced by Kantianism and Edmund Husserl. In 1923, while a professor at Marburg, he published a section of *Being and Time*, which would become his major work. From 1928 to 1951 he held the Chair of Philosophy at Freiburg, having succeeded Husserl.

Although he is called an "existentialist," Heidegger rejected this term. He stated that the main philosophical concern is the problem of being and of what it means to be. Heidegger analysed human existence as it is connected with time and temporality. He maintained that there are two kinds of being, human existence and physical reality, composed of nonhuman objects.

Heidegger considered himself to be the first thinker in Western philosophy to raise the question concerning the "sense of being." He believed that the crisis of Western civilization can be laid to the "forgetfulness of being" on the part of the masses.

93. NORBERT WIENER

The small group of students at Massachusetts Institute of Technology are gleeful. Their professor, Norbert Wiener, is about to enter the room. The year is 1960. They have worked for over a year on a secret project implementing his research in cybernetics, a new branch of science he developed during the 1940s.

As Wiener enters the room he is confronted by a noisy array of four robots. Immediately, the students sense he is displeased, although obviously impressed by the rich deployment of sophistication. Only a decade or so ago at the Macy Conferences in New York, he had spent many hours in the first tentative discussion of the possible uses of cybernetics with such colleagues as Warren McCulloch, Gregory Bateson, Margaret Mead, and John Von Neumann.

Wiener walks forward to inspect the robots. All have name tags: Jim, Tobi, Marc, Les. They are assembled around a big conference table. Tape recorders, located inside, can be activiated for automatic conversation. Each robot has been programmed to perform a different task. Jim plays with a pencil, Tobi asks questions, Marc adds very large numbers, and Les jumps like a frog and sweeps the room.

Despite the sophistication, Wiener does not like what he sees. He has always been gravely concerned with the implications of his work in cybernetics. He realizes that his students have no concern over what the future holds. They are simply electrical engineers, not interested in what they consider to be "social problems."

Wiener has cautioned them to pay attention not only to what something can do, but also to what kind of reflection it is on the human condition. He considers the word cybernetics to be a serious term since it means someone who steers, someone who creates an apparatus that can respond to the needs of the external world and adapt its functioning accordingly.

The students are ashen faced as Wiener walks behind the robots and, one by one, pulls out their plugs. He turns to the young men and says . . .

(A) "Science is a way of life which can only flourish when men are free to have faith. A faith which we follow upon orders imposed from outside is no faith, and a community which puts its dependence upon such a pseudo faith is ultimately bound to ruin itself because of the paralysis which the lack of a healthy growing science imposes upon it."

(B) "Let us try and describe ourselves exactly to each other. We shall find that we can do better than by trying to speak of ourselves as inhabited by a number of pseudo-things such as consciousness, mind, experience, and the rest of them. Of course, this is making the situation out at its worst. Few people speak of the mind as if it were a simple thing. It is a truism that our powers are compounded from many sources. The suggestion is that we should now fully recognize this, face the multiplicity of ourselves and speak less as if we were inhabited by a semi-thing—the mind."

(C) "Perhaps the most important task facing us today is the regeneration of our environment and institutional structures such as school, government, church, etc. With increasing sophistication has come the recognition that institutions are not sacrosanct and that they have but one purpose and function—to serve as a framework for the actualization of human potential. It is possible to evaluate both the institution and the contribution of the institution by asking this question: To what extent does the function of the institution foster the realization of human potential?"

Answer (A):   CORRECT! From Norbert Wiener's *The Human Use of Human Beings.*

Answer (B):   From J. Z. Young's *Doubt and Certainty in Science.* Young (1907–   ) is a biologist.

Answer (C):   From Herbert Otto's *New Light on Human Potential.* Otto writes about the human potential movement in the United States.

Norbert Wiener (1894–1964), American mathematician, was born in Columbia, Missouri. His father was a well-respected scholar. Wiener could read at three, entered Tufts University at eleven, and received his doctorate from Harvard at eighteen.

In 1919 Wiener joined the faculty of the Massachusetts Institute of Technology. He worked as a mathematician, designing anti-aircraft defense systems and developing improvements in radar and Navy projectiles during World War II.

By 1947, he had decided to dedicate his energy to the study of the influence of automation on society. His work is summarized in the book, *Cybernetics,* in which he reformulated biological and social problems in engineering terms. In 1959, Wiener was appointed Institute Professor at MIT. He returned in 1960 and in 1964 was awarded the National Medal of Science. He died the same year.

Wiener was responsible for the development of the science of cybernetics (from a Greek word meaning "steersman"), which is the application of mathematics to the communication of information and to the control of such information.

94. R. BUCKMINSTER FULLER

"I had a choice, in 1927, as to whether I would dedicate myself to making enough money to support my wife and child or dedicate myself to try to do those things which seemed to need to get done. I chose to dedicate my time to the realizing of patterns that seemed obvious enough but were never considered or acted upon. I worked to make a representation of the earth that was not distorted if it changed from spherical to flat. This became my dymaxion map. I tried to discover a new geometry. This became synergetic geometry. I tried to find the most efficient housing solution, one which would give the most space using the least amount of materials. This resulted in the geodesic dome. I tried to find a way to demonstrate that all the resources of the planet should be considered before any wasteful acts are perpetrated. This resulted in the "world game." There have been so many other inventions and ideas which all arise out of, and become part of, the idea that we must use our energy and minds to create a world where the possibilities of the imagination can soar for everyone."

R. Buckminster Fuller is concluding a marathon lecture to a rapt New York audience of 2000 people. The year is 1975. They have listened to him for hours. Attention wavered from time to time, but at the lecture's end, they are amazed at how the threads of this man's thoughts all intertwine, a great weaving. They rise and give him a thunderous ovation.

Fuller, eighty years old, is traveling around the world more than ever, constantly telling everyone that they must reinvest their lives with the energy necessary to create and to work at sustaining a world in which everyone can find time to be creative and expressive.

As the applause dies out, Fuller turns his hearing aid back on. An eager crowd surrounds him, asking questions, trying to get closer to the energy and force radiating from this man. A young woman asks him for one last thought to remember before she returns to the tedium of college. Bucky winks at her and whispers in her ear . . .

(A) *"The rarer seen, the less in mind, the less in mind, the lesser pain."*

(B) *"Dare to be naive."*

(C) *"I am two fools I know,
For loving and for saying so."*

Answer (A): From Barney Googe's "Out of Sight, Out of Mind," in his *Ecologues, Epitaphs, and Sonnets.* Googe (1540–1594) was a popular English poet of his day.

Answer (B): CORRECT! From R. Buckminster Fuller's *Synergetics.*

Answer (C): From John Donne's "The Triple Fool." Donne (1573–1631) was an English metaphysical poet.

R. Buckminster Fuller (1895–   ), inventor and designer, was born in Massachusetts and educated at the United States Naval Academy and Harvard, although he never completed his studies at either place.

Fuller was appointed Research Professor at Southern Illinois University in 1959. In 1961 he instituted the World Design Science Program at the Congress of the International Union of Architects. He inaugurated the "world game" at Southern Illinois University in 1966. Recently, Fuller became World Fellow in Residence at the University of Pennsylvania.

In 1929, Fuller invented the dymaxion house; in 1935, the dymaxion car. He has invented a dymaxion bathroom, a dymaxion projection of the world, and is the inventor of synergetic geometry, geodesic structures, and tensegrity structures.

He has been the recipient of numerous honors, including honorary doctorates in design, science, and art. In 1968 he was awarded the Royal Gold Medal for architecture by Queen Elizabeth and the Gold Medal Award of the National Institute of Arts and Letters.

95. WERNER HEISENBERG

Two physicists, one young and robust, the other old and frail, have finished dinner. They year is 1940. Werner Heisenberg, thirty-nine, is very pleased to welcome Max Planck, eighty-two, for this visit to his Leipzig home.

As the colleagues enjoy cigars, Planck walks to the billiard table and attempts to stack the balls on top of one another. "It interests me that this structure is very similar to that of a molecule. By stacking the balls higher, we can make a larger molecule and see if we can determine anything from its properties."

"Max, if the Nobel committee could see us now, they would demand the return of our prizes. That's how frivolous your analogy is." Heisenberg tries to aid Planck in his endeavor. Before Heisenberg was born, Planck had laid the groundwork for modern physics, a path that would be followed by Albert Einstein, Niels Bohr, Max Born, Louis de Broglie, Heisenberg himself and all the others.

"Frivolous or not," he says, "we examine things for many reasons, one of which is an attempt to find flaws."

"But, if you begin by using a model in your mind that includes the flaws, you can barely get beyond that beginning point."

Planck is visibly upset by these words. The war has made him nervous as it is. Neither he nor Heisenberg likes the Nazis, but there is nothing they can do about the situation. Losing his calm, he places a ball in the wrong position. The entire pile collapses. Planck is livid. Heisenberg smiles.

"Heisenberg, the logic of indeterminacy, whereby a thing which is known in position cannot be known in time, is brilliant. But I must say that on a personal level, your tact and sense of humanity are minimal."

Heisenberg is taken aback. His whole life is such a complete absorption with his uncertainty principle that he often neglects the emotional events that occur. He realizes that he has angered the old master. Perhaps a clear statement about his recent thinking on quantum mechanics will soothe and astonish Planck. "Max," he begins . . .

(A) "The representation of motion in its full allegorical sense is therefore as impossible in science as it is in painting, or, for that matter, in a literary work. The need to use civilized mathematical functions is incongruous with respect to the discontinuous nature of self-conscious experience: and conversely, the need to take data during experimentation is incongruous with respect to the continuous nature of the processes which are being investigated."

(B) "To be able to appreciate justly in each case the considerations of convenience and economy which present themselves, to be able to recognize the most important of those which are only subordinate, to adjust them all suitably, and finally to reach the best result by the easiest method—such should be the power of the man who is called on to direct and coordinate the labors of his fellow men, and to make them concur in attaining a useful purpose."

(C) "In atomic physics . . . all previous concepts have proved inadequate. We know from the stability of matter that Newtonian physics does not apply to the interior of the atom: at best it can occasionally offer us a guideline. It follows that there can be no descriptive account of the structure of the atom: all such accounts must necessarily be based on classical concepts which, as we saw, no longer apply. You see that anyone trying to develop such a theory is really trying the impossible. For we intend to say something about the structure of the atom but lack a language in which we can make ourselves understood."

Answer (A): From Gerald Holton's *The Thematic Origins of Scientific Thought*. Holton (1922–   ) writes about the relation of science and culture.

Answer (B): From Sadi Carnot's *The Second Law of Thermodynamics*. Carnot (1837–1894) discovered important energy relationships for physical science.

Answer (C): CORRECT! From Werner Heisenberg's *Physics and Beyond*.

Werner Heisenberg (1901–1976), German physicist and one of the founders of the quantum theory, was born in Duisberg. His father was a professor of history.

In 1926 he developed a form of quantum theory called "matrix mechanics." In 1932 he was awarded the Nobel Prize in physics for his work on the quantum theory and nuclear physics.

Heisenberg, as a student, was an assistant to Max Born, and later became a close associate of Niels Bohr. From 1927 to 1941 he taught at the University of Leipzig, and from 1942 to 1945, at the University of Berlin. In 1958, he became the director of the Max Planck Institute for Physics and Astrophysics in Munich.

Heisenberg is the founder of the uncertainty principle, which states that it is impossible to accurately determine both the position and momentum of subatomic particles such as electrons. This principle transforms laws of physics from statements about absolute certainties to statements about relative probabilities.

96. JEAN-PAUL SARTRE

Someone at a nearby table is humming loudly to the music being played by the two-man band at the sidewalk cafe. This irritates the group of men sitting at the next table, yet none of them complains or even mentions it. These Parisians wear serious faces. They smoke strong, stubby cigarettes and talk about the nature of existence. Still, whenever an attractive woman walks by, the conversation ceases abruptly as they carefully appraise her and her parts: legs, breasts, ass. They know the limits of possibility in the world, the anguish of never really being with a woman, or, for that matter, anyone else. After a few lingering moments, they shift back to their intense discussion about existentialism.

The group is dominated by Jean-Paul Sartre. The year before, in 1964, he had declined the Nobel Prize for literature, saying that the award would lend too much weight to a writer's influence. "The anguish arises," he says, hearing the man at the next table, "out of our constant inability to use the moment to be in, rather than to observe."

His compatriots nod in silence. The man continues to hum and annoy them. His presence becomes a metaphor of the problem. "If a man hums in a crowd," Maurice says, "when others wish to be in peace, he is forcing his presence on them and refusing them the freedom to be who they are since they must attend to his wishes."

"Ah no," Giles disagrees, "we must respect his universe. He is being in the music and is oblivious to our needs. He exists outside of our world. We must exist outside of his."

Sartre, who has been listening, gets up and goes to the next table and asks the man to stop humming as it is disturbing everyone. The man is offended. He instructs Sartre in no uncertain terms to perform various acts upon himself. Sartre shrugs and returns to his table. He puffs on a cigarette and becomes one with the music. He is trying to grasp the essence of his being and express it to his friends. He carefully removes his glasses, looks at Maurice, Giles, and the others, and begins. . . .

(A) "If he lives in human dignity, man can sustain a happy and peaceful life on very little material wealth. We do not need most of the wasteful trappings of the highly industrialized civilizations. We should learn, from the sorrows of today and their deep anxieties about the future, to be content to fulfill our basic needs and to further enrich our life from the cultural resources we have inherited.

(B) "And I too, wanted to be. That is all I wanted: this is the last word. At the bottom of all these attempts which seemed without bonds, I find the same desire again: to drive existence out of me, to rid the passing moments of their fat, to twist them, dry them, purify myself, to give back at last, the sharp, precise sound of a saxophone note."

(C) "Knowledge is a passion for perfection resulting from the union of an intelligible and an intellective power. And this is its ground reason in the mode by which it is generated or is made in the understanding. But in the mode by which it is as it is in fact, it is a condition by which the true is discerned from the false and by which one of them may be judged to be true."

Answer (A): From Mochtar Lubis' "Voices for Life." Lubis (1922–   ) is one of Asia's best-known journalists.

Answer (B): CORRECT! From Jean-Paul Sartre's *Nausea*.

Answer (C): From Pseudo-Grosseteste's *The Summa of Philosophy*. The work is by an unidentified follower of a follower of Robert Grosseteste, who was never identified and so given the above designation. Grosseteste (c. 1170–1253) was a philosopher.

Jean-Paul Sartre (1905–   ), French existentialist philosopher, was born in Paris. In 1929 he began teaching in secondary schools and traveled. He studied with Edmund Husserl and Martin Heidegger in Germany, which had a great effect upon him. In 1938 his novel *Nausea* was published, and in 1939, *The Wall*, a volume of short stories. Both works are concerned with human experiences of meaninglessness.

Sartre joined the army in 1939. A year later he was taken prisoner in Alsace and spent nine months in captivity before escaping to Paris. He resumed teaching and became a member of the French Resistance. His play, *The Flies*, was produced during the Nazi occupation in 1943. *No Exit*, another play, was produced the following year. In 1946 Sartre founded *Les Temps Modernes*, a political and literary periodical.

Sartre was the leader of a group of intellectuals who met at the Café Flore. The group included Simone de Beauvoir and Albert Camus. Sartre was interested in Marxism until the Soviet intervention in Hungary in 1956, which disillusioned him. He is still an avid socialist.

His major philosophical work, *Being and Nothingness* (1943), is an elaborate exposition of his existentialism.

97. HANNAH ARENDT

The gray-haired woman is taking a leisurely walk through New York's Greenwich Village. The year is 1967. She is returning to her office after her morning lecture at the New School for Social Research, where she is a professor. At sixty-one years of age, this sociologist still avidly looks around at the world in which she lives.

Coming to a playground, she stops, fascinated by the young boys frolicking on the seesaws and jungle gym. Secretly, she giggles with them at the power they have over each other. As their eyes become aflame with this power, she is frightened by it as well. In their eyes, she recognizes the seeds of the lover of power. "How long before they move from seesaws to machine guns and rockets?" she wonders.

Returning to her office, her secretary is ready to take dictation, listen, and argue, all part of the process of writing her new book. She is constantly writing texts of warning. She clearly sees the demise of the world. The problems lies in the unchecked, uncontrolled search of the ever-adventurous mind. The roar of the rockets that propel men into space frightens her, just as she fears the power lust of the children at the playground. It is the power lust of those who will one day reach out into the universe and abdicate their responsibilities on earth. Part of her concern is over changes of such scale and depth that the climate of mind and interaction of mortals will be forever altered.

The secretary picks up a notepad as Dr. Arendt begins to dictate with forcefulness, erudition, and humanity, always returning to the issue of people. At one particularly gloomy thought, the secretary interrupts her to ask, "Professor, is the world doomed?"

Hannah Arendt smiles, then frowns, her expressions reflecting her feelings. She answers slowly and thoughtfully. . . .

(A) *"The difficulties and complexities involved in such a challenge are considerable: the mere existence of innate mechanisms for meeting them does not mean that the odds are in favor of success. Human history is replete with evidence that de-evolutionary processes also operate, with deterioration of the human condition, unless foresight, imagination, ingenuity, determination, and wisdom are brought to bear, to increase self awareness and self discipline in the choice of ends as well as means. To be able to prevent such deterioration, principles will be required by which to live, and by which to intervene judiciously in the process of biologic and metabiologic evolution with knowledge of the de-evolutionary as well as the evolutionary consequences of each action or nonaction when we face issues that affect our well-being individually and collectively."*

(B) *"If we compare the modern world with that of the past, the loss of human experience involved in this development is extraordinarily striking. It is not only and not even primarily contemplation which has become a meaningless experience. Thought itself when it became 'reckoning with consequences' became a function of the grain, with the result that electronic instruments are found to fulfill these functions much better than we ever could. Action was soon and still is almost exclusively understood in terms of making and fabricating, only that making, because of its worldliness and inherent indifference to life, was now regarded as but another form of laboring, a more complicated but not a more mysterious function of the life process."*

(C) *"Consideration for posterity has throughout history operated as a motive of conduct, but feebly, occasionally, and in a very limited sense. With the doctrine of progress it assumes, logically, a preponderating importance: for the center of interest is transferred to the life of future generations who are to enjoy conditions of happiness denied to us, but which our labors and sufferings are to help bring about. If the doctrine is held in an extreme fatalistic form, then our duty is to resign ourselves cheerfully to sacrifices for the sake of unknown descendants, just as ordinary altruism enjoins the cheerful acceptance of sacrifices for the sake of living fellow creatures."*

Answer (A): From Jonas Salk's *Survival of the Wisest.* Salk (1914–   ) discovered the polio vaccine and founded the Salk Institute, which conducts research into other diseases and into basic scientific thinking.

Answer (B): CORRECT! From Hannah Arendt's *The Human Condition.*

Answer (C): From J. B. Bury's *The Idea of Progress.* Bury (1861–1927) explores here the idea of progress, its history and its growth in modern times.

Hannah Arendt (1906–1976), German political philosopher, was born in Hanover. She received her bachelor's degree at Konigsberg in 1924 and her doctorate at Heidelberg in 1928.

In 1941 Arendt immigrated to the United States and was naturalized in 1950. From 1952 to 1953 she was a lecturer and Guggenheim Fellow. She went on to become the first woman to be appointed to a full professorship at Princeton. She was a visiting professor at Columbia in 1960 and taught at the University of Chicago from 1963 to 1967. That year she went to New York to teach at the New School of Social Research.

Arendt's book *Origins of Totalitarianism* (1951) examines national socialism and communism, two forms of twentieth-century totalitarianism, tracing their origins to nineteenth-century imperialism and antisemitism.

Eichmann in Jerusalem (1963) is an analysis of Nazi war crimes, based on the trial of Adolf Eichmann. *The Human Condition* was published in 1973.

98. SAMUEL BECKETT

Two men are sitting at a sidewalk café in Paris. The year is 1952. "The romance of the past disgusts me. You hate it, too, don't you, Sam?" asks William Tindell, one of Beckett's most continuous and longstanding admirers and critics. He has come to Paris for the opening of *Waiting for Godot*, Beckett's new play.

Beckett does not answer.

"I remember asking you in a fifteen-page letter about all the ideas I was having about your work. I was interested in how minimal description was very poignant, how basic things like mud and debris were more real than horses and meadows, how the body was like a bag, how the mind was merely the place to store other people's actions. You answered me with fifteen words, seven yesses and eight no's. Won't you expand a little on these ideas now that we are spending some time together?"

Beckett does not answer.

"Look, you are certainly not like Henry James, who kept one hand in his pocket the whole way. I mean, you are really breaking new ground. Using subtraction, rather than addition, to describe the world. Sam," Tindell continues, "your world is not a very happy place, is it?"

Beckett smiles.

"I am quite sure it is interesting to hear someone reflecting on your work, but is it also very trying? Do your characters try? Or are there characters in your work at all? I mean characters of flesh and blood."

Beckett does not answer but scans the street and the plaza near the café.

"Perhaps my annoying questions will prod you into a new thought," says Tindell, who, with resignation, pays the bill, bids Beckett *au revoir*, and wanders away.

Beckett does not change the focus of his gaze. "Every gesture in the world is rich," he thinks, "so by focusing, one can learn more. Words are so interesting, they should be shared with the reader. Also, the reader should share in the creation of the whole of the text. Books should be games to play, not to watch."

Beckett takes pen and paper out of his coat pocket and writes. . .

(A) "But why can't we see the facts as they really are? What is this reality which seems to get out of focus as soon as we try to bring moral judgments to bear? Well the trouble is that moral judgments are about social relations and relations have no material existence. We can only observe social relations indirectly by interpreting other people's behavior, and we can only do this if we first invent an artificial code which attaches social meaning to cultural facts."

(B) "Perhaps the men of genius are the only true men. In all the history of the race there have been only a few thousand real men. And the rest of us, what are we? Teachable animals. Without the help of the real men, we should have found out almost nothing at all. Almost all the ideas with which we are familiar could have never occurred to minds like ours. Plant the seeds there and they will grow: but our minds could never have spontaneously generated them."

(C) "If at least he would dignify me with the third person, like his other figments, not he, he'll be satisfied with nothing less than me, for his me. When he had me, when he was me, he couldn't get rid of me quick enough, I didn't exist, he couldn't have that, that was no kind of life, of course I didn't exist, any more than he did, of course it was no kind of life, now he has it, his kind of life, let him lose it, if he wants to be in peace, with a bit of luck."

Answer (A):   From Edmund Leach's *A Runaway World?* Leach (1910–   ), a British anthropologist, discusses the evolutionary humanist's position.

Answer (B):   From Aldous Huxley's *Young Archimedes and Other Stories.* Huxley (1894–1963) is best known for his quasi-science fiction novels like *Brave New World.*

Answer (C):   CORRECT! From Samuel Beckett's *Stories and Texts for Nothing.*

Samuel Beckett (1906–   ), Irish novelist and playwright, was born in Dublin. He studied and taught in Paris, finally settling there in 1937. He was a good friend of James Joyce.

His first novels, *Murphy* (1938) and *Watt* (1944), were written in English. Thereafter, he wrote in French and then translated his works into English.

Beckett's work has been called the "literature of the absurd." He portrays his characters in odd scenes and situations, often farcical and grotesque, and the only freedom they are granted is the freedom of the mind.

Molloy (1951), *Malone Dies* (1951), and *The Unnamable* (1953) are three novels which form a trilogy. Some of his best-known plays are *Waiting for Godot* (1952), *Endgame* (1957), and *Krapp's Last Tape* (1959).

99. SIMONE DE BEAUVOIR

Simone de Beauvoir and Jean-Paul Sartre sit in their bathrobes having breakfast in a Paris apartment. The year is 1952. Simone's recent book, *The Second Sex*, has been translated into English and is about to be published in America. It is a profound analysis of the status of women.

The couple are in a large room. They sit opposite each other, around a small table, eating croissants and jam, drinking coffee. Last night they had argued. This morning they are not talking. They are not talking to each other, that is.

"Did you see who won the American election for President?" asks Simone.

"I'll have a little more coffee," responds Jean-Paul.

"Who would you have voted for?"

"I said I wanted more coffee."

"I think I would have voted for Stevenson."

"You know, these croissants are stale."

"They certainly seem to take their elections seriously." Simone is being obstinate in ignoring Jean-Paul in the same way as he has been ignoring her.

"Please pass the jam," asks Jean-Paul without lifting his head from the morning newspaper.

"I think that France can use some real elections. I would like to see a woman run for office," Simone says.

"Simone, I have asked you for three things and you have not given me any of them. I realize that we are existentialists, but we are also living in the same house. We have to work together and function as a team. If you will not listen to me, you deny my presence and so we are not really anywhere. Now, will you please pass the jam and pour some coffee."

"You know, Jean-Paul the American presidency is one of the last vestiges of the revolutions of the eighteenth century."

Sartre gets up in a huff, reaches across the table for the coffee and the jam, and sits down again. He pours his own coffee as Simone looks him in the eye and says. . .

(A) "I may not word this as memorably as I'd like to, but I'll write you a letter about it in a day or two. Then you can get it all straight. But listen now, anyway. This fall I think you're riding for, it's a special kind of fall, a horrible kind. This man falling isn't permitted to feel or hear himself hit bottom. He keeps falling and falling. The whole arrangement is designed for men who, at some time or other in their lives, were looking for something their own environment couldn't supply them with. So they gave up looking. They gave it up before they ever really got started."

(B) "It goes very deep this culture of control. Indeed, some anthropologists and mythologists believe that the only time of complete freedom for women was in prehistory, before paternity had been discovered, before there were any motives for such control. It was thought then that women, like trees, simply bore fruit when they were ripe, a mysterious gift that was proof of their superiority. In religious ceremonies men worshipped and imitated the act of childbirth. A variety of cultures may have prevailed but all of them were gynocratic. The gods were female gods."

(C) "Here is miraculous balm for those afflicted with an inferiority complex, and indeed no one is more arrogant toward women, more aggressive or scornful than the man who is anxious about his virility. Those who are not fear ridden in the presence of their fellow men are much more disposed to recognize a fellow creature in woman; but even to these the myth of woman, the Other, is precious for many reasons. They cannot be blamed for not cheerfully relinquishing all the benefits they derive from the muth, for they realize what they would lose in relinquishing woman as they fancy her to be, while they fail to realize what they have to gain from the woman of tomorrow."

Answer (A): From J. D. Salinger's *The Catcher in the Rye*. This novel about youth by Salinger (1919–) has become a classic.

Answer (B): From Gloria Steinem's "The Feminist's View." Steinem (1934–) is an American feminist.

Answer (C): CORRECT! From Simone de Beauvoir's *The Second Sex*.

Simone de Beauvoir (1908–), French novelist, essayist, and exponent of existentialism, whose life is closely linked with Jean-Paul Sartre, was born in Paris. She taught philosophy at college. In 1943, with the publication of her first novel, *She Came to Stay*, she gave up teaching entirely to write.

Between 1946 and 1955 de Beauvoir published three novels—*All Men Are Mortal* (1946), *The Blood of Others* (1947) and *The Mandarins* (1955)—all of which are concerned with existential themes, as well as with Sartre and his colleagues. In 1949, she published *The Second Sex*, which is her analysis of the position of women in the contemporary world. This book has become a classic modern-day feminist statement. De Beauvoir's later works—*Memoirs of a Dutiful Daughter* (1958) and *The Prime of Life* (1968)—are autobiographical.

100. MARSHALL MCLUHAN

The still darkness of the auditorium is illuminated by the blinding, stroboscopic lights. A bank of eighteen movie and slide projectors blazes images on the screens surrounding the dazzled audience. Huge loudspeakers blast eight tracks of sounds, voices, singing, and musical instruments. The psychedelic multimiedia era has arrived at this college auditorium in Rochester, New York, in 1964.

After the performance Marshall McLuhan walks backstage to greet his friend Gerd Stern, the multimedia artist and poet. Stern is one of the first avant-garde artists to be fascinated by the Canadian thinker's study of new technologies as an instrument of cultural change, which, in turn, leads to perceptual changes in the society constituting the culture. In McLuhan's words, "the medium is the message," and the message conveyed by a new technology indicates the need for an appropriate change in the patterns of daily life in the society in which the technology is activated.

"But what does all this have to do with me?" a bewildered McLuhan asks of the hirsute artist. He has spent years as a serious literary critic. Some of his own books, straight descriptive texts, seem to contradict the ideas he professes.

"Now Marshall," Stern says, "you taught us that the form of a medium influences the way it affects its audience. A typical theatrical performance tells what the real world is. The members of the audience don't have the opportunity to discern it for themselves."

"I still don't see the connection," McLuhan says.

"Don't you see," responds Stern, "we're organizing an environment that allows you to create your own experience, to create your own perception and understanding of the event. The form of the event changes the way you can understand it. If you'll excuse the expression, Marshall," he continues, "it's McLuhanesque!"

"Well, I just don't know," the professor sighs as his feet become tangled in the dozens of wires sprawled on the floor. He shakes his head in silence as a young hippy couple approach Stern. "Far out!" the girl swoons. "Psychedelic!" exclaims her date.

"Look," says Stern, turning back to McLuhan who is dressed in a gray business suit, "it comes straight from you. There's a passage in *Understanding Media* that explains the point I'm trying to make." He pulls a well-worn copy of McLuhan's book out of his overstuffed briefcase, quickly finds the page, and begins to read. . . .

(A) *"The continuity of existence has the smooth amplitude of a plane or a sea. It has the marvelous simplicity of free space. But this simplicity engenders a complication. For I am at the same time he who contemplates and the object of this contemplation. On the one hand, I exist in the place and the moment in which I am looking, and on the other hand, I see my own look traversing and possessing an expanse and duration that are still myself. I am he whom I see: I am he who is seen, sometimes at the extremity of the line of my look; and I am he who, by the movement of the vision, is able, in some way, to rejoin and see myself."*

(B) *"No matter how the conditions of the workers were altered the workers did more and better work. Whether the heat and light and leisure were arranged adversely or pleasantly, the quantity and quality of the output improved. The testers gloomily concluded that testing distorted the evidence. They missed the all important fact that when the workers are permitted to join their energies to a process of learning and discovery the increased efficiency is phenomenal."*

(C) *"Conventionality has nothing to do with calculated simplification (as in modern designing) or with degeneration from representation (as often assumed by the historians of art). It is unfortunate indeed that the word conventional should have come to be used in a deprecatory sense with reference to decadent art. Decadent art is simply an art which is no longer felt or energized, but merely denotes, in which there exists no longer any real correspondence between the formal and pictorial elements, its meaning as it were negated by the weakness or incongruity of the pictorial element; but it is often, as for example in late Hellenistic art, actually far less conventional than are the primitive or classic stages of the same sequence. True art, pure art, never enters into competition with the unattainable perfection of the world, but relies exclusively on its own logic and its own criteria, which cannot be tested by standards of truth or goodness applicable in other fields of activity."*

Answer (A):   From George Poulet's *The Metamorphosis of the Circle*. Poulet is a contemporary French literary critic.

Answer (B):   CORRECT! From Marshall McLuhan's *Understanding Media*.

Answer (C):   From Ananda K. Coomaraswamy's (1877–1947) *The Transformation of Nature in Art*. Coomaraswamy was an art historian and keeper of Indian and Islamic art in the Museum of Fine Arts, Boston.

Marshall McLuhan (1911–   ), Canadian cultural historian, was born in Edmunton, Alberta. His family was Scottish-Irish. McLuhan was educated in Canada and England. He received his doctorate in English literature from Cambridge University. He taught at the University of Wisconsin and at St. Louis University. In 1967–1968 he held the Albert Schweitzer Chair in the Humanities at Fordham University. He has also been the director for the Center for Culture and Technology at the University of Toronto.

His works include *The Gutenberg Galaxy* (1962), *Understanding Media: The Extensions of Man* (1964), *The Medium Is the Massage* (1967), and *War and Peace in the Global Village* (1968).